Bardsey
Now and Then

Photographs and Text
Jean Napier MA arps

Gwasg Carreg Gwalch

First published in 2018
© Jean Napier MA arps / Gwasg Carreg Gwalch

Published by Gwasg Carreg Gwalch,
12 Iard yr Orsaf, Llanrwst, Conwy, LL26 0EH.
tel: 01492 642031
email: llyfrau@carreg-gwalch.cymru
website: www.carreg-gwalch.cymru

ISBN: 978-1-84524-287-9

Cover photos: Jean Napier

Jean and Jes: photograph Ken Bridges

Previous Books

Jean Napier
Rhinogydd – Ancient Routes and Old Roads
ISBN 978-1-84524-271-8
Rhosydd – A Personal View/Golwg Bersonol
ISBN 978-0-86381-470-9

Jean Napier with Alun John Richards

A Tale of Two Rivers	ISBN 978-0-86381-989-1
Two Snowdonia Rivers	ISBN 978-0-84527-206-7
The River Conwy	ISBN 978-1-84527-288-3

All published by Gwasg Carreg Gwalch, Llanrwst

***This book is
dedicated to all
who cherish
Bardsey Island –
Ynys Enlli***

Contents

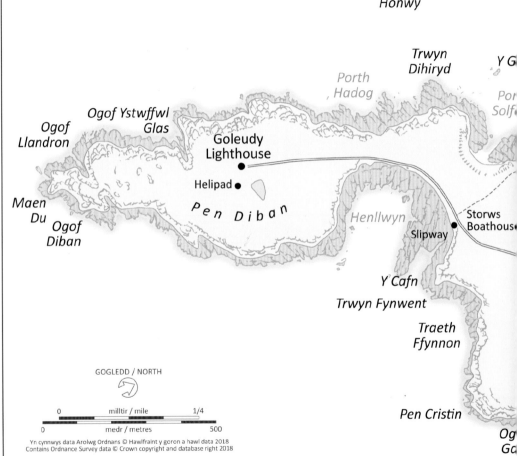

Carreg yr Honwy

Trwyn Dihiryd

Y G

Porth Hadog

Por
Solf

Ogof Ystwffwl Glas

Ogof Llandron

Goleudy Lighthouse

Helipad

Pen Diban

Maen Du

Ogof Diban

Henllwyn

Storws Boathouse

Slipway

Y Cafn

Trwyn Fynwent

Traeth Ffynnon

Pen Cristin

Og
Ga

GOGLEDD / NORTH

| 0 | milltir / mile | 1/4 |

| 0 | medr / metres | 500 |

Yn cynnwys data Arolwg Ordnans © Hawlfraint y goron a hawl data 2018
Contains Ordnance Survey data © Crown copyright and database right 2018

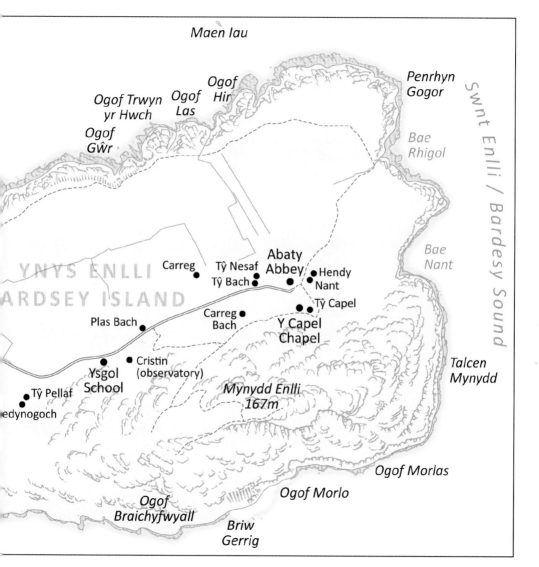

Introduction

The main part of this book are the fine photographs of Jean Napier, a Bardsey visitor in all seasons and all weather since 2006. In her essay, *Bardsey Now and Then*, she illustrates why the island and its people have come to be such an important part of her life.

Moving back in time from the present, two further texts have been selected to portray past lives on the island. Gwenda Waltson was the headmistress' daughter in the 1930s and still attends the annual general meetings of Bardsey Trust. Tomos the Islandman is a very popular text translated from Welsh. Jennie Jones, a Botwnnog teacher, transcribed Tomos Jones' memories in 1964 when he was eighty-six years old.

In his introduction of a new edition of the book, John Rees Jones wrote: 'I remember being spellbound by the book when it was first printed, and although almost forty years have passed since then, its spell lingers still.

Here is an old man relating the story of his life on Enlli in the closing years of the nineteenth century and the beginning of the twentieth century. My own ancestors also lived on the island throughout the nineteenth century, and naturally the book is of considerable interest to me. They came to the mainland a few years before the First World War because, according to the story, Uncle William became disillusioned with the island when his mother died before the doctor could get to her. (A fact that was greatly overlooked was that the old lady was well into her eighties at the time of her death!)

When I was very young, I also heard, from different members of the family, many stories about the inhabitants of the island and their peculiarities. There were the three who lived in Cristin – Harri, Mari and Wil – all unmarried. It is said that Mari was on the island for twenty-six years without once setting foot on the mainland, When Harri died, Mari's complaint was that he died after eating and egg for breakfast and having a clean shirt to wear that morning. Understanding her reasoning could be dangerous territory, but it is fair to think that an egg for breakfast and a clean shirt was some treat. Her brother Wil's reasoning when Mari herself became ill is unbeatable. 'Doctor,' he said, 'Have you anything for Mari? Remember, I don't want to spend too much on her; she's become quite old.'

The last king of the island was Love Pritchard. It is said that he went to the National Eisteddfod in Pwllheli in 1925, and that Lloyd George welcomed him as one of the Exiled Welsh, drawing an enormous cheer from the audience. Another time he went to Liverpool, and when a waitress asked him, 'What will you have love?' Love proudly turned to his friend and said, '*Diaist i*, they recognize me here as well'.

To our sophisticated world, the old inhabitants of the island were naïve and simple, and it is likely that the people of the mainland thought the same of them in the old days; yet, few of us would last a month living as they did with the hardship and isolation. Determination and tough endurance was needed for that. They said that the people of Enlli only had two masters: one was the owner of the island, Lord Newborough, and the other was death.

In his memories, Tomos o Enlli does not overstate the hardship of life. He remembers the odd happenings and moments, and the fun of going from house to house relating stories. His language in describing the society is also interesting; it is a simple language that richly describes the life he led. While putting it all on paper, Jennie Jones succeeded in being true to the nuances of the speaker. She is to be greatly thanked for her priceless endeavour.'

Myrddin ap Dafydd

Bardsey Now and Then

Bardsey – A Few Facts

Bardsey, or to use its Welsh name – **Ynys Enlli** (*Island in the Current*) is the farthest point west in North Wales and lies 2 miles off the tip of Llŷn. The only permanently occupied Welsh island, it is just over 1½ miles wide and 2½ miles long with Mynydd Enlli, its highest point, rising to 167 metres (548 feet). An important religious site since Saint Cadfan built the first monastery in 516, legend says that 20,000 saints are buried here and the North Wales Pilgrims' Way finishes on the island.

Bardsey, managed by the Bardsey Island Trust (BIT), is a National Nature Reserve, a Site of Special Scientific Interest (SSSI) and is safeguarded by many other environmental and conservation protection orders. Its unique position attracts migrant birds and it is one of the most important staging posts for birds in

below: Grey seals;
right & overleaf: Y Capel graveyard

the Irish Sea. The Bird and Field Observatory (Obs) was founded in 1953 and one of its main functions is to ring birds in order to collect data on their migration patterns. In addition, the island is a unique place to see grey seals at close quarters with 25-30 pups born each autumn.

Much has been written about Bardsey; some of which are listed at the end of this book. My favourite by far is 'Bardsey' by Christine Evans – full of exquisite detail about living on Enlli as well as beautiful poetry; she also includes a comprehensive history of the island.

Reminiscences of Past Visits

I first came here in 2006 for a week's silent retreat with 6 friends staying at Carreg, one of the big stone houses. At the time I was undertaking a 3-year course to become a Yoga and Meditation tutor and a week of silence seemed a useful experience. An amazing 7 days of stillness and contemplation with just the sounds of nature for company, my trip left an indelible mark on me – I was smitten by the island's magic, arriving back home a revitalised and renewed person!

Since then I have returned many times, mostly to stay with a great friend, Carole Shearman, who runs a variety of traditional art and craft workshops on the island during the summer. In 2016 the Bardsey Island Trust allowed me to stay for 3 weeks in Carreg in order to produce a film for them. I can remember endlessly trudging up to the Warden's shed with all my electronic equipment to charge it for the next day's filming via batteries fed by voltaics (there is no electricity on the island!).

One very early morning during that particular visit, I climbed up the mountain in order to catch the sunrise over Bardsey Sound on film (the channel of water between the mainland and the island). It was a truly spiritual experience; the Sound was awash with golden light as the sun rose over the mainland. The air was filled with birdsong and the crash of waves on the rocks far below me.

This was also the first time I heard

Manx shearwaters returning from the sea back to their burrows in the ground. Thousands of them pour in at night, when it is not too bright, in order to evade the gulls that lay in wait for them. I sat quietly in the dark at the north of the island with the air all around me full of their cries – a deafening mixture of strangled choking and loud gurgles – as they called to their mates in their burrows. The birds were invisible in the darkness, but I could feel the disturbed air on my face from their

above: Manx shearwaters burrows;
right: Manx paintings; opposite: Jean's tapestry

wings as they flew in directly over me.

I have a strong memory of huddling into a deep cleft in the rocks at Maen Du, the southern-most point of the island, whilst trying to shelter from the violent wind and rain to eat my lunch. I watched gannets fishing close by, plunging like arrows into the vast waves forged by the storm blasting around the headland.

In more tranquil weather, I whiled away a peaceful, sunny afternoon sitting on the slopes of Mynydd Enlli with a woman from the Whale and Dolphin Conservation Society, watching out for porpoises and dolphins. I saw, for the first time, a pod of magnificent Risso's dolphins pass through Bardsey Sound below.

I will treasure an extremely wild and bumpy fishing trip around Bardsey with Colin on his boat, experiencing the joy of catching my first ever decent-sized fish – a beautiful wrasse!

It was also a privilege to spend a lazy day crafting a wall-hanging made from Bardsey fleece on a peg loom in one of Carole's workshops. I wove into it 'found objects' – shells and dried seaweed – from Porth Solfach (the only beach) and ceramic pieces I had created from beach

clay, fired in a kiln built by Carole. It hangs here at home on my wall – a reminder of that special day. Carole also wove for me a made-to-measure meditation rug from Bardsey fleece during this visit.

I have visited Bardsey at least a dozen times over the years since 2006 and I am here again now for a further week to finish filming for the Trust, to talk with the residents and capture final photographs for inclusion in this book.

JEAN'S JOURNAL

April 2018

Saturday 21 April

My first day back on Bardsey and it is idyllic! I am sitting looking down on Hellwyn, a craggy bay that is a favourite spot for grey seals. Dozens are lounging on the rocks below me, snoozing in the warm sun. I find if I sing to them (a sort of doggy howl) they sometimes sing back (probably saying "shut up"!). Occasionally they squabble and bicker as their perches are overrun by waves from the incoming tide

left: Wrasse; opposite: Grey seals

– it will soon be time for them to return to the sea once again to fish.

The piping cry of oystercatchers accompanies me as I stroll down towards the lighthouse where I come across many carcases of golden plovers and lapwings scattered around this part of the island. Billy Dykes, one of the Bird Observatory Assistant Wardens, tells me later that, as they were unable to feed off the frozen ground during the prolonged cold and snow of last winter, these birds died of starvation.

above: Oyster catchers;
left: Golden plover carcass;
opposite: Bardsey storm

Sunday 22 April

Today sees a big change in the weather and I am drenched by the rain and spray whilst trying to film the waves sweeping around Penrhyn Gogor rocks at the north end of the island. Attempts to use my tripod for filming are futile in the strong gusting wind – I crouch low behind the bird hide, my camera on my knees, trying in vain to create a steady platform! I recover from mild hypothermia with two hot water bottles in bed back at Cristin (the Obs house) where I am staying this week.

Monday 23 April

I am starting my interviews with the residents today, beginning with Siân Stacey, the Island Manager, and Mark Carter, Assistant Warden. Siân talks to me about her feelings for the island and how hard it is to keep on top of all the work that needs to be done. I also hear fascinating stories about the past inhabitants' way of life. I meet Mabon their sheepdog – such a lovely, friendly creature – he helps out 'shuffling' the lambs (he is just learning and only a year old!). Being with him makes me realise how much I miss Jes (my sheepdog) – only dogs of residents are allowed on the island.

I also spend time with Gwenllian Jones (a Bardsey 'old timer') and Heather Hayward (her first visit) – two volunteer gardeners from Borth spending a week here tending the house gardens, and making a great job of it too. Over tea and biscuits, they explain to me the reasons they have come and talk about their passion for the island.

This evening, in the Obs Shop, I am giving an illustrated talk about the Rhinogydd mountains (the topic of my latest book) for a few of the residents and

top right: Mark Carter; below right: Mabon; above: Siân; right: Volunteer gardeners

volunteers. We have a generator going for a couple of hours each evening so it is also an opportunity to recharge my equipment batteries.

Tuesday 24 April

A special treat today – two guided walks! Billy is leading a nature tour for a group of us around the south of the island. We have a list to tick off of all the birds we see – my favourite one is the whimbrel, a beautiful bird, similar to a curlew, that I have not seen before. Billy carries a telescope to enable us to watch the seabirds nesting around the back of Mynydd Enlli. We watch gannets diving in Porth Solfa on our return and Billy gets excited as he had never seen this before!

In the afternoon I rejoin Siân, who gives a group of us a fascinating historical tour around the northern end of the island. She explains the history of Saint Cadfan and how the monks of St Mary's Abbey lived – the remains of the abbey tower can still be seen. In Y Capel we examine ancient remains of stone crosses and Siân rings the bell up in the chapel

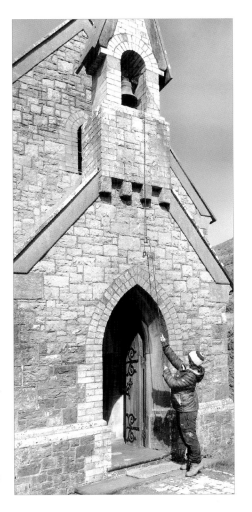

left: Siân Stacey ringing Y Capel bell;
opposite: Inside Y Capel

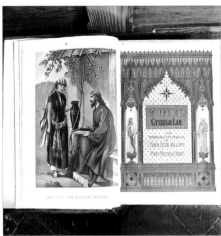

tower. Siân also talks about evidence of prehistoric habitation that has recently been found on the island.

Wednesday 25 April

The island is having an 'off day' and is shrouded in a thick, damp sea mist – I can't even see the top of the lighthouse! I decide it is a day for editing films and photos. Also it is time to recharge my own batteries! Continuously walking the island, even though it is small, carrying all the

left: Betws Oratory; Y Beibl;
above: Billy's nature walk

heavy film and photographic equipment is exhausting, especially with my damaged knee.

In the afternoon I manage to interview Steve Porter, the farmer, who said to catch him when it was raining – and it still is! It is cosy and warm sharing tea and biscuits (a common occurrence here!) with him at Tŷ Pellaf, the farmhouse, where he tells me about his family and their experiences of living and working on the island.

I also manage to grab a lengthy conversation with Steve Stansfield, Director of Operations for the Obs, and his wife Emma. I learn a great deal of in-depth information about how the Obs is run including their interaction with the Bardsey Island Trust and the RSPB, as well as their thoughts about living on the island.

Thursday 26 April

The weather seems more settled today and not too windy for a change, so I am making another attempt at filming and photographing the seals. I find if I sit quietly until they settle down, I can gradually creep closer without disturbing them. I love watching the interaction

between them, the arguing over a rock and the mock (I think!) fights. They sleep floating upright in the sea with just their heads visible, bobbing about in the water; their eyes are closed and they have such peaceful expressions.

I have a short chat with Billy Dykes and Ephraim Perfect about their roles on the island. They are both Assistant Wardens who are helping out at the Obs at the moment. I am enjoying sharing the

left: Grey seals; above left: Billy Dykes; above: Ephraim Perfect

facilities at Cristin with these two young lads this week.

Friday 27 April

Colin Evans, the boatman, is coming over to the island this morning and has promised to show me the properties around the lighthouse that he has purchased from the Trinity Lighthouse Service. I am looking forward to hearing what his plans are as the little he has told me so far sounds exciting and enterprising for both him and the island.

I shall spend my final evening on the island taking a last walk around saying a goodbye to the residents and, of course, the seals (I promise them I won't sing!).

Saturday 28 April

I am on the 10.00am boat back to Porth Meudwy on the mainland, feeling sad to leave as it has been a wonderful week. Luckily, I have achieved most of what I wanted regarding filming, photographing and interviewing.

As I alight from the boat there are

above: Colin Evans the boatman;
below: Lighthouse sign;
opposite: Lighthouse; Marathon runners

about ten people clad in bright lycra (not the usual Bardsey garb!) waiting for the boat back – I find out they are going over to run the 3rd Bardsey Marathon which is 9½ laps of the island! Well, at least the weather is kind today for their race.

I manage to catch Gareth Roberts and his family at Cwrt Farm where my car is parked for the week. He and his wife, Meriel, discuss with me (yes over more tea and biscuits!) their thoughts and ideas for when they take over running the farm on Bardsey after the Porters leave this October.

Later, I visit Colin's mother, Christine Evans, on the mainland, as I need to catch her before she returns to Bardsey next week where she will stay until October. We have an interesting conversation talking about the island, Ernest (her husband) and Colin, amongst dozens of other topics. I feel a real affinity with her. Ernest kindly pumps up my car tyres as they are looking ominously flat.

I am going to take a walk at sunset up to Mynydd Mawr, a high point at the end of Llŷn from where I can see Bardsey across the Sound. It will be a good opportunity to capture some final images of the island from the mainland.

I have found an excellent B&B in Aberdaron that will cater for a very early breakfast, as I will be taking a day trip back to Bardsey tomorrow.

Sunday 29 April

It is 6.45am and I wait at Porth Meuddy close by Aberdaron (the port near Cwrt Farm where Colin the boatman picks up nearly everything and everybody destined for the island). I am heading back to the island on the cattle boat when it returns

Loading cattle; Cattle in transit; Arriving Bardsey

from its first run to Bardsey. Blackbirds are singing all around me, gentle waves lap onto the slipway. I am accompanying Colin, Carwyn Evans and Raymond Grindle (Colin's employee), who are returning the welsh black cattle to the island that have been wintering at Cwrt Farm. I am told that today the conditions should be ideal – little wind and a high tide on the slipway to aid loading the cattle onto the boat.

Despite their reassurances, it is a turbulent crossing on the flat-bottomed ferry and the cattle are not looking too happy either – lots of mooing! Soaked, frozen and covered in cow poo, I think I still manage to get some reasonable photos – all in a day's work!!

Monday 30 April

Back home on the mainland I walk with Jes, my dog, down to the end of Afon Dysynni where it flows into the sea. It is a beautiful, clear evening and I can see Bardsey as a dark shape on the horizon across Cardigan Bay. There is a Welsh word – *hiraeth* – that describes how I am feeling at this moment – a sense of longing from the heart – a nostalgia for home. I will return ...

Who's Who on Bardsey Today

There are now only four permanent residents on the island all year but many others live there from March to November. An army of volunteers, both skilled and unskilled, short and long term, who come each year are an absolute Godsend for Bardsey. They undertake the myriad of jobs needed to maintain the houses and other vital work. During my recent visit, I interviewed all the people staying on the island. This included residents, volunteers and also other people that are a mainstay for the island, such as Colin the boatman, Gareth who farms Cwrt on the mainland and holds the tenancy for the farm on Bardsey from BIT, Christine Evans, the mother of Colin, a writer and poet, and her fisherman husband Ernest, both of whom usually live on the Island from May to October.

The Island Management

On Bardsey all year round are Siân Stacey, the Island Manager, and her partner Mark

below: Siân Stacey launching Colin's boat from Y Cafn; right: Plas Bach

Carter, Assistant Warden. Siân had been visiting the island for 21 years before she became manager in 2015. Her mother, Mel Stacey, runs writing courses on the island – the Bardsey community is a real family! Her partner Mark, a passionate 'birder', first came to work at the Obs in 2012 and worked there until 2016 – he and Siân met on the island. Siân says, "We both have a passion for the island, its wildlife and its heritage (built and living) and it feels like home. We are keen to further improve the island's facilities in a sensitive way and we have to be multi-skilled to cope with all the different jobs that need to be done.

This winter we spent days scraping and preparing the floors in most of the houses and used over 75 litres of paint. There is the odd Mabon paw-print on some of them as they took ages to dry!" Siân and Mark constantly need to take into account weather conditions, the tide and the seasons when planning the hundreds of jobs – including checking guttering, cleaning out water tanks and fixing compost bins – that are necessary to maintain the eight stone houses in

below: Tŷ Pellaf; top right: Steve and Jo Porter; below: Steve Porter

preparation for the holiday season. "When Storm Ophelia was raging this February, we had to don hard hats for trips to the toilet with slates flying off roofs!" Siân says.

The Farmers

The other all-year round residents are Steve and Jo Porter who currently run the farm at Tŷ Pellaf. They have been living here for 11 years, having previously been coming to Bardsey for family holidays for 6 years before they decided to apply to take over the farming on the island. Steve had past experience helping out his father on their sheep farm. His early misgivings prior to applying for the job were overruled by his family, and they were interviewed by Gareth Roberts of Cwrt Farm who holds the tenancy on behalf of the Bardsey Island Trust and who employs the Porters. Steve keeps bees and the honey is sold in the small shop. He says, "As Bardsey Island is a nature reserve, the farming has to work hand in hand with conservation objectives to benefit wildlife and biodiversity. This has been a rewarding challenge, although not easy at times, especially when so much is dictated

by the weather, tides and the season. Also everything has to be brought over by boat including the sheep and cattle!"

Jo, a Botanist, is monitoring habitat and collecting data on the island for Natural Resources Wales and the RSPB. In addition, she runs the small café/shop during the summer for visitors. An accomplished craftswoman, she creates a variety of hand-made rugs from Bardsey fleece and willow baskets that are sold there.

opposite: Bardsey bees; above: Island shop

Their children, Rachel and Ben, were home-schooled since arriving on the island. Steve says, "Both Rachel and Ben have Bardsey to thank for their passion for environment they were brought up in. Rachel's drawing and painting reflects the beauty of the natural world and Ben is finishing a degree in Falmouth on Conservation Biology." Ben's photographs of wildlife are some of the best I have seen!

The family have decided to leave running the farm on the island this October to live on the mainland but intend to keep a close connection with Bardsey. Maintaining the farm will then be taken over by Gareth and his wife Meriel Roberts.

The Bird Observatory Team

Steve and Emma Stansfield, along with their son Connor, live at Cristin (the Observatory, or 'Obs'). They are in residence from early March to November and often return for Christmas. Steve is the Director of Operations for the Obs,

above: Steve, Emma and Connor Stansfield;
right: Bird information boards;
Mark Carter ringing Manx Shearwater;
Manx Shearwater chick

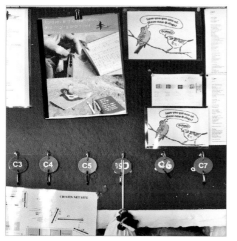

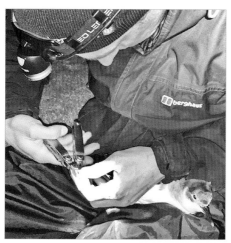

and his role covers a multitude of different responsibilities including the compilation of the 'Bardsey's Wildlife' report and collation of data collected by the Obs on migration and breeding bird numbers.

Since arriving on Bardsey in January 1998, Steve has developed a real affinity with the island. He says, "It is freeing being away from the mainstream, to work in harmony with the weather, tide and seasons. Also, there are no distractions and we have the freedom to make any changes that become necessary along with the flexibility to implement them. A recent highlight for me was being awarded the prestigious Marsh Award for Local Ornithology from the British Trust for Ornithology (BTO) – the Award carried a prize of £1,000 and a special ceremony in London!"

Steve and Emma met on the island in May 1998 (yes, a common occurrence!) and Steve asked her to come back as a volunteer the following September. Emma explained to me that, as Y Capel is not licensed for weddings, they had to get special permission from the Archbishop of Canterbury to marry on the island in 2007. Before giving his consent, he required amongst other things, permission from both of their parents to show that they approved of the wedding. Connor was born in 2002 and home educated until 2016. He now receives tutoring on-line via video conferencing and is about to take his GCSEs – I am told he is doing very well at his studies.

Billy Dykes and Ephraim Perfect, Assistant Wardens at the Obs, both arrived this March and will stay until November. Billy had previously volunteered at the Lulworth Cove Ranges and Skokholm

above: Bird Observatory sign;
opposite: Colin Evans's lighthouse project

Island. He showed me the moth trap he sets up each night – filled with egg boxes – a daily record is kept of numbers and names. Billy also leads a series of nature walks around the island for visitors.

Ephraim first came to the island in 2015 as a guest, then volunteered for a 3 months stint in 2016 prior to being offered his current job in 2017. His passion is the birds and, like Billy, he spends a great deal of time each day recording numbers and species of bird visiting and breeding on the island. Birds are caught in nets positioned in different parts of the island. They are then ringed by Ephraim (he holds a Bird Ringing License) and released. Ephraim is also an avid bird photographer and his images are amazing.

The Boatman

Colin, who ferries almost everything and everybody to and from the island in his boat, has a long historical link with Bardsey. His great-grandfather, John Evans, took the tenancy of Cristin in 1926 and he can trace his lineage on the island back to 1770. Colin has a great compassion for Bardsey and feels his family has a responsibility to the island. He is concerned that the island is now at its lowest ebb and has been reduced to just being a tourist destination relying on grants to survive.

He has now purchased many of the buildings around the lighthouse and plans to set up a business which will hopefully add enough value to traditional island produce and thus enable farming and fishing to continue in the old ways. He wants to implement a variety of factors to enhance the island's economy and financial viability. Colin says, "I want to help Bardsey become more sustainable in the future without degrading the island's unique character and I wish to attract and

Bardsey Now and Then

empower young people to set up family units here with prosperous occupations. If the island is to continue to attract and, more particularly, sustain, skilled and self-reliant residents, there needs to be well-paid employment and a quality product to be proud of."

One absolute necessity, Colin says, is "We have to develop and increase the transport service to the island, especially in winter, in order to make these changes viable – I am currently building a new boat to help make this happen". Colin built the current ferryboat, named Benlli III, as well as a large landing craft that carries livestock and machinery to Bardsey. "As boatman for the island I spend my working life focussed on that which lies between island and mainland, on a Sound changing by the quarter-hour, trying to meet its challenge and to second guess what is coming next. Some twelve million tons of water pass through Bardsey Sound in a minute: the boat weighs just three."

The Poet and the Fisherman

Christine and Ernest Evans, Colin's parents, live on the island for the fishing season from May to October, in Rhedynogoch next to Tŷ Pellaf. Christine first came to Bardsey for a week in 1968, stayed for three and has spent every summer there since. She is an accomplished writer and poet with many books to her name – 'Bardsey' is an excellent example, full of stories and poems about the people, history and wildlife of the island.

Christine explains, "I was hooked by Bardsey; after 40 years I am still hooked. Since that first week, the island has become either 'here' (when I am on it) or

above left: leaving Bardsey;
below left: Y Cafn – Bardsey harbour;
right: Ernest Evans

'there' when I am away from it. I have landed and walked up the stony track many times, not always with delight but invariably with a sense of coming home. It is the great fact of my life, the place that chose me and where I became the person I am, or the better part of it". She adds, "I discovered a way of doing things properly that could enhance the task and make one feel in touch with the generations who had evolved it. I learned weather signs and sayings: that an easterly wind blows by the hour but gwynt gogledd wrth y dydd, a northerly lasts all day; when it was best to plant potatoes, sow broad beans and set a hen to sit on a clutch of eggs."

Like many other couples linked to Bardsey, Christine met Ernest on the island and her book tells us the story of how Ernest took her down to the Seal Cave for their first outing. Ernest's father Will hoped that Ernest would take over the farm at Tŷ Pellaf but Ernest preferred to fish – he was said to have an instinctive knowledge of the currents. He was also a natural mechanic and worked at the lighthouse after leaving school. Christine

left: Christine Evans;
right: rough seas on west coast

informed me that, back in the Seventies, Ernest was offered the farm tenancy but he had always said 'One farmer can't manage'; he knew the effort involved in bringing everything to the island, coping with the demands of the farm, as well as lobster fishing. There was no ferry service then, each island family had its own boat. Ernest keeps his fishing boat 'Pedryn' (Storm Petrel) at Porth Meudwy when he is not on the island, and has been the Royal Mail postman for 50 years.

left: Heart rope; above: Lobster pots; opposite: Gareth and Meriel Roberts

Christine concludes, "I love – yes, it's not too strong a word, not just gush – I love being here because of that feeling of losing myself in impressions: the timelessness that comes from floating, immersed in the moment. On all but the calmest days the air is moving around the island and there is the sound of the sea, like breathing, its movement and that of the light on it, encircling. Cloudscapes are richer, and more dramatic; the sky dominates the view and we lie in the path of all the weather from the south-west."
I completely understand what she means.

The Farm Tenancy Holder

Gareth Roberts has held the overall tenancy for farming on Enlli for the Bardsey Island Trust (BIT) for 10 years. I sit with him and his wife Meriel at their kitchen table and he tells me, "My connection to Enlli goes back nearly 50 years, and I'm still as keen to step onshore now and spend time there as I was as a young boy when I did that for the first time. Another honour is being responsible for the practical husbandry that strives to develop the environment so that the unique plants and creatures can thrive,

thus contributing in my own way to the varying mosaic of experiences that make Enlli such a special place".

Gareth and Meriel are looking forward to taking back the running of the farm on Enlli when Steve and Jo Porter (who are currently employed by Gareth to managing it) leave this October, and they have plans to develop the farm as part of a living and sustainable community. He says, "We have to avoid Enlli becoming a cold and impersonal museum. We can't depend on industry and yesterday's methods to do this, so we have to be inventive and work together, whilst at the same time showing due respect – intelligently and sustainably – to what exists already and create structures that can support a community and our inheritance as well as the island's history and habitat."

The Artisan on the Island

Carole Shearman first came to the island in 2003 on one of Christine Evans' writing courses. She spent time at the Obs in 2005 undertaking her own artwork inspired by

left: Welsh Black cattle; Goat and kid; Sheep and lamb; right: Carole Shearman; Spinning Bardsey fleece

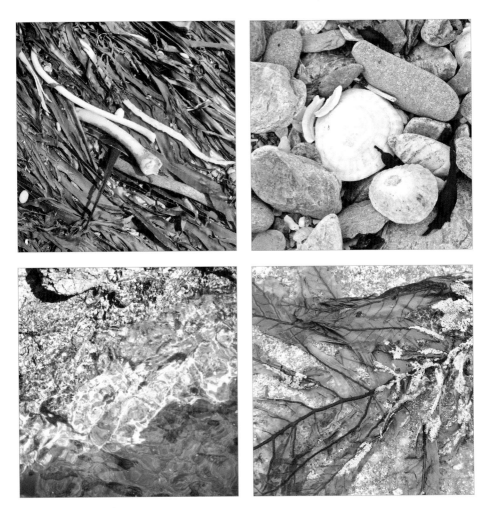

the island – she then applied to, and was accepted by, BIT to run art and traditional craft workshops during the summer months – she has been back here every year since.

Carole says, "I have space here to be creative with others. Working with the fleece and clay from the island and the recycled materials of the visitors, is a real 'hands-on' experience for them. There is a sense of giving and receiving with the workshops – an authenticity that comes from the use of the island materials. It is an inspiring place to be and it is such a privilege to be here. The island is both contained and expansive, bringing together silence, solitude and simplicity. Each time I arrive on Enlli, I find my true self waiting for me – it is my home".

A Magical Island

The beautiful words spoken by both Carole and Christine concerning their feelings for the island evoke a deep resonance in me – yes, Bardsey does weave a magical spell when you are there. The Welsh have another unique word – *heddwch*. It means more than just peace, it

is about having a heart-felt sense of harmony with your surroundings and contentment with where you are in that moment. This word describes exactly how I feel when on Bardsey, regardless of the variety of extreme weather it can throw at you all in one day!

I hope after reading this little book you are encouraged to pay a visit to this unique and wonderful island so that you too can be smitten by its special qualities – its magic.

above: Maen Du; below: Solfach beach

Enlli Headmistress's Daughter
The reminiscences of Gwenda Watson

Traditionally, the minister's wife was the schoolmistress on Enlli. When an unmarried minister was appointed to the island, the authorities had to find someone else who was qualified for the post. When my mother, May Murray-Williams was first appointed headmistress there in 1932, my brother and I were destined to experience a very special childhood.

Reverend William Jones was minister on the island for fifty years. Back in 1875, Lord Newborough – who owned Enlli at the time – offered the island occupiers a choice: a new mill or a new chapel. They chose a chapel. It's a handsome building at the northern end, near the old abbey. The building was constructed around a large Italian pulpit. The pulpit had been intended for another church, but when it arrived there, it was too big to fit through the door. The deacons had refused to widen the door and the pulpit's donors had refused to cut it down in size. A request was sent across the Sound for it,

and it was given to the islanders. It was installed on the foundations and the chapel was built around it. At a later date Megan Lloyd George presented the chapel with an organ.

Reverend William Jones was succeeded by Owen Jones. He was a tailor from Garndolbenmaen who had converted during the Revival of 1904–05. He administered the island's spiritual needs while his wife took care of the children's education – despite never having received any kind of training in the field. The couple were followed by Rev. R. M. Evans and his wife, but they left after a short period to answer a call to the Welsh Chapel in Rochdale, Lancashire. The next couple to look after the chapel and school were Rev. Owen Jones and his wife – they stayed for seven years, during which time

1. Mother standing, schoolchildren enjoying special treat 1934;
2. Tŷ Capel & Y Capel;
3. The old school

INTODUCTION.

Bardsey is the bigges
island off the Caernarvonshire
coast. It has no trees, so you
would use drift-wood for your
fire. It has no rivers and the
islanders would fetch their fresh
water from 7 wells. The island
11 miles long, 3/4 of a mile wide
and the mountain reaches
548'. All the houses are made
from the stones of the

Lighthouse East. Bardsey Island.

the school was brought under the supervision of the Education Board. Owen Jones and his wife left in 1930 and for two years the island was without a minister, with only a supply teacher in the school.

Once again a couple was advertised for – a residential minister to take care of the chapel and a wife to be responsible for educating Enlli's children. Ultimately, the services were secured of Rev. Edward Evans B.D. who had been a missionary in Nigeria for over twenty years. However, he was a bachelor, and so the teaching position at the school remained vacant.

The education authority advertised for a qualified teacher. My mother telephoned the director, David Thomas.

'I understand you're looking for a teacher for Enlli?'

'Yes. Who are you?'

'Mrs Murray-Williams.'

'Oh, you're married? We don't employ married women.'

1. Gwenda Watson's childhood notebook with memories of the island;
2. Bardsey lighthouse in the 1930s;
3. My brother Gordon on holiday with us on Enlli – Gordon is between me and Jane Tŷ Pella in the front

'You offered the job to the minister's wife, so why not offer it to someone else's wife?'

'Um … OK. Come and see me in the morning.'

The background to the move to Enlli was that my father had gone bankrupt in the shop in Cwm-y-glo. Our home was part of the shop, so when he lost it, he lost everything. We initially had to move to Groeslon to live with Nain – my paternal grandmother. Then Mam decided to return to teaching in order to sustain the family. When she approached the education authorities in Caernarfon, she said she was homeless and that she needed a job in a school with an attached house if possible. The authorities saw their chance and offered her the position on Enlli.

The outcome was that my mother, my father and we two small children crossed the Sound for the first time in our lives. My brother Gwyn was born on 6th June, 1929 and I arrived on 5th November, 1930.

My father was one of five boys and had had to leave Groeslon school at a young age, as his father had died in a cholera plague while working as a stonemason in Penmaenmawr. He'd never been anywhere near Enlli. Although my mother had spent most of her life in Pwllheli before working as a teacher in Oldham and Groeslon, she had never set foot on Enlli soil either.

Mam was a Pwllheli girl – her grandfather, John Murray, had come from Scotland to work in the Carreg yr Imbyll granite quarry, where her father, Robert Murray, had risen to become manager. My mother's mother – Agnes Clemence – was originally from Cornwall, and Mam was one of five daughters: Margaret Olive, Judith May, Edith Emily, Lucy Agnes and Helena Clemence. If you were friends with Mam you would never utter the name 'Judith'. Because Murray was such a foreign and exotic surname in Pwllheli, and Williams was very common, when Mam got married the surnames were joined – and she was Mrs Murray-Williams to everyone afterwards.

For the migration, it was a still and quiet day and we had no trouble crossing or carrying our furniture onto the island in summer 1932, according to Mam. And that's just as well, because some items of 'Enlli furniture' are in my home in Manchester today and I never cease to be amazed at how the big Caernarfon grandfather clock and the massive chest of drawers were transported to the island and back. My father, John Ellis Williams, had crossed ahead of us to prepare the house, assisted by the islanders and Rev. Edward Evans. The sea was smooth as glass and we were all bemused by all this nonsense about the Sound being so difficult to cross. We were carried over in a small motor boat presented as a gift to the islanders through the kindness of the late Frederick Wynn, Glynllifon. It only took an hour – much quicker than rowing in one of the old Enlli double-bowed boats.

However, we wouldn't be there long before coming to understand that the strait was full of treacherous currents. In the old days, it was nothing for the islanders to be trapped on Enlli for six weeks or more. On one occasion, we children and Mam had gone over to Pwllheli for Christmas. When January came, it was too stormy to return, and Mam spent seven weeks doing supply work in Llŷn schools.

The boatmen at that time crossed from Aberdaron beach, not Porth Meudwy. What you had to do was go past the old St Hywyn's church to the beach and walk over the sand to the water's edge. The men would be waiting for you there. They would have already crossed back and forth a few times carrying fodder for the cattle and hens and essential goods and coal for the homesteads. There would be rowing boats where the waves broke on the beach and the motor boat would be a bit further out into the bay. Enlli men would carry the passengers on their backs donkey-fashion if they were men, but women and children would be carried in their arms to the rowing boat. We were there for more than six years, but no two crossings were ever alike. You never knew what to expect – sunshine, rain, wind, sea mist, undertow, wild waves, a lovely tranquillity or serious seasickness.

When I was born, Dad was a shopkeeper in Cwm-y-glo while Mam baked bread at the back. Very early on, it was noticed that I had something wrong with my leg – my foot was limp. I was taken to Nain's at Groeslon and the doctor was called. My parents were informed that I was suffering from infantile paralysis (polio) but that there was nothing they could do there and then. Mam took me to see a specialist in Liverpool in November 1934 when I was four years old and I returned there to Heswall Hospital on 2nd January, 1935. I was there until 22nd November that year – I underwent three operations but they were unsuccessful. The journey there was quite a saga for a five-year-old girl – Mam couldn't take me, so a chain of escorts was arranged to look after me. One of the Enlli boatmen took me to Aberdaron and transferred me to the care of people at Tŷ Newydd, Aberdaron. I sat on a chair there until the Pwllheli bus came. Auntie Magi came to meet me on the Maes in town and took me to her home in Church Place until it was time to go and catch the train. Then the guard was entrusted to care for me all the way to Liverpool where Auntie Meri and Uncle Dic awaited to meet me and take me to the hospital.

Visitors were allowed on the first Saturday in every month – but Mam only managed to come and see me once, on the first Saturday in August which was a school holiday. I had to have a splint on my leg while I was growing up – one leg was a good five inches shorter than the other. But my mother always drummed into me that I was no different to anyone else.

As we settled into our new home, Plas Lleuddad (Chapel House), Gwyn was of school age and so he'd be there with Mam. But within six months my dad fell ill – he suffered from TB, and had to return to the mainland to live with Nain in Groeslon. There was no option then but for me to follow Mam and Gwyn to school. Immediately before Dad left, Mam had become pregnant with Gordon, who was born in one of the little cottages in Aberdaron on 15th January, 1933. Once the baby was born, he was taken to be nursed by Nain and Taid in Pwllheli and Mam returned to Enlli to carry on working at the school. My father died that summer – August 1933 – and Gordon was baptised on the same day as Dad was buried.

When we came to live on the island, there were 35 adults and 17 other children living there. When we left in 1938, we left just seven adults and three children. It was Mam's decision to leave to ensure secondary education for us children. Our family had been dealt two cruel blows by the depression of the thirties – we'd been bankrupted and a few months later our father had died of tuberculosis.

The school on Enlli consisted of one room, containing about fifteen of us aged 2-14, the older children helping with the infants. Every one of the children could read at four years of age. There was also a gramophone, piano, pianola and a small museum of island life containing amazing things like an ostrich egg, pink coral and foreign coins. While I was there, the children's classic *Llyfr Mawr y Plant* had just been published for the first time, and it was a great favourite of ours.

There was a top-quality HMV gramophone in the school as well as a wireless radio set. The wireless was used to teach English – one of the daily tasks for the older children was to record the Weather Forecast on a slate – the forecast was read at a speed that could be transcribed on paper in those days. The other purpose of this exercise was that it allowed Mam to listen to the forecast and then go and report it to the Cristin family after school.

We loved having visitors on the island

1. The class of 1934 with Mam in front of the school; 2. Tom Nefyn and George Davies; 3. Aunty Amy, Peter Scott (Prof C. H. Dodd's son), Tom Nefyn (with me in his arms), Lockley and George M. Ll. Davies

– it broke the monotony of a one-teacher school. Quite a few were occasional visitors: C. H. Dodd, George M. Ll. Davies, the minister and pacifist, and Tom Nefyn the preacher. Others weren't so popular. Twice during my mother's time as teacher the schools inspectorate tried to come over to assess the school, and twice they failed. This was how it went:

● The HMIs would contact the schoolmistress noting the date of the visit and asking her to arrange a boatman to come and get them from Aberdaron beach at a specified time.

● The boatman would wait on the beach and when the inspectors inquired whether the sea was all right for them to cross, the boatman always replied: 'Yes, I'll take you over there. But d'you see those clouds to the north-west – the wind will be picking up towards the end of the morning and that's that then. We won't be bringing you back for at least three days.'

● And the inspectors' response each time was: 'There we are then. We'll leave this for some other time.' They were men who liked solid ground underfoot and they preferred to return empty-handed to Caernarfon than to venture out to the island. But they didn't know anything about clouds, either!

George M. Ll. Davies was a minister in the Aberdaron area and he valued the character of the place and its people. He wrote about the openness of the local people in *Y Ford Gron*:

> I remember hearing of an Enlli minister arriving on the Mainland and greeting Wil Saer (a carpenter) who was working on the church roof. Wil had dabbled with various denominations before ending up with the Scotch Baptists.
>
> 'What are you now, Wil?' the minister inquired.
>
> 'High Church,' said the old wag nonchalantly.
>
> 'Goodness gracious, how so?' said the minister.
>
> 'Well, I'm doing a bit of repairs on

the Church roof and so I'm higher than any of them,' replied the old Carpenter.

In those days a craftsman was a man and not a machine, and was known by his craft: Wil Saer [Carpenter], Betw'r Gegin [Kitchen maid], Rhisiart y Crydd [Cobbler], and Huw'r Felin [Miller]. Happily the old Welsh way still lives on today in Aberdaron in the face of the 'modern method' which tries to level men by their names so that every servile milksop claims the title of 'Mister'.

He also refers to burial rituals on Enlli:

One by one the old family of fishermen passes away; one by one the old residents of Enlli come to the place of their eternal home. But the old funeral song before pushing the boat out to sea in Enlli still holds its ground:
  Farewell, beloved friends so dear,
  For a moment we depart from here,
  All hail the day we'll meet again
  Around the table in Salem.
I can't imagine that I have a better idea of heaven than the greetings of the family and the welcome of the pure and simple community found amongst the Saints, ancient and recent, in Aberdaron and Enlli:
  In the frailty of my old age
  I would wish, be privileged
  To spend there in peace
  Of tranquil retreat
  The feeble final years
  Of my life in God's sanctuary.
  To live there, to live for Him
  To be content and at peace
  And hold communion with the waves
  A world away from worldly things;
  No earthly crowds, no horizon
  But the blessed blue-green ocean.
  Of all the world, Enlli
  Is the wholesome land for my demise.

The condition of the houses was good – they were sturdy buildings with high protecting walls to shield the yards from the weather. Every one bar one – Carreg Bach – was built around 1850, with many of the stones, regrettably, pilfered from the ruins of the old abbey. There are approximately 444 acres of arable land on the island, and the inhabitants depended on the small fields and the sea for their sustenance. Lobster-pots caught plenty of crabs and lobsters which were sold to the Trinity House boat that ferried back and forth to the lighthouse. Occasionally, that boat would leave Enlli directly to Liverpool, when good prices would be obtained for the produce.

The island had no mill, smithy, shop, tavern, cobbler or any specific craftsman. But all the men were practical and could turn their hand to all kinds of work. I learnt how to live independently on Enlli.

Ready-made horseshoes were purchased on the Mainland but it was the job of one Enlli man – with no blacksmith's training – to shoe the horses. Before our time, the men had constructed a boat which had won the race at Aberdaron Regatta.

All the island's inhabitants were one big family – of necessity. Every adult was addressed by their first name and the name of their house – Nel Tŷ Pella, Lizzie Kate Cristin, Jane Nant and so on. None of the doors on the island were locked, night or day, and no-one would wait on the doorstep for an answer – just knock, lift the latch and walk in to the middle of whatever was happening in the house at the time. Very little attention was paid to the décor and condition of the house in winter but once the days started getting longer and lighter, major spring cleaning would get under way. The catalogues would arrive and the wives would order new bedclothes, towels, overalls and aprons. Oxendales and J. D. Williams' catalogues were the favourites.

Produce from the land and gardens was shared as well. If a furrow of new potatoes was ready on one farm before the others, everyone had a share of the potatoes until more became available. It was exactly the same with a good catch of fish. We used to share our eggs because Mam only kept hens.

The only commodity not considered common property was driftwood. The men watched the tides and currents, moon and wind with eagle eyes, and would often set out to collect driftwood with lanterns. Taking a piece of wood that had been dragged higher than the high tide line was an unforgivable crime. If two men were combing the beach at the same time, the prize belonged not to the first man to see the driftwood, but to the first to lay hands on it. Planks, entire hatches and good pieces of wood of all sizes – these were all very common on the island's shores, together with all kinds of other junk thrown into the sea from the Irish Sea steamers.

The driftwood bug had gripped Mam and us children as well. It was very exciting to be allowed to go and collect the driftwood, jumping up and down between the rocks and looking underneath them for fragments. Very soon we became expert at knowing where the best coves were. We had no use for the biggest pieces of wood but we'd drag them home happily and give them to whoever needed them. Our requirements were met by the smaller splinters of firewood. Enlli is a bare, treeless island – it boasted just one small, shapeless maple in the 1930s and one apple tree. There was plenty of gorse on the mountain and in the embankments but sawing gorse wood meant spending ages extracting prickles from the hands and fingers afterwards. So driftwood from the sea was a very welcome energy source.

Every house used a coal-fired oven for all its cooking, of course. You can't beat an old-fashioned brick oven over a hot fire for baking bread. That was a weekly task – one day, all day. Cakes were never bought – everything was home-baked using home-made butter and free-range eggs. After baking, a dishful of rice pudding would be put in the oven and left overnight. By morning it would be thick and creamy, crisp-skinned and wonderful.

Life on the island was wonderful and romantic for Mam and ourselves, and peaceful beyond words – but it was awfully hard too. Although quiet, it wasn't a lonely place. It offered solitude rather than loneliness. Even at the top of Mynydd Enlli, I didn't feel I was alone. Mam had lived in Manchester for seven years and had experienced loneliness in crowds as she walked through Deansgate and along Market Street. No-one was lonely on Enlli.

The only ones on the island who had a regular income were Mr Evans the minister, the lighthouse men and Mam. When a catalogue arrived, Mam would take the orders of the other island dwellers and pay for the goods herself; they would then repay her as they could. I remember

1. An animal in the 'Horse Boat' in the Cafn landing area; 2. Rev. Edward Evans, Enlli minister, in the stern of the boat returning to the mainland with two visitors; 3. In front of Cristin

Mrs Williams, Nant coming to our house and asking for this and that from the catalogue as if it were a letter to Santa Claus. Mam finally had to say of one item – 'I can't get this for you'. I had no understanding of this as a child, but now I can appreciate how difficult things were then. Anyway, what Mam used to do was add one box of chocolate biscuits to the list, so that when the order reached the island and everyone congregated in Cristin to receive their goods, Mam would open the biscuits and let everyone choose their favourites. I remember the dilemma in my head on such occasions – should I pick a chocolate biscuit that I could see or one of those wrapped in silver paper that I couldn't see.

The catalogues were recycled too – one Oxendale catalogue page torn in half was enough to wrap one egg! Every other house on the island had a pig in a shed – apart from ours, so all the scraps and food waste from our house went to the chickens. As a result, they were very good layers – our hens were the only ones to lay eggs throughout the winter. Because of this, we had a market that paid well at the time, as we were suppliers of eggs to the lighthouse men. Mam would get sixpence a dozen for them in spring and up to two shillings a dozen in winter. There being plenty of hens, chicken meat was very common – as were crab and lobster – and not a festive treat as it was elsewhere.

A lot of labour sharing went on, of course – everyone would join in together for sheep washing and shearing. The sheep used to graze on the mountain common land, and when the time came to gather them, someone from every family along with every dog on the island would start from one end and gather all the sheep together. The wives would be constantly knitting at home – socks, gloves and such items.

The drawback of the island was that we were entirely dependent on crossing back and forth to the Mainland for certain

1. Mam keeps an eye on us in school. Mary Nant (right) with me in the front; Jane Tŷ Pella behind us and my brother Gwyn behind her; Gwilym Nant and Wil Cristin next to Mam;

2. A group of day visitors to Enlli. This is also a good photograph of some of the islanders' boats;

3. Two visitors watch Wil Cristin treating a horse's shoe on Cristin farm

necessities. Sometimes, after days of stormy weather and blustery gales, provisions would be in short supply in the houses. The island has no river – but it does have twelve springs. Every house had its own well and some had interesting names – Ffynnon y Brenin (King's Well), Ffynnon y Barf (Bearded Well), Ffynnon y Baglau (Crutches Well). This water was like gold and was kept for drinking only. We collected rainwater too for other requirements. The well had to be cleaned at least once a year – and that was a very long day.

We had no newspapers (but for a pile that would arrive every three weeks or so), no policeman, no motor car of any kind or telephone on the island in the thirties. There were three radio sets on the island – in the school, Plas Lleuddad and Cristin. Still, while we were living there, we saw no-one in need either. If one house ran out of tea leaves, everyone would share what they had left and as sure as night follows day, the storm would have passed before the last spoonful had gone into the pot.

A supply of yeast was another concern, but as long as there was flour available, all would be fine. Every family kept a little of the previous week's dough in case the yeast ran out – but we never had cause to use it, so I can't vouch whether that worked or not. When a lull came in a storm, a boat would be pushed into the water and a crossing made to Aberdaron to get the bare essentials. Sometimes a boat would reach Trinity House – the Beacon – with fresh supplies for the lighthouse men and they would share the goods with us. The most fervent thanks were given for cigarettes and tobacco for the men and yeast for the women!

The craving for tobacco was a terrible thing. A day or two after the stock was used up, the men would refuse to do anything. It was hard on the women at those times. They'd be willing to try anything – drying tealeaves, coltsfoot leaves, and more – to let the men have a smoke. Mam used to keep packets of cigarettes and a box of tobacco in reserve for the other island women on such occasions. She learnt to stock up on goods from Pwllheli too – a sack of flour, a hundredweight of sugar, a chest of tea, boxes of fruits, tinned meats and fish and packets of biscuits and sweets and so on.

In the old days, the minister was the

principal leader of society. Enlli was a close community of nine families, and as happens in families, there would sometimes be fierce disputes and disagreements. Traditionally it would be the minister who would settle such matters and keep the peace, but Mr Evans wasn't accepted by the people of Enlli to continue with that part of his calling. Apparently he was impossible to talk to. So they used to come to Mam and let her try and smooth things over. The island people thought the world of her. But I can only imagine how hard it was for Mam in those years – a widow, with responsibility for the school, two small children at home and a baby on the Mainland.

The police used to visit the island about once a year. If the men found bones as they ploughed the fields, they put them to one side and saved them for the police visits. Then they'd be taken away to confirm that they were ancient, and that no-one had buried a recent corpse on the island.

It was always easy to get a good price for an animal reared on Enlli but loading the bullocks and heifers was hard work, especially with the more stubborn creatures. No matter how ardently and diligently they were pulled and pushed, one or two would refuse point blank to jump into the 'Horse Boat' – Enlli's big boat. A few cargos could be fun too – the island women would take a day's holiday when the animals were being loaded, and especially so when the pigs were loaded. They used to leave their tasks and come down to the Cafn landing area to watch the high jinks.

The women were far more trapped than the men. While the men crossed to Aberdaron, the women remained on the island to look after the animals. Mam used to take that opportunity to lend a helping hand with the milking in the neighbours' cowsheds. Having said that, some women preferred to stay at home even when presented with the opportunity to go to the Mainland. One woman stayed on the island for fifteen months, and another for two whole years. The reason for that was poverty – they had no money to leave even for a day. Life can't have been too bad there, though, and many times during my life thereafter I would have been willing to return to the island under the same conditions as were there in the thirties.

Life on the island was very healthy for us children. But occasionally there was no option but to call for medical attention from the Mainland. I remember one of the children having appendix pains and having to be rushed over sea and land to Bangor hospital. The method of communicating an emergency of that kind to the Mainland was by lighting a beacon on the top of Mynydd Enlli. Once the message was received a doctor would be summoned from Pwllheli. Apart from that, we relied on home-made remedies – wormwood, treacle and sulphur, a tin of coal-tar and a hot poker, goose-grease on brown paper, soap and sugar, tincture of rhubarb, castor oil, and syrup of figs.

1. *Enlli people believed that seaweed had properties that would alleviate my lameness. Men used to bring loads of seaweed to our house and I'd have to sit still and let them wrap it around my leg. We weren't allowed to go swimming in the sea as children – the currents were too dangerous around the island and nobody on Enlli could swim, as that would be tempting fate. But we were allowed to go and sit in the odd pool sometimes – seaweed pools, of course!;*
2. *One of the Cristin boys with his catch*

There were no foxes, rats, snakes or frogs on Enlli. But there were plenty of mice and seals and an abundance of rabbits in the thirties. There were all kinds of birds of course, scores of them attracted by the light and flying into the lighthouse walls. The coast was dangerous in some places for us children. There are forty-four caves on the island, many of them with interesting names – Ogof y Gaseg (Mare's Cave), Ogof Ystwffwl Glas (Blue Pillar Cave), Ogof y Morlo (Seal's Cave), Ogof y Lladron (Robbers' Cave), Ogof Diban and Ogof y Crancod (Crabs' Cave).

I remember one awkward incident arising from all the demands made on Mam. She used to let Gwyn and me leave school at 11.45 to walk across the island to our house to light the paraffin stove so that we could have a cup of tea with our lunch. Dinnertime was twelve until one, and it was a bit of a squeeze for Mam to get everything done and walk back and forth to school within that timescale. Before starting back for the afternoon shift, she used to put a match in the cold fireplace – after dampening it with a drop of paraffin – so that the house would be warm when we returned from school at the end of the afternoon. One day when I, a seven-year-old girl, decided to light the fire after lighting the stove, my only intention was to ease Mam's workload. Unfortunately I spilt far too much paraffin on it and once I lit a match the flames leapt to my face scorching my hair and eyebrows. I took fright and ran to hide in the understairs cupboard – but Mam found me and I received another clout on top of the burns.

Mam only used to bake on Saturdays, but other women baked bread two or three times a week. So in midweek I used to be sent to Cristin after school to fetch a fresh loaf. On one of those occasions Lisi Cêt gave me a hot buttered crust there before sending me on an errand to Mr Evans the minister. I didn't want him to see my crust, so I left it on the wall before walking up to the house – but when I went to get it, it was covered in ants. I can remember to this day how I cried at that.

No other island in Wales has the same appeal as Ynys Enlli. The age of the monks and saints has long gone – but they haven't left the island either. The last king was a real character who was loved by all. The place is more familiar than ever these days – and through it all it remains a mysterious and spiritual island. This was the 'Rome of Britain'. It stands apart, like a citadel in the waves keeping watch over the tempestuous seas on behalf of the Mainland. This is one of the most magical places I've ever experienced.

Here are some of the old remedies of Enlli:

Common cold – spread goose-grease on brown paper and grate nutmeg over it, then wrap it onto the back and chest.

Sore throat – wrap a dirty sock around the neck and swallow a spoonful of black treacle and yellow sulphur.

Pimples – mix a poultice of soap and sugar and apply it to the pimple. Leave in place until the pus seeps out.

Stomach ache/Indigestion – wormwood; there was a bush in every garden on the island; boil a few leaves in water and drink the bitter infusion.

All kinds of illness and disease – asafoetida; this was guaranteed to heal all illnesses – it tasted so disgusting, every sick person very soon felt better after taking it, just to avoid having to face another dose of the stuff.

On 12th August, 1993, our family experienced another memorable day – we got to return to the island. Since leaving the place in 1938, I hadn't been back once. Fifty-five years is a long time to go without returning. Over the years I'd lived in various areas and foreign countries – we moved to live in Bryn Pydew first, where I attended John Bright secondary school, Llandudno, and then I lived in Leeds, Stokesley, Panama, London and Manchester. Wherever I went, everyone would have heard me speak very nostalgically about the island. But the longer I delayed crossing back over the Sound, the more difficult it was for me. The great bugbear was fear. I was afraid that the memory and the happy, evocative picture I had of my childhood would be shattered into smithereens. I was afraid of losing my childhood dreams. But I needn't have worried!

Mam passed away in her beloved Pwllheli in March 1993, aged 93. I decided I should take her ashes to be scattered either on Mynydd Mawr, Uwchmynydd or on Enlli. I wrote to the island trust asking their permission to do this and received a positive reply stating that I needed to contact Dafydd Thomas. That was no easy task but the arrangements were finally made and the pilgrimage was set to take place on Thursday, 12th August.

That year's summer was pretty poor and we didn't know if the boat would be able to take us until the last minute. My family – all but one of them foreigners from England – stood on Porth Meudwy beach trying to catch a glimpse of Bugail Enlli coming around the headland from Pwllheli. The strangers couldn't understand what all the fuss was about the weather. They're Mainland people with dry feet – they could see nothing but the tranquil waters of Porth Neigwl and they knew that only about three miles of sea separated us from the island. What was the problem? They'd heard me go on about the Enlli boat breaking through enormous waves as it ventured across the Sound – but that must have been a child's imagination. Old Gwenda was letting her memories run riot!

At last, there was Bugail Enlli, with Dafydd Thomas at the helm. The modern boat looked like a whale compared to the little sprat of a boat with an engine in its middle and a steering blade in its stern that used to take us back and forth to the Mainland in the 1930s. Under the old regime we'd be carried in boatmen's arms and transferred from one boat to the other like a sack of potatoes. But today there was a smooth rubber dinghy to take us ashore from the boat. Was this the beginning of the shattering of my dreams?

With the eleven of us – from 65-year-old Taid to 8-month-old Bethan – having boarded the Bugail Enlli, and having listened to Dafydd Thomas' firm and stern instructions, we were ready to start. The boatman warned us that we faced a rough crossing. After another ten minutes' plain sailing, we hit the surge of the Sound's currents and had one of those unique experiences. The waves were like cliffs and yes, it was a rough crossing. But thanks to the boat's power and the boatman's skill, we came through it. My childhood memories hadn't exaggerated the picture after all!

We emerged from the troubled waters of the Sound to the island waters' tranquillity. I was so excited – there's the mountain; there's the lighthouse; and there's the Cafn. Yes, I could step off the boat and stand on a jetty now, rather than be carried through the shallow water. But there's the old boathouse and the lobster pots just like the old days.

The experience almost proved too much for me. Time had stood still. I was a five-year-old girl once again. The memories flowed back. I could see Tŷ Pella and 'Dyno Goch' (nobody said 'Rhedynog Goch') ... and the school ... and Cristin ... and Plas Bach and ... and ...

Here's Plas Lleuddad and the Chapel. My first home. They were always one place in my mind. The two are so close together. There's my old bedroom window in Plas Lleuddad looking out onto the mountain. And the pantry, with the same slate that kept our milk and butter cold fifty years ago. And the Chapel with its massive pulpit where Rev. Edward Evans delivered his lengthy sermons and drawn-out prayers. The harmonium is different – but it stands in exactly the same spot as the one played by my mother all those years ago.

Brother Raphael joined us for the Chapel service – he'd met my mother in Pwllheli. We sang her favourite hymns and I felt the presence of the saints I'd known on Enlli as a child, and all the families in whose bosoms I'd grown up, and my grandfather – Robert Murray – and Tom Nefyn and George M. Ll. Davies. I still have photos of them holding me in their arms, a little child on the island.

My mother's ashes were scattered and it was time to return to the Mainland. Leaving was hard because there was so much to show and to talk about. Childhood memories had been revived and I saw that the place hadn't been spoilt by the big modern world. Thanks to all the volunteers for their care and to workers like Gwydion who carried us from the Cafn to the Chapel in the back of his tractor and Haf who was working for the Trust at the time, for facilitating all the arrangements. It was a never-to-be-forgotten pilgrimage.

Looking around my home today, I feel the presence of my childhood filling the house. Enlli apples, thrift and fuchsias from Enlli grow in the garden. There are two granite stones from Carreg yr Imbyll quarry too. In the hall is a barometer that was in our home on Enlli – the weather controlled everything there. There are pictures of the island on the walls and there's also a grandfather clock, a chest of drawers and a round table that were transported to Enlli and back during our time living there.

The Cristin family with visitors to the island

Tomos the Islandman

This story was told to me by Tomos Jones, an eighty-six year old bachelor. Tomos was born on Ynys Enlli and it was there that he spent most of his life.

He is a small, gracious man with the salt of the sea in his voice.

He now lives on the mainland with his cousin, in a tidy house without a woman near the place.

Jennie Jones, preface to the original Welsh publication, 1964

Enlli's children, 1881

Bardsey Islanders 1934

Early days

I was born on Enlli eighty-six years ago, in a farmhouse called Tŷ Newydd or Tŷ Nesa, the farm nearest to Tŷ Bach.

Enlli was very different at that time from what it is today. At that time there were living there, between adults and children, about a hundred and fifty people, and all of them Welsh. Today, there are only some two Welsh families living there; the remainder are English and a mixture of all countries.

At the time when I was a child there, Enlli practically lived on its own produce. Only tea, sugar, wheat flour, tobacco, matches and beer came from the mainland.

Duwc annwyl! if you could only see the corn that grew there – it was bent almost down to the ground with the weight of the grain.

I was saying that beer came there. Some old woman kept the pub in her kitchen – but the beer would not last long.

As I was saying, my home was a farm, but my father was a farmer and a fisherman, just like all the other farmers.

There were six children in our house, and everyone got a good bellyful of tasty home-made food. We used to kill two pigs every year, salt them, and hang them from the kitchen ceiling. When we wanted fresh meat we would kill a sheep, and with six children and neighbours, it did not last very long. We also used to kill one cow a year, salt it, and store it in a big barrel.

What tasty food we used to get then – 'brwas' (a sort of thin gruel) for breakfast, and 'potes tatws' (potato broth) for lunch – it was no wonder that Enlli people were strong. *Bobl bach!* you should have seen the bacon – about half a yard of thickness on the bone.

We had home-made bread that had been raised with home-made barm. I must tell you how to make the barm. This is what was in it: barley, oats, hops and 'pys llwydion' (grey peas).

It was only in Enlli that these 'pys llwydion' grew. We would get 6 pounds a hobbet for them on the mainland.

We had to clean the barley well from the husk, and the way we would do this was to pour the barley onto a clean floor, and take off our clogs so that we would not soil it. Then take a tool – it was called a 'gluddwr' – a square of iron with teeth in it that was fixed to a long wooden stick like

a broomstick. Then flail it and flail it until all the husk had gone from the barley. (Tomos Jones got up and went through the motions of flailing barley.) Having got the husk away we had to sift the barley three times through a sieve.

Boil a basinful of barley, oats and the peas, and a handful of hops with water in a pot. When it was boiled enough, strain it and pour into a jug. Then put the jug on a warm hearth after putting a handful of sugar and wheat flour in it. Leave it then for a day or two to ferment – and it would be ready for bottling. It was so strong that it sometimes broke the bottles.

If only you could have had bread and butter with Mother's bread! There was bread for you, *bois bach*, bread worth eating. A loaf from a tin nearly as big as the top of the little round table, with a crust as yellow as a sovereign. Sometimes the cat would go on top of the table and walk over the loaf. You could hear the crust crackling under her feet. 'Scram,' cried Mam, flicking it with the dishcloth. Baking day was a busy one for Mam, wanting to make enough bread to fill eight healthy stomachs. She used to have two big wooden tubs, scrubbed clean. Wheat flour in one and barley flour in the other. The

opposite: Old boat by harbour;
above: Old Enlli fishermen 1886

above: Carreg Bach;
right: stone in the graveyard

bread used to be baked in the outside kitchen, a little way from the house. There was a big chimney there and no oven.

On a big round iron griddle, fixed to a tripod, she used to bake the bread. Firstly, she would rub the griddle with bacon, then the lump of dough was put in the middle, and a big iron pan placed over it. She wrapped turf around the pan and then burned bracken under it until it was hot.

She always used to make the last loaf in two colours: a lump of white dough and a lump of barley dough. What good bread and butter it was, with home-made butter on it, and Enlli butter was better than butter from anywhere else!

After baking was finished, I used to have to carry the bread home in a white linen sack on my back. It was heavy too and I struggled with it.

'Don't shake that bread, Tomos,' shouted Mam, 'or you'll be sure to break it.'

'But Mam bach, it is heavy,' I would say.

After getting to the house, Mam would keep it in a wooden tub, scoured clean.

The Strong Man

One of the strongest men on the island was William Huws. Wil Huws he was called. *Duwc annwyl!* there was a giant of a man for you. All the Enlli men were strong at that time, but Wil Huws was the strongest. One of his hands was as big as two ordinary hands. No one dared to cross him because no one could stand up to him. He was a cousin of my father's He has been buried since many years in 'Mynwent y Seintiau' (the Graveyard of the Saints).

Are there any saints buried there, I can hear you asking. Yes, indeed. The island is called 'Ynys y Seintiau' (Island of the Saints). There are twenty thousand buried there, all over the island and their bones in every corner of it. When ploughing the fields, many skulls and bones come to light – brought up by the ploughshare.

Wil Huws was a farmer and a fisherman, the same as every other man there. The Enlli men had big strong boats that were able to withstand any storm. At the time of catching herring, the men used to be away for days. They had a loft above some stable in Porthdinllaen where they used to clean and salt the herring. After a

good catch of herring they used to bring them to the loft, and after cleaning and salting, like I said, would pack them tightly in wooden casks, then send them to various markets. They would send them to Anglesey, Chester, Liverpool and many other places.

One man would usually go with them, and bring the money back to be divided amongst all the fishermen. One time one of the men went with the casks to Liverpool, and after selling all the herring he went on a spree and spent every penny. When he sobered down, he was afraid to come back to Enlli, so he ran away. The boys had a pretty good idea where he had gone – to Traeth Coch in Anglesey. They often went to Traeth Coch to fish and to sell herring.

'Do you know where he is, boys?' said one, scratching his head. 'Upon my life! He's in Traeth Coch.'

'Out with the boat, boys,' said another. And out in the boat they went, setting out for Anglesey.

Having reached Traeth Coch they saw a man in a field near the beach. One of the boys went to him and asked,

'Do you have a stranger working for you?'

'Yes,' said the farmer, 'he's down on the beach somewhere mending nets.'

The boy went back to the boat and told the others what the farmer had said. Out onto the beach they all crowded.

'Yes! upon my life, it's him boys.'

'Just you wait, my lad, 'till I get my hands on you,' said another.

They dragged him into the boat, and back they went to Enlli without further ado.

When we stayed in Porthdinllaen, Wil Huws used to stay behind in the loft to look after things and to cook the food. When the men came in for food, there would be fresh herring, fried, and put out on each plate, and a hunk of bread beside each plate, ready for them. As I said, Wil Huws was a strong man, and he was able to eat as much as two men. Having eaten one side of the herring, we then turned them over, only to be faced with just the bone. Wil Huws had eaten the underside of every herring! But nobody dared complain or raise his voice – Wil Huws was the boss!

Fish were a large part of our food on Enlli. We used to dry herring and 'gwrachod' (wrasse – a rock fish) in the sun, and when they were hard, put them

on a line and hang them from the kitchen ceiling to be used when we wanted. Boiled herring or 'gwrachod' like this, on top of jacket potatoes were delicious. I preferred the 'gwrachod'. Wooden bowls with brass rims were what everyone had for eating.

Duwc annwyl! I must tell you how to make 'Potes Penradell' (Penradell Broth) – dough made with barley flour, salt and water. Put it into boiling water and boil it on the fire until it becomes like pudding. When it had boiled enough, everyone would be waiting with their wooden bowls. The bowls were called 'hodad'. At the bottom of the bowls we would have bacon fat, and then break pieces of the hot dough into it, and beat it well with wooden spoons.

I remember, once, Wil Huws flying into a rage. He had beaten the dough so hard that there was a hole in his 'hodad'. He was so furious that he threw the bowl and its contents into the farthest corner of the kitchen, and out he ran through the door and refused to eat for days. A new bowl was found for him and he came to himself in his own good time.

Plas Bach (centre) and Cristin (on the right)

Clogs and Clothes

Everyone on Enlli wore clogs at that time. Home-made clogs. The soles were made from hazel wood, and the uppers from dried sheepskin. We would put straw inside to keep our feet warm.

Clothes were very scarce there, especially clothes to protect us from the sea water and rain. What we would do about this was to put coal-tar on our trousers and our coats, and let them dry. They were so hard they would practically stand up by themselves, but, believe me, not a single drop of rain or sea water came through.

At that time there were rumours that the Irish intended to attack Enlli and the mainland. Everybody was very frightened. No one dared go out after dark, and everyone locked all doors and windows. Soon after all these rumours about the Irish, the Enlli boys went fishing in Nefyn bay, and, as usual, landed to buy food. Each one was in his 'coal-tar' clothes, with little round hats on their heads, and long dark beards almost hiding their faces, and their skins were dark – coloured by the sea. And I must confess, they looked terrifying.

I can't help laughing, remembering the occasion. The gang all went together to Nefyn. When the Nefyn people saw them, they stared for a second in terror, and then ran home for their lives shouting 'The Irish have come! The Irish have come! Run home for your lives'. And everyone ran in and locked their doors.

The Enlli boys went along to a food shop. When the shopkeeper saw them she flung up her arms and cried, 'Oh dear, Oh dear, what shall I do? Take whatever you like but spare my life'.

'Whatever is wrong with you woman? We are the Enlli boys come to buy bread.'

And the woman said, shaking with laughter, 'Well, *hogiau bach*, thank heaven! I thought you were the Irishmen'.

The boys went from there laden with supplies. And they talked a lot about this incident.

We used to have fearful storms around Enlli, and many ships were wrecked on the rocky shores. One frightfully stormy night, with waves like big mountains pounding the rocks, a ship was wrecked under the lighthouse. All the crew were drowned except one. The sea flung him onto the shore in his night clothes. He climbed up the hill somehow, and dragged himself to

a farmhouse. He knocked on the door. The farmer shouted from his bed, 'Go home you wretched creatures, instead of waking people up at this time of night'.

He thought that it was the Enlli boys making a row. It was nothing for them to be up at two or three in the morning. But the poor fellow went on knocking. At last the farmer got up and opened the door. The poor sailor fell into his arms, almost dead with cold. The farmer's wife got up and made hot food and a warm bed for him.

Next morning all the people on the island went down to the wreck. There was nothing left of it except splinters, but on the shore, thrown up by the waves, was a barrelful of brandy – the best sort. But after smashing the top of the barrel, it dawned upon them ... plenty of drink but not a glass to drink from! They looked at each other glumly for a moment.

'Hey,' said one, 'what are we waiting for?' taking off his clog as he spoke. Everyone took off their clogs to fill them from the full barrel, and went on drinking until the barrel was empty. You can imagine what it was like – everyone reeling drunk, all except two – the minister and the little farm servant of fifteen.

There were tins of meat scattered everywhere over the rocks.

'Look John,' said the minister, 'neither you nor I want the drink, but it is a sin to leave all this food to go to waste on the rocks. We will take it home.' The two went home with as much as they could carry in their arms. And who could blame them? It was best that the men, and not the fish, ate the beef.

At that time there were one or two cottages on Enlli, and in one of them lived a spinster called Siân. She was nearly dead from wanting a husband. The way she tried to win a man was to make a delicious 'pwdin tatws' – potato pudding. And a tasty dish it was indeed! This is how she made potato pudding. Put a slice of bacon at the bottom of a tripod crock, then boil the potatoes, mash them, or as some would say 'stwnsio', and put salt and pepper in them. Then put the mash on top of the bacon, cover the mash with more bacon and bake it on a griddle. When the pudding was ready she used to make a sauce with white flour, salt, a bit of butter and milk, and put it on top of the pudding when we ate it.

To this feast she would invite the island boys. She usually invited the king – an old batchelor – perhaps she expected to be made queen! 'Nol' was the name of every dog belonging to the king and every time Siân saw him coming she would say, 'Old Nol is coming boys'. One day he was not invited and what he and another boy did was climb onto the roof and put a torch of burning gorse down the chimney. *Bobl bach!* what a commotion there was – everybody terrified and pushing for the door. The dresser caught fire and the window was broken, but the fire was put out before much damage was done. Siân never made pudding for them again.

Ghosts and Fairies

'Were there ghosts there, Tomos Jones?'

Duwc annwyl! yes of course, with so many buried there. They were not only buried in the little graveyard, but all over the island, as I mentioned before. *Hiswy bach!* they were everywhere. I'll tell you about one ghost I heard with my own ears. One quiet Sunday evening my mother and father had gone to chapel. My brother, Dei, was reading his Bible by the table, and I lay and dozed on the settle by the fire.

'Tomos,' said my brother suddenly, in a whisper, 'wake up. Do you hear something?'

I sat up immediately and listened.

'Yes,' I said in a whisper, shaking like a leaf, 'someone is groaning in the bedroom.' The groaning went on in an unearthly voice. We were both nearly faint from fear – afraid to move hand or foot. And the voice went on groaning.

Soon we heard the footsteps of our mother and father returning home from chapel. Oh! what a relief to hear them open the door and come into the kitchen. Mam stared at our faces.

'What's wrong boys?' she asked. 'Are you ill? You are as white as chalk.'

'There's a ghost in the bedroom,' we said together.

My father took a candle and went to the bedroom to have a look, but the groaning stopped at that moment. It wasn't a dream, this is perfectly true because I heard it with my own ears. I never tell lies.

Here is another story for you. There was a miserly old spinster living by herself in one of the houses. Her sister and her family lived on a farm nearby. The spinster kept her money in a stocking, a long long stocking. She died, and after her burial, the house was searched from top to bottom for the money, but not a single penny could be found anywhere. Some time after her burial her spirit began to wander from her own house to her sister's house along a path that led from one house to the other. When they were in their beds and everywhere was quiet and locked, she would slip into the house, and upstairs to the bedroom. She would pull the bed-clothes off them, shake the foot of the beds, and pull the brass knobs off – they were iron beds at that time. Then she would slip out and disappear like mist out of their sight. She had hidden the money there, somewhere, and she was trying to tell them where it was. I don't know whether they found the money or not.

There are many caves on Enlli. There was one on the mountain that no one dared go near after nightfall. 'Ogof y Tylwyth Teg' (The Fairies Cave) it was called. One evening a farmer was going home from another farm. It was not very dark, and having gone part of the way, he heard someone walking lightly beside him. He saw no one to begin with, then suddenly he heard a girl's voice singing sweetly– the sweetest-sounding voice he had ever heard. Then he heard bells like silver, ringing somewhere. The bells sounded as if they came from the cave. As he neared the cave he saw the owner of the voice – the most beautiful girl he had ever seen. She was all shining and her hair like gold on her head. Suddenly she disappeared down into the cave. The farmer did not know how he got home that night, so great was his fright.

There is an old lime-kiln on Enlli, idle since a long time. The fishermen usually got up at two or three o'clock in the morning to go out to their nets, but one morning the nets had to stay where they were. When the fishermen were going one night, or rather in the early morning, and getting nearer to the kiln, they saw blue flames rising from it. They were like tongues of fire reaching up to heaven and lighting the whole place. The men stood astonished for a moment, then turned and ran for their lives back to their houses and shut their doors. They never again went near the old kiln after nightfall.

Enlli Pirates

As I said earlier, Wil Huws was the strongest man on the island. One day he was ploughing in a field above the sea. On the rocks below he saw a big white sack full of something. He left the horses in the field and went down to the rocks. He had clogs on his feet. When he got to the sack, he saw that it was a sack of wheat flour. He lifted it and threw it over his shoulder, and carried it up the rocks safely. How much, would you guess, was the weight of that sack of wheat flour? Two hundred and eighty two pounds. There's a feat for any man.

All the Enlli men were strong at that time. Their arms were as stout as the waists of ordinary men. They had thick hair on their arms and chests, and each one had a long thick beard. They never shaved their faces, that was the fashion at that time. When they sold animals – a cow, a horse, a sheep or a pig – on the mainland, they had to be carried over the sea in a big strong boat. You can imagine that the boat had to be strong and solid. They could lift a cow – four men, one at each leg – as easily as lifting a sheep. Then tie it in the boat.

It was a rather dangerous task to bring a horse over on the boat. I remember one horse getting unruly and falling into the sea. It drowned too, and the men almost drowned with it.

At one time, many years ago, there was a mansion on Enlli and it was called Carreg Plas. In this mansion all the inhabitants of Enlli lived. There were two pirates who lived there also, before the lighthouse was built. These pirates were under the influence of the landowner on the mainland, that is Aberdaron and the district around. He was called 'The General' and lived at Bodwrdda. The pirates would attract and plunder ships, and he would take the money and everything that they had stolen. They would light torches to draw the ships onto the rocks, and then kill the crew and steal the cargo.

A ship was once drawn onto the rocks and all the crew were killed, but the captain managed to escape and swam to Aberdaron. The sea was certainly narrower at that time. The captain found the parsonage, knocked on the door, it was opened for him and he fell in nearly dead. The priest looked after him and gave him lodging and every welcome. He was there for some time recovering, and he told the whole story to the priest. One day, who

came to the parsonage but 'The General', full of boasting, but he turned pale when the priest told him who the stranger was and what had happened. He realised that he would no longer be able to get any more plunder from Enlli. The authorities came and caught the pirates. They were hung as far as I know, and 'The General' was lucky that he did not get the same treatment.

Remember that this was before my time, but I have heard the story often from the old people. Life was very interesting on Enlli in my time, going to each other's houses, listening to and telling old stories and tales.

Enlli Place Names

Here are the names of some of the points and caves that are around Enlli:

Y Cafn	Trwyn Fynwent
Trwyn Rhonllwyn	Trwyn Maen Saer
Trwyn Melynion	Trwyn Du
Trwyn Chwith	Y Meindy Pendiban
Sgers	Trwyn y Llanciau
Trwyn Dihiryn	Trwyn Main
Maen Iau	Maen Melyn
Trwyn Penrhyn Gogor	Trwyn Golchach
Ogof Diben	Ogof Stwffwl Glas
Borth Fadog	Porth Sol'ach
Higol Pwll Du	Ogo'r Gŵr
Ogof Hir	Twll Dan Ddaear
Ogof Wilbod	Ogo'r Nant
Twll Halen	Ogof Morgan
Ogof y Gaseg	

Here are the stories of some of the points and caves:

Y Cafn: This is the entrance to Enlli. It is to this place that the boats come. The water is too shallow for steamers to come in; people and goods have to be brought ashore in boats.

Trwyn Fynwent: A ship was wrecked here. Her captain was Tomos Williams. He was my great-grandfather. His daughter was with him in the ship and she was drowned and all the crew.

Trwyn Rhonllwyn: A ship went down here too. Her captain was James Coesau Preniau (*James Wooden Legs*). His legs had been frozen while he was sailing in cold countries. He was very wealthy but I do not know who got his money.

Trwyn Maen Saer: A ship went on this point too – but was able to get away from there. I am sure there are lots of birds on it, because we used to hear the cock crowing loudly in the early morning.

Trwyn Chwith: Here is where we used to catch plenty of crabs and lobsters. Their holes were everywhere but one had to use his left hand to pull them out. And that is why the point got its name.

Y Fuddai: Here is another good place for crabs. It got its name from being in the form of a churn.

Sgers or Ogof Ladron: Here was the place where the pirates used to come in to Enlli.

Trwyn y Llanciau: There was a great disaster at this point. Three brothers drowned here together. They were the sons of Tyddyn Mawr, Penllech. The three brothers lived with their sister in Tyddyn Mawr. This was the time that Howel Harris had to hide himself in a cupboard there because his enemies were after him.

One fine day the three brothers went to fish for mackerel to Enlli. When they were near this point a big storm arose suddenly. The boat was thrown against the rock and the three were drowned.

Borth Fadog: Named by some boy from Porthmadog. He came to Enlli with a small boat and landed safely at this point. It was here that Wil Huws found his sack of wheat flour.

Trwyn Dihiryn: Outside this point there is a large stone called Ona's stone. A ship carrying coal was broken into fragments against this point and the island people had enough coal to last for months. Everyone went down the rocks and filled their sacks. It is said that some coal still appears there.

Porth Sol'ach: This is where the fishermen kept their crab creels and boats.

Higol Pwll Du: This is the place where the ship *Leah of Scotland* went down. All the crew went into the boats and rowed towards land. The captain stayed in the boat until the end, but he was forced to leave her when she had sunk practically out of sight. The crew wanted him to come with them. 'No,' he said, 'you go in the boats; I will come ashore somehow.' He grasped his clothes-bag, and put an oar under each arm, and let himself go into the sea. The oars kept him up fairly well. The sea nearly overcame him but he managed to drag himself onto the shore somehow. One boat turned upside down, but the crew were able to hold onto it until they were rescued by the Enlli boat. Amongst the crew there was an Irishman and when he saw the Enlli boat coming towards them, he shouted 'Boat-a-hoy, Boat-a-hoy'. Everyone was saved and landed in Porth Sol'ach. One of the Enlli boats nearly turned over as well, because it was a frightful storm. The Enlli king was in one of the boats and he was horribly frightened; he thought he would never reach the shore safely. When the crew got to the shore the Irishman was very alarmed. He saw the walls of Cristin and thought we were going to put them in prison.

Ogo'r Gŵr: It was in this cave that the poor old mare fell and drowned. The mare's name was Nel, and Dic was the name of the old man who owned her. The reason for the name of this cave is that a husband and wife were having frequent rows, and to find peace, the husband would come to this cave to hide until his wife's temper had cooled down.

Ogo'r Twrch Fawr: There is a strange story about this cave. There was some lad in trouble over one of the girls of the island, and he treated her badly. A policeman was sent for to deal with him, but the lad escaped and hid in this cave. When they came to search for him he was nowhere to be seen. In the far end of the cave there was a large hole, and he had been able to climb up into it and hide.

'There's no-one here,' said the policeman. 'Only a crow or a seagull could hide in this place.' And back he went to the mainland. His family carried food to the lad, and he was there for a long time.

Somehow he escaped from there without anyone seeing him. He went to Liverpool, but he was caught there, and said to those who caught him, 'Well indeed, its not worth me hiding any more, the little feet have caught the big feet'.

Before his time was up he became a ship's captain and went to live in Australia, and married a girl from there.

Trwyn Main: This is the place for 'gwrachod' (wrasse). We used to catch hundreds of them there every year.

Ogof Tan y Ddaear: This is the longest cave on the island. It goes a long way under the ground. It is said to reach under the hearth of one of the farmhouses, and that the pirates used to carry their loot there.

Maen Iau: Many ships were wrecked on this rock. A large anchor was found here, and quite a bit of trouble was had dragging it away.

Twll Tan y Ddaear: This is a kind of a small cave. There is a hole in the top of it like a chimney, and when the tide comes in white foam comes up through it like smoke.

Maen Melyn: Evan Nant had a ship called *Pesant*. She had one mast, and a white sail on it. It used to carry earthenware pots and coal to the island. It would stay outside Maen Melyn, and then the boats would go out to carry the goods. Every time it came within sight of the island one old boy used to say, 'O'r brenin!' (literally 'Oh! the king') 'a one mast ship for me, boys! *The Pheasant* is the one, boys!'

Every time it came we used to get plenty of hard cakes. 'Sgledan galed' we used to call them. This was the sailor's food at that time, and you needed sharp teeth to eat them. Siân Tŷ Pella used to make a hole in them and put a thread through and hang them from the kitchen ceiling, just like the herring.

Ogo'r Nant: A ship was wrecked here too. It was a ship from Ireland called the 'Prince of Wales'. It was said that it was brought here purposely to be wrecked. It was an old ship and dangerous to sail in her.

Twll Halen: Salt was scarce and dear at this time, and it was taxed. Enlli boats used to go all the way across the sea to Ireland to fetch salt, and bring it back to the shore at Twll Halen. Then it was hidden in a hole high up in the hill, out of reach of the sea, covered against the rain. When we were unable to get salt, we used to boil sea-water in a bucket over the fire, let it boil dry and then collect the salt from the bottom of the bucket. They say that the stones that were used to build the tower or belfry that is on the island are from Twll Halen.

Ogof Morgan: It is said that the famous Captain Morgan, the pirate, landed in this place and hid some of his treasure.

Springs on the Island

There are no streams on Enlli, only trickles from the springs. There are plenty of springs there and these are some of them:

Ffynnon Corn: This is one of the most important and it is in a rock. There is a strong wall built around it. The water in this spring never dries up, and is cold and pure. It was the monks that excavated this spring, and built the wall that is around it.

Ffynnon Uchaf: The water in this spring is not as pure as that in Ffynnon Corn. The water in it used to dry up in hot weather; it is extremely hot on Enlli in the summer; everyone's skin is dark from the sun and sea.

Ffynnon Barfau: There is a story about this one too. I heard my grandfather say that it was at this spring that the monks used to shave their heads. I should say that there are two Ffynnon Barfau on Enlli. They are in the form of a skull. There are holes in the rock above the spring, like shelves, and in these holes the monks used to keep their razors.

Well I must mention the farms, their names and their stories. Here are their names:

Tŷ Bach and Tŷ Nesa	Tŷ Newydd
Nant	Carreg Bach
Cristin Uchaf	Cristin Isaf
Tŷ Pella	Rhedynog Goch
Tŷ Capel	Hen Dŷ

There is only one road on Enlli, reaching from Y Cafn to the far end of the island, that is, from the south of the island to the place where the Abbey is. The farms

are spread out along both sides of the road, from one end to the other, in the shadow of the mountain. The farmhouses are big and strong, built with stone and with big strong walls around them. The houses and the walls are made with stone from Anglesey, and the paving with round stones (cobbles) from the shore at Aberdaron, all carried across in boats.

Life was very agreeable on Enlli when I was a boy – going to each others houses in the evening and telling old stories and tales. There was a lake on the mountain where we, as children, used to go and play little boats, and our mothers said every time, 'Don't go near the precipice', thinking of the steep drop from the mountain to the sea.

All the farms kept a pig, or pigs. Morris y Nant used to ring everyone's pigs. It was quite a cruel method too. A hole was punched first in the pig's nose with a sacking needle. Then a peg was put into it.

I remember a lot of fun once with Morris ringing the pigs on one farm. One big pig escaped from him, and everyone ran after it. Old Morris lost his clog while running.

'Well, there, I've had it,' he said, scratching his head. 'Hey you devil, come back. This is no bargain for Morris,' he said, whatever that meant. They all used to swear there until they were appointed deacons. In Siân's house, who was an aunt of mine, everyone used to shear their sheep. What a place there was, and Siân with a cup of tea for everyone.

I remember the time when we used to catch oysters on Enlli. Very hard work it was too. One had to scratch underneath the water for them, with something rather like a harrow. Iron teeth that combed the bottom under the water. I did this many times. I don't think there are any oysters there now.

There was another good fish there – the red pouch. One had to catch this one very carefully because all around its mouth was very fragile and inclined to break with the hook. These were caught at night, and girls usually would go out in light rowing boats when the sea was calm. The light from Cristin would lead them to the right place. They used to catch a great many sometimes, and you can imagine the feast we had the next day.

Burials and Keepers

As you know, Ynys Enlli belongs to the Wynne, or Newborough, family. As far as I know this is the only place where one does not have to pay rates on the houses. As well as the twenty thousand saints buried there, there is also a family grave belonging to the Wynnes. It is an underground chamber with steps going down into it. The coffins of the dead have been placed on shelves. This tomb is near the Abbey. When the late Lord Newborough died, he was buried first in the graveyard at Boduan Church. A year later he was dug up and brought to the burial place on Enlli.

I remember a very funny occasion. You remember me talking about John, the young farmhand, with the tins of meat? Well, here is another story about him. He wanted to see Lord Newborough's coffin. He took a candle, lit it and went down the steps into the vault. When he was beside the coffin, something made an unearthly noise above his head. His hair stood straight upon his head and in his terror, the candle fell from his hand, leaving him in darkness. He ran out for his life and up the stairs. What was there but a meddlesome old sheep, with its head down, bleating 'me-e' all over the place.

But John was really terrified; it was enough to scare him too.

Enlli lighthouse is at the southerly point of the island. There are three men looking after it. One is on duty for four hours, one is free for four hours, and one is in bed for four hours. There is a wall around the lighthouse and a wide gate leading to the surrounding yard.

I must tell you a funny story about one of the watchmen. It was a quiet foggy night, and he was sitting with his back to the window, reading. Suddenly he heard a strange sound at the window behind him, a sound that he had never heard the like of before. He turned to look. He got to his feet in alarm. What was that grey-black creature that was moving backwards and forwards across the window pane. It was like an enormous slug a foot long. At last, he plucked up courage to go nearer the window to see what this creature was. What was behind, attached to the slug, but a big black bullock! The 'slug' was the bullock's tongue licking salt from the window pane. The watchman had been very frightened but he laughed when he saw what the bogey was. Someone had left the gate open and the bullock had wandered inside.

A Good Catch

In one of the houses on Enlli there is furniture that belongs to Lord Newborough. It is to remain there as long as he lives, or really as long as they last. Today the house has been given to 'Ieuenctid y Groes' (a youth group) and they go there for weeks in the summer.

I am afraid that I have not told the stories of half the ships that were wrecked on Enlli. One boat was lost returning home to Enlli. It went down at Trwyn Dwm. All the crew except one were drunk. The plug of the boat came out and the one sober man put an ounce of tobacco in the hole, but to no purpose. They all drowned except him. He was able, the sober one, to swim to the shore.

Enlli is bare of trees; there is only one tree there – an ash-tree growing behind Cristin. There is plenty of scrub growing there, osiers and twigs as well as brambles. There were plenty of blackberries there, and Mam used to make good tarts on the griddle with them. The same flowers grow there as on the mainland. As I was saying, there are plenty of twigs there and on winter evenings everyone would be busy making creels with these sticks. They were round baskets with a hole in the top leading down into the basket like a little passage. Once a crab or lobster went in, it could not come out again. Having made a good catch of crabs and lobsters we used to keep the pots in the water not far from the shore, with weights to keep them there. *Duwc annwyl!* I remember one evening when we had a good catch and they were ready to be carried to the mainland to be sold the next day. But when we went to look for them, there was nothing there – they and the pots had gone. A French ship had come there during the night and stolen every one! The Enlli people could speak only a very little English when I was there as a boy. William Williams lived in Cristin, and he could not speak much English either. One day one of the men from the lighthouse, an Englishman, was having a chat with him.

'Can you tell me anything about this chapel, William Williams?' asked the Englishman.

'Oh yes,' said William Williams. 'Tad fy nhad, grandfather to me cododd this chapel, and rŵan, there is gwellt glas wedi tyfu round the chapel you know.' But they understood each other very well.

Enlli Candles

In the year 1914, on a fine quiet morning, with a slight mist on the sea – it was Easter morning I remember well – a big sailing ship went aground in Tŷ Mawr bay, on the mainland. She was on the way from Liverpool to Australia and carried a mixed cargo – spirits (rum and whiskey), all kinds of crockery, pianos, candles, matches and all sorts of things. It stayed there, undamaged, for a few days, but they failed to refloat it, and it was wrecked, and its cargo was scattered everywhere along the rocks. What drinking there was afterwards! There was cotton in it too, and this is what I was about to say: we saw a big bale sailing ashore at Enlli. Sitting on top of it was a large rat, which had made a hole like a nest in it, where it was perfectly safe and dry. But it was killed by one of the boys. There were once on Enlli hundreds of rats in the rocks by the sea, but a great storm came one night and drowned them all.

As you know, one side of the mountain falls straight to the rocks and the sea. It is a very dangerous place to go near the precipice. I remember a great loss that one farmer had. He had three horses grazing on the mountain; somehow the three ran towards the precipice and fell into the sea and drowned. Everyone sympathized with him very much. A committee was formed, and it was decided that a collection of money would be made for him. The minister undertook to go and collect on the mainland, and he got a good sum of money for the poor farmer.

One of the lighthouse men fell down this precipice too; he fell down onto the rocks. He was hunting and went too near the precipice. He was alive when they got him. He was taken to Holyhead but he died three days later.

The people of Enlli used to make rush candles and tallow candles. To make rush candles – there were plenty of rushes growing there – one had to peel off all the green skin except one thin line to hold the white pith that appeared. As a rule it was the women who used to do this; their hands were lighter. The pith was dipped in fat or oil. A bottle, or something similar, would be used as a candlestick. Some

people had something like pincers for this purpose. This is how they made tallow candles. Thin linen threads were tied to poker-like iron. They would tie about six candles. Then they would dip them into boiling fat or tallow which was in a bucket above the fire. Dip them in, then lift them out for a bit for the tallow to boil, and then dip them again and again until the candles were thick enough. They were dirty old candles too, and one used to have to cut the top of the wick often with scissors.

Skates

Duwc annwyl! I haven't told you about the skates, enormous big fish. I remember us catching one nine feet from one 'wing' to the other – big enough to capsize the boat if we were not careful. With a line, a 'long line' we used to catch them. Big strong hooks were fixed on it and it was cast into the sea, close to the shore. Underneath the wing fin of the skate there are scales with hooks in them, and these would get tangled in the line – in addition to the hook that went in his mouth. They have big mouths and strong teeth. One had to turn the skate flat on its back before one was able to catch it, or it would push the head hard down. I can remember falling flat on my back under one. Having turned over the skate we had to push our fingers into two holes at the side of its head, and then quickly bite hard on its nose while another fisherman would stab it.

We only ate the fins, and very good food it was too, tasty white meat. I remember one skate breaking a boat hook right off with his teeth; I don't know whether he swallowed it or not – we saw nothing more of him after. It was a hook belonging to old king Nol too, and we threw the shaft into the sea.

'Have any of you seen my hook, boys? I can't find it anywhere,' he inquired. But he didn't get an answer from us.

I remember three kings in Enlli. The first was John Williams, Cristin. He was crowned with great pomp and honour. A warship came there with important men in it. All the people of Enlli gathered together, and John Williams knelt down in the centre. Then the chief held a sword over his head, saying, 'John Williams, I crown you King of Enlli, to govern justly and righteously'. Then a beautiful yellow crown was placed on his head – I don't know whether it was gold or not. The crowning took place above Ogof Gunan. Then he was given a big strong boat from the Trinity company, and he would be responsible for goods for the lighthouse. He had to go to Holyhead often. His end was through drowning in an accident, falling from his boat when it was not far from the shore. This was a great calamity for his wife. The day previously their only son had been born.

John Williams was the son's name too, and when he was grown up he took the place of his father to become king. There is not much news worth telling about him. He was called to the mainland, and that is where he died. He had £3,000 on leaving Enlli but he died in poverty and no one knows where the money went.

Enlli had no king now. One day Love (Love Prichard) said, 'I am going to be king now'. He invited everyone to come to the level green place that is above Y Cafn, and he announced himself as king. He also died on the mainland. The crown is in the mansion of Boduan today.

The Chapel

There is a chapel and a school on Enlli, both closed by today. When I was a boy there, everyone went to chapel on Sunday. There was always a minister there. William Jones was the minister when I was there. He was a pious little man. He had a big family – nine children – and some of them live on the mainland today. There is a handsome pulpit in the chapel, carved in a valuable wood, a present from Egypt, I think. They had to build the chapel around the pulpit.

I remember several ministers on Enlli.

Here is one funny story for you. When there were special meetings in the chapels on the mainland, everyone went to them in boats, from Enlli, in their best clothes. When the Enlli boats arrived in Aberdaron, they were too big to come completely to the shore, and the sailors had to carry the passengers to the shore. Once, while carrying the minister's wife ashore, and, *duwc annwyl*, she was a grand one too – the sailor stumbled and down into the water they both fell! They were as wet as fishes when they reached the shore. The minister's wife was so wild with fury that she would almost have beaten the poor sailor, who was as wet as herself. Someone stepped into the breach, as they say and she was given dry clothes in one of the houses, until her own clothes were dry.

People think that there are no snakes on Enlli, but this is not altogether true. In one half of the island there are snakes, but not a single one in the other half, and this is the half where the monastery is. Some say that earth carried over from Ireland is in this part.

I often heard my father tell of a big Eisteddfod that was held on Enlli once, and about all the fun and turmoil that was there. The sea around the island was dotted with ships, having come from Caernarfon and everywhere. Directing the Eisteddfod was Mynyddog, Hwfa Môn and several other famous people. In addition to the Eisteddfod there were all kinds of other things. It was like a big fair there – tables of 'India Rock' and all kinds of other worthless wonders. But the strangest thing that once came there was a hurdy-gurdy, played by two Italians. They had two little monkeys dressed in red coats, and red caps on their heads, and they would hand fortunes to people for a penny. There were many spinsters on Enlli at this time who had never been away from the island, nor seen an Italian, nor a monkey, ever before. There were two sisters with faces almost as dark as the Italians – because soap was very scarce there then. When they saw the yellow men, one said to the other, 'Tell me, did you ever see such ugly men before?'

'Don't mention that,' said her sister, 'did you ever see anything as ugly as their children?' She was thinking of the two little monkeys!

Well, indeed, I think I have told you all my tale. Huh! you will be asking me why I never got married. *Duwc annwyl!* my dear girl, I am still searching for a wife!

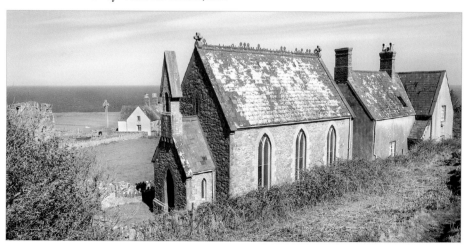

About Jean Napier

Born in the East End of London, Jean has lived in the Snowdonia National Park since 1991 and the magnificent variety of scenery and the coast within Eryri is the main inspiration for her work. Man's archaeological and industrial influences on the landscape are a recurring theme in her exhibitions, films and books.

Her primary motivation is to promote photography as an artform; using the camera as a creative tool to explore and interpret, not just a means for recording moments in time.

Her work has been widely exhibited in the UK, as well as in the USA and Australia. She runs photography workshops for people of all ages and abilities throughout the UK including a long-standing series of Landscape Photography Workshops at the Snowdonia National Park's Study Centre at Plas Tan y Bwlch, Maentwrog.

She holds a Masters with Distinction in Fine Art (Photographic & Film Studies) and is an Associate of the Royal Photographic Society.

Jean is also a Qualified Yoga Teacher and Stress Counsellor.

www.jean-napier.com

Acknowledgements

Creating this book has been a real delight; the sharing of many chats with the people of Enlli over tea and biscuits. The in depth discussions with my dear friend Carole Shearman and Christine Evans were especially thought-provoking, as was hearing Christine's vast knowledge of Enlli's history.

I have listed below people I would like to thank for all their help and contributions in putting this small book together.

Ken Bridges
Mark Carter
Myrddin ap Dafydd
Billy Dykes
Carwyn Evans
Christine and Ernest Evans
Colin Evans
Raymond Grindle
Gwenllian Jones
Heather Hayward
Annie and Phil Horsley
Ephraim Perfect
Steve and Jo Porter
Gareth and Meriel Roberts
Siân Stacey and Mabon
Steve, Emma and Connor Stansfield
Carole Shearman

Also Alison Davies for creating the beautiful map of Bardsey.

Not forgetting a special mention of the person who has, yet again, spent hours editing my stumbling words into something suitable for publishing:
– Kate Coldham!

Enlli Headmistress's Daughter – The reminiscences of Gwenda Watson

A chapter from *Pobol Enlli*, 20th century autobiographies of Bardsey island people; translated from Welsh by Sue Walton; published 2015.

Tomos the Islandman

by Jennie Jones
First published as *Tomos o Enlli* in 1964; translated from Welsh by Gwen Robson.

Further Reading / Contacts

Between Sea & Sky
Images of Bardsey
Peter Hope Jones & R S Thomas

Bardsey
Christine Evans & Wolf Marloh

I Know an Island R M Lockley

Tomos o Enlli
Tomos The Islandman
(Bilingual Welsh-English) Jennie Jones
Illustrations by Kim Atkinson

Enlli Ddoe A Heddiw
Bardsey Past & Present
(Bilingual Welsh-English)
Peter Hope Jones

Pobol Enlli
Myrddin ap Dafydd
(Welsh)

Enlli, tu hwnt i'r Swnt
Marian Delyth
(Welsh with photographs)

Ynys Enlli H D Williams
(Welsh)

Contacts for Booking Accommodation and Boat Trips on Bardsey:

Bardsey Island Trust
www.bardsey.org
Bardsey Bird and Field Observatory
www.bbfo.or.uk
Bardsey Boat Trips
www.bardseyboattrips.com

The puplishers wish to acknowledge their gratitude for these images:
John Thomas Collection – National Library of Wales
© **Steve Stansfield** *p. 45 x2*
© **Marian Delyth** *p. 52*

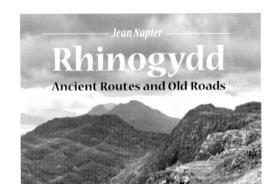

Jean Napier

Rhinogydd
Ancient Routes and Old Roads

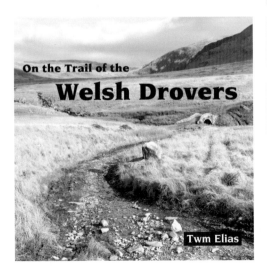

On the Trail of the
Welsh Drovers

Twm Elias

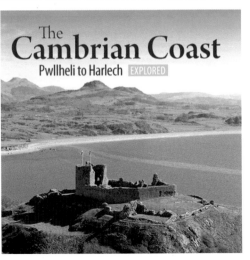

The
Cambrian Coast
Pwllheli to Harlech EXPLORED

arge of the mortgage, you need to check that the person named
t as making the payment was the person who then owned the
roperty. If he was, the receipt does discharge the mortgage. If
he receipt does not discharge the mortgage; instead it trans-
p of it from the original lender to the person named as making
This is why care is needed in dating the receipt. Suppose that
ackacre, which is mortgaged to the Northlands Bank. She con-
Blackacre free of the mortgage to Catherine, and the sale is
6 March. Part of the purchase price is used to pay off the
ink endorses the receipt on the mortgage deed and names
g made the payment. It is correct to name Bella rather than
he arrangement in the agreement for sale was that the mort-
e discharged by the seller before Blackacre was conveyed to
e receipt must be dated either 6 March or earlier. If it is dated
is not at that date the owner of the land. The receipt trans-
ige from Northlands Bank to Bella. Although in theory Bella
ken a transfer of the mortgage, probably nothing would have
lear the title. If the conveyance to Catherine said that Bella's
rom incumbrances', Bella would be estopped from asserting
see *Cumberland Court (Brighton) Ltd v. Taylor* [1964]).
l not operate as a transfer if the receipt provides otherwise.
ociety will use the form of receipt allowed by the Building
986. This merely acknowledges receipt of the money. It does
erson making the payment, and cannot operate as a transfer.

gage As has already been mentioned, banks and building
mes refuse to execute the receipt in advance of completion.
s solicitor may accept undertakings as discussed in section

e

part of the land in an unregistered title, the lender may
from the mortgage.

ching

n section 7.4(c). A purchaser will not see a receipt on the
nortgagee who is selling, nor on any subsequent mortgage.
tle, the power of sale is implied into any mortgage by deed
of Property Act 1925).

hing a Title by Adverse Possession

blish that he has a good title by proving adverse posses-
must establish not only that he (and possibly his prede-
n in possession of the land, but also that the possession

One is where the transaction between the attorney and the person dealing
with the attorney is completed within 12 months of the date of the power.
The other is where the person dealing with the attorney makes a statutory
declaration before or within 3 months of the subsequent purchase that he
did not at the material time know of the revocation of the power (s.5(4) of
the 1971 Act).

Example An example might help. Vimto has agreed to sell Blackacre to
Pedro. Vimto gives his solicitor, Alexis, a power of attorney to execute a
deed of conveyance and to complete the transaction.

Alexis executes the deed and completes on 1 October 1989. The conveyance to Pedro will be valid unless Pedro knew that Vimto had by then
revoked the power, or become bankrupt or insane or had died.

Pedro later sells to Quentin. Quentin can conclusively presume that
Pedro did not know of any revocation, provided that the power came into
effect in the 12 months preceding 1 October 1989. Quentin will *not* raise
any requisition as to Pedro's knowledge. He will simply compare the date
of the power and the date of the conveyance. If the 1989 conveyance was
executed by Alexis more than 12 months after the date of the power, Pedro
will be asked to make the statutory declaration.

Again, the requisition to Pedro is not 'did you know of any revocation?'
but is 'supply the statutory declaration'. Pedro may be lying in his teeth
when he makes the declaration, but the title he gives to Quentin will be
sound.

(g) A Power of Attorney Delegating a Trust

Section 25 of the Trustee Act 1925 (as amended by s.9 of the Powers of
Attorney Act 1971) provides that a trustee (including a trustee for sale) can
by a power of attorney delegate the exercise of his trust and powers for up
to 12 months.

The power of attorney must be executed in the presence of a witness, and
notice of it must be given to the other trustees.

A trustee cannot delegate to his fellow-trustee if there are only the two
of them. One of three or more trustees can delegate to a fellow-trustee. Nor
can a trustee use the statutory form of power of attorney under s.10 of the
Powers of Attorney Act 1971 even if the trustee is also a beneficial owner
(see *Walia* v. *Michael Naughton Ltd* [1985]).*

So if A and B own the legal estate on trust for sale for themselves as beneficial co-owners:

 (i) A cannot appoint B as his attorney;
(ii) If A appoints X as his attorney, the power must comply with the Trustee
     Act 1925, otherwise it will be void.

N.B. At the time of writing, the Trustee Delegation Bill is before Parlia-
ment. If enacted, it will, among other things, provide a statutory form of
power of attorney to be used by a trustee. It will also distinguish between

trustees who hold in trust for others, and who will have to comply with restrictions when delegating the trust, and trustees who hold in trust only for themselves, who will not.

(h)   The Application of these Rules to Registered Title

Although this chapter is on the subject of unregistered title, this is a convenient time to consider the application of these rules to a registered title.

A transfer by the attorney of the registered proprietor will again be valid, provided that the person dealing with the attorney did not know of the revocation of the power. The transferee will then apply for registration of the transfer. It is now the *Registrar* who is concerned as to whether the transferee did or did not know of any revocation. Therefore, if the transfer did not take place within 12 months of the power, the Registrar will require the transferee to provide the Registrar with a statutory declaration that at the time of completion the transferee did not know of the revocation of the power. If the power is a security power, the transferee must declare that he did not know that the power was not in fact given by way of security, and did not know of any revocation with the attorney's consent. The power, or a certified copy of it, must also be filed (Rule 82 of Land Registration Rules 1925, as substituted by Land Registration (Powers of Attorney) Rules 1986).

This declaration must also accompany an application for first registration.

(i)   The Enduring Powers of Attorney Act 1985

The purpose of this Act is to enable a principal to appoint an attorney whose authority will not be revoked by the principal becoming mentally incapable. The power must be created while the principal is of sound mind, and so long as he remains mentally capable the power operates as an ordinary power of attorney. It may confer a general authority on the attorney, or empower him to do only those things specified by the power. An enduring power is effective from the moment it is executed, so the attorney is empowered to dispose of the principal's property even while the principal is still mentally capable. It can be made clear in the power that it is only to become effective when the principal becomes mentally incapable if this precaution is felt to be necessary. The power must be in a prescribed form (see the Enduring Powers of Attorney (Prescribed Form) Regulations 1990 SI No. 1376). It must, for example, contain an express statement that the principal intends the power to continue notwithstanding any later mental incapacity, and the principal must confirm that he has read this statement. The power must be executed by the principal and the attorney in the presence of a witness.

When the donor becomes mentally incapable, the attorney is under a statutory duty to register the power with the court, and his authority to deal with the principal's property is suspended until the power is registered. Once the power is registered, the principal cannot revoke the power unless has extinguished the title of the true owner (see Re *Atkinson and Horsell's* contract [1912]). This means that the title of the true owner must be deduced, and the extinction of that title must be proved. It is not sufficient merely to prove possession, for however long, as the effect of the possession cannot be gauged unless it is known whom the possession has been against. If, for example, the land is subject to a ninety-nine year lease, possession for over twelve years may have extinguished the tenant's title to the lease, but will not have extinguished the landlord's title to the reversion, as time does not start running against a landlord until his right to possession arises at the end of the lease.

It will often be impossible for a seller to prove the title of the true owner, and a special condition in the contract will be required, limiting the evidence of title to, for example, a declaration by the seller that he has been in undisputed possession of the land for however long it is. If the condition specifies what evidence of title will be supplied, the seller will be in breach of contract unless he supplies that very evidence. In the case of *George Wimpey & Co Ltd* v. *Sohn* [1987] the sellers promised in the contract to give the purchaser a statutory declaration that they had been in undisputed possession of the land for twenty years. However, the sellers could not make the declaration, as their possession had been disputed. The sellers then claimed that they had been in adverse possession for twelve years, and had thereby extinguished the title of the true owners. The purchaser could refuse this title, as he had not been given the evidence of title he had been promised.

9.8 Minors

It is not usual to raise a requisition as to the age of a purchaser under a past title deed. This is because there is a *presumption* that a party to a deed is adult. If, however, it becomes known that land was conveyed to a minor then the following principles apply:

(a) A minor cannot hold a legal estate, either beneficially or as a trustee.
(b) If land is conveyed to a minor for the minor beneficially, he does obtain the equitable interest. The legal estate remains with the transferor. The conveyance operates as a declaration that the land is held in trust for the minor (Trusts of Land and Appointment of Trustees Act 1996 Schedule 1 para. 1(1)).
(c) If the legal estate is conveyed to an adult and a minor as beneficial co-owners, the legal estate will vest only in the adult. He will hold it in trust for himself and the minor (*Ibid* Schedule 1 para. 1(2)). He can overreach the minor's interest by appointing a second trustee (see Chapter 11).

9.9 A Voluntary Conveyance

A deed of gift or a conveyance at an undervalue can be set aside under the Insolvency Act 1986. A donee may therefore have a voidable title. Under s.339 of the Insolvency Act 1986, a trustee in bankruptcy can apply to have the deed set aside if made within the two years prior to the presentation of the petition in bankruptcy. If the two years are past, but five years have not yet passed, it can be set aside providing the donor was insolvent at the time of the gift, or became insolvent as a result. It will be up to the trustee to prove the insolvency, unless the donee was an associate of the donor (as defined by s.435 of the Act) e.g. a spouse, in which case there is a rebuttable presumption of insolvency.

These provisions of the Insolvency Act have the potential to affect a third party who acquires the gifted property from the donee. If the donor were to go bankrupt within the relevant period, the property, or its value, could be clawed back from the third party by the donor's trustee in bankruptcy.

However by virtue of s.342 (2A) of the Insolvency Act 1986 (inserted by s.2 Insolvency (No. 2) Act 1994), a purchaser for value in good faith from the donee is safe from any such clawback. The Act defines a purchaser in good faith as a purchaser who either has no notice that the transaction was a gift or was at an undervalue, or has no notice of the donor's insolvency.

If a registered title is transferred, the register of title does not disclose whether the transfer was a by sale or gift. A later purchaser from the donee will therefore be in good faith, as he will have no notice that the registered proprietor acquired by way of gift. If an unregistered title has been given away, and this has not led to first registration of title (see 3.2), a purchaser will know he is buying from a donee. He will only be in good faith if he has no notice of the donor's insolvency. Such a purchaser should, therefore, make a bankruptcy search at the Land Charges Registry against the donor's name. The search should begin with the year of the gift and end with the year in which the purchaser intends to complete his purchase.

If a gift of land does lead to first registration, the Registrar will put a note on the register of the title, warning of the possibility of clawback by the donor's trustee in bankruptcy. Again, a purchaser should make a land charges search against the name of the donor.

9.10   Bankruptcy of the Seller

Bankruptcy proceedings are started by the presentation of the petition in bankruptcy, usually by a creditor. If the court is satisfied that the debtor is unable to pay his debts it will make a bankruptcy order. This has the effect of vesting the bankrupt's property in the official receiver. This would be followed by an appointment of a trustee in bankruptcy. When the trustee is appointed, the bankrupt's estate vests in the trustee and it is his duty to collect and distribute the bankrupt's assets (ss. 305 and 306 of the Insolvency Act 1986).

As soon as the court makes the bankruptcy order, any disposition by the bankrupt made between the time of the presentation of the petition and the time when his assets vest in his trustee in bankruptcy is void (s.284 of the Insolvency Act 1986). Therefore, a conveyance made by the bankrupt in this period would be void. So a purchaser who is alerted as to the presentation of the petition will not accept a conveyance from the seller, but will await the appointment of the trustee and take a conveyance from him. This may mean delay, and a purchaser who is unwilling to accept the delay could terminate the contract by serving a completion notice (see Chapter 19). If the purchaser suffers loss through the delay he will have to prove in the bankruptcy. If he ends the contract, he will also have to recover his deposit. There will be no difficulty if this is held by a stakeholder. If it had been paid to the seller's agent the purchaser would have to prove in the bankruptcy, unless he can rely on his lien (see section 5.9(a)).

It is possible for the trustee in bankruptcy to disclaim the contract and as a result cease to be under any obligation to fulfil it. However, it is unlikely that the seller's trustee would do this. The equitable interest in the land would have vested in the purchaser as a result of the contract and disclaimer of the contract would not restore this interest to the trustee, who would, therefore, lose both property and price.

The purchaser should be alerted to the bankruptcy of the seller by the pre-completion search. If the title to the bankrupt's land is unregistered, the petition in bankruptcy is registrable under the Land Charges Act 1972 in the register of pending actions and the order in bankruptcy is registrable in the register of writs or orders. If the title to the bankrupt's land is registered under the Land Registration Act 1925, when the petition is presented *and* it is ascertained that the bankrupt does own the registered land, a creditor's notice will be registered in the proprietorship register. When the order in bankruptcy is made, a bankruptcy inhibition is entered preventing the registration of any disposition other than by the trustee (s.61 of the Land Registration Act 1925).

It is very unlikely, in the case both of unregistered and registered title, that the registration will not be made, as the registration is applied for by the staff of the Bankruptcy Court on the filing of the petition in bankruptcy. If it should happen, however, a purchaser would as the result of the non-registration take the property free from the claims of the creditors and of the trustee in bankruptcy (see s.6 of the Land Charges Act 1972 and s.61 of the Land Registration Act 1925).

9.11 Bankruptcy of the Purchaser

The trustee in bankruptcy could disclaim the contract if it is unprofitable (s.315 of the Insolvency Act 1986). Otherwise, he will have to complete it.

Section 284 of the Insolvency Act 1986 again presents a danger. A payment by the purchaser of the purchase price will be a disposition and therefore void, so that the trustee could reclaim the purchase price. The seller might be able to claim the protection of s.284(4) which provides that a payment received by a person before the order in bankruptcy is made, in good faith, for value and without notice that the petition has been presented, shall be valid.

9.12   The Purchaser's Pre-completion Search – The Last Stage in the Investigation of Title

(a)   The Search at the Central Land Registry

A search should be made against the name of every estate owner revealed by the abstract of title. The search form (K15) must:

(i) Specify the name against which the search is to be made. If variations of a name appear in the abstract, a search should be made against every variation of the name, e.g. Edward Smith, Edward John Smith, Eddie Smith, Edward Smyth.

(ii) Specify the county in which the land is situated. This means not just the county in which the land is now, but also any county in which it has been during the period covered by the search. The difficulty can be illustrated by looking at Sidcup. The postal address of a house in Sidcup is Sidcup, Kent. But Sidcup is in the London Borough of Bexley, not in Kent. It was however in Kent until the creation of Greater London in 1965.

(iii) Specify the years to be searched. For example, if Edward Smith bought the house on 1 June 1960, and sold it on 12 August 1964, the form would specify 1960 to 1964 inclusive.

The registry will issue an official search certificate, saying either that there is no adverse entry against the name or that an entry does exist:

e.g: Edward Smith
Dii No 40 dated 1 June 1960
Land at Greenstairs, Kent

If the purchaser's solicitor finds an unexpected entry, he can ask the seller's solicitor to certify that the entry does not affect the land contracted to be sold. (This could be because it affects other land in the county owned by this Edward Smith, or because the registration is against a different Edward Smith.) If either solicitor feels doubt on the matter, he can obtain an office copy of the entry on the register, and from this find the name and address of the person who owns the benefit of the interest that has been registered.

Advantage of an official search certificate

(i) The official search certificate gives the purchaser a priority period of 15 working days from the date of the certificate. If the purchaser completes his purchase within that period, he will take free of any entry made on the register after the date of the search and before completion. Purchaser is defined to include someone who takes a lease or a mortgage. It also presumably includes anyone who claims through the purchaser. So suppose Vera owns a freehold house. She arranges to borrow money, and to grant a mortgage of her house in return. On the Monday before the completion of the mortgage, the lender obtains a certificate saying there is no entry against Vera's name. On Tuesday, Vera's husband Horatio registers a class F land charge. The mortgage is completed on the Friday. The mortgage is not subject to Horatio's rights of occupation. If Vera fails to keep up her mortgage payments, the mortgagee may exercise his statutory power of sale. The purchaser from the mortgagee also takes free from Horatio's rights.

(ii) The certificate is conclusive (s.10(4) of the Land Charges Act 1972). This means that if the Registry staff makes a mistake, so that the certificate fails to reveal the D(ii) registration against the name of Edward Smith, the purchaser will take free of the covenants leaving the incumbrancer to the chance of redress from the Chief Land Registrar. There is no statutory right to compensation in these circumstances, which seems strange, but it seems that an action against the Registrar for negligence would be possible. However a purchaser can only rely upon the certificate if his application for the search was in order. If the D(ii) is properly registered against the name of Edward Smith, a certificate issued in the name of Edward Smyth, because that was the version of the name supplied by the purchaser, confers no protection against the registration. The purchaser will take subject to the covenants (see section 4.5).

Section 10(6) states that there is no liability on the part of the registry staff for a discrepancy between the particulars in the application for the search, and the search certificate itself. So if the purchaser searches against the name of Edward Smith, and receives a certificate saying there is no registration against the name Edward Smyth, the purchaser must realise that this certificate is not reliable, and ask for the search to be repeated. So when reading a certificate of search, you must ask yourself, 'Is this the name I asked for the search to be made against?'

Past search certificates   As a matter of courtesy, the seller's solicitor usually sends with the abstract of title any past search certificates that exist. If the protocol is being followed, the seller's solicitor must supply search certificates against the names of past owners revealed by the evidence of title. The purchaser's solicitor needs to check on the reliability of any such certificate. He must check that the search is against the correct name, that it covers the period of estate ownership and that completion took place within the priority period given by the search. Try problem 1 in the workshop section.

(b) If the Seller (or a Past Owner) is a Limited Company, is a Search of the Companies Registry Necessary?

A search at the companies registry in the file of the company concerned may be essential. A fixed charge created by a company before 1 January 1970 could be protected against a purchaser *either* by its registration at the companies registry, *or* (if unprotected by deposit of title deeds) by its registration as a land charge. Therefore, a clear land-charge search certificate against the company's name does *not* clear away the possibility of there being a pre-1970 fixed charge capable of binding a purchaser on completion. A fixed charge created by a company after 1969 and unprotected by deposit of title deeds must be registered as a land charge if it is to bind a purchaser for value.

A floating charge created by a company at whatever date is not registrable as a land charge. The purchaser will require a certificate of non-crystallisation signed by the company secretary, or better, by the chargee, to be handed over at completion.

A search must also be made for evidence of the commencement of winding-up proceedings. In a winding-up by the court, any disposition of the company's property after the commencement of the winding-up is void (s.127 of the Insolvency Act 1986). The winding-up of a company by the court is deemed to commence at the time of the presentation of the petition for winding up (s.129(2) of the Insolvency Act 1986). The *order* for the winding-up will be filed in the company's file, but the petition is advertised in the *London Gazette*, so a search must also be made in the *London Gazette*.

It is also important to discover the appointment of an administrator or administrative receiver.

The company's file can only be searched personally, so this will be done either by the solicitor, or by a law agent instructed by the solicitor. The search gives no priority period, so should be done only shortly before completion.

(c) A Bankruptcy Search at the Central Land Charges Registry against the Name of the Purchaser

This has been explained in section 7.6(b). It is made on behalf of the mortgagee who is lending money for the purchase. It has nothing to do with the seller's title, and has been added here simply to complete the list of pre-completion searches.

Case Note

Walia v. Michael Naughton Ltd [1985] 1 WLR 1115

Three people, X, Y and Z owned the legal estate in land on trust for sale for themselves beneficially. X appointed Y to be his attorney. The power of attorney was expressed to be given 'in accordance with s.10 Powers of Attorney Act 1971'. A transfer of the land in favour of P was executed by Y personally, by Y as X's attorney and by Z. The transfer was held to be void as the power did not authorise Y to execute the transfer on behalf of X. Although X owned part of the equitable interest and to that extent was a 'beneficial owner' the function that he was delegating was his power to convey the legal estate, and his ownership of the legal estate was that of a trustee. The power of attorney, being given in accordance with s.10 of the 1971 Act, was not effective to delegate his function as a trustee.

Workshop

Attempt these problems yourself, then read specimen solutions at the end of the book.

Problem 1

You are investigating an unregistered freehold title. The seller Anthea Grumble has supplied you with a search certificate. The date of the certificate is 1 June 1992. It reveals that the search was against the names of William Faulkner and Anthea Grumble, and says that there were no subsisting entries against these names. She also supplies you with a copy of the conveyance dated 1 July 1992 by which William Faulkner conveyed the property to her. Does the search have to be repeated against these two names?

Problem 2

Alan Brown is acting for Vesta Smith, who is selling Rosedene, a large property in the village of Leadlode. The title is unregistered. The conveyance to Vesta, dated 1970, describes the property as the 'piece of land together with the dwelling-house standing thereon known as Rosedene, as the same is for the purpose of identification only outlined in red on the plan annexed hereto'. Alan used this description in the contract, and a copy of the 1970 plan and deed were sent with the draft agreement for sale to Paula Prentiss, the purchaser, for approval. Paula looked at the plan, and has told Alan that it does not show the current boundaries of Rosedene. She feels that the site of the large water-garden and summer-house is not, according to the plan, part of the property conveyed by the 1970 deed. What should Alan do?

Problem 3

You are investigating the title to Blackacre. The abstract of title gives you details of the following deeds:

1. 1 October 1983 – a conveyance on sale from Agnes to Bertha.
2. 4 December 1989 – a power of attorney given by Bertha to Sarah, her solicitor,

authorising Sarah to execute all documents and deeds connected with the sale of Blackacre.
3. 23 December 1990 – a conveyance on sale from Bertha, executed by Sarah as Bertha's attorney, to Charles.
4. 14 March 1991 – grant of letters of administration to the estate of Charles, the administrator being Delia. Delia is the seller.

Is this title in order?

Problem 4

This question is taken from the Law Society Examination, Winter 1985.

Your firm acts for James Brown who has just contracted to purchase 23 Chestnut Grove from the West Building Society. The contract incorporates the standard conditions. The Building Society is selling the property in exercise of the power of sale given by a mortgage dated 24 June 1982 executed in their favour by Donald Smith. The root of title is a conveyance on sale dated 6 July 1974. The XY Building Society is to lend Mr Brown £20 000 towards the purchase price of £25 000 and your firm has been instructed to act for them. You have taken over the conduct of the transaction from a colleague who is on holiday and you have just received the replies to his requisitions on title which include those shown below.

(a) Comment on these requisitions and the replies and briefly explain whether or not the replies are satisfactory. If not, state what further action is necessary and whether or not this can be left until your colleague returns from holiday.
(b) List and briefly explain the steps you will take up to the completion of the transactions once you are satisfied with the replies to the requisitions on title.

Requisitions on Title

1. The conveyance of 23 August 1974 is insufficiently stamped and this must be rectified before completion.
2. A land charges search has revealed a C(i) entry against Donald Smith registered on 10 September 1982. This must be discharged on or before completion.
3. Please supply a copy of the plan annexed to the conveyance dated 4 March 1960 to which reference is made in the conveyance of 6 July 1974.

Replies to Requisitions on Title

1. See the special condition in the contract prohibiting requisitions on stamping of documents.
2. The Purchaser is not concerned with this.
3. This pan is annexed to a pre-root conveyance and the purchaser is not entitled to a copy.

10 Personal Representative: The Passing of a Legal Estate on Death

10.1 The Death of a Sole Beneficial Owner

Suppose that Albert is the sole owner of the legal estate in Blackacre, and he owns it for his own benefit – i.e. not as trustee for someone else. When Albert dies, Blackacre will be owned by his personal representative. His personal representative may be his executor, i.e. the person appointed by Albert in his will to manage his affairs. If Albert has not appointed an executor, his personal representative will be the person, probably a member of his family, who applies to the probate registry for a grant of letters of administration. Both executors and administrators are known as personal representatives, and their statutory powers of disposing of Albert's assets are the same. The powers include a power of sale (s.39 of the Administration of Estates Act 1925).

10.2 Buying from the Personal Representative

If you are buying Blackacre from Albert's personal representative, when investigating his title you must check his identity, the number of personal representatives, and whether or not any memoranda are endorsed on the grant.

(a)   The Identity of the Personal Representative

Look at the grant of representation to confirm the identity of the personal representative. The grant is the only evidence that is acceptable.

An executor would actually have become the owner of Albert's property as soon as Albert died, as his position of executor derives from his appointment by the will. Despite this, you must not complete the purchase until the executor has obtained a grant of probate of the will, naming him as executor. The grant is conclusive evidence of his status. The will is *not*. (Remember the will may turn out to be void, or to have been revoked by a later one. Of course, the will may be challenged after probate has been granted, and as a result, the grant of probate itself revoked, but a dealing with an executor who has obtained a grant usually remains valid despite the later revocation of the grant, s.37 and s.55(1)(xviii) of the Administration of Estates Act 1925). It is possible to enter into the contract with the executor before probate, but the grant must be obtained before completion.

An administrator would not have become the owner of Albert's property, nor would he have any powers over it, until he had obtained the grant of letters of administration. The point is that it is *the grant* which makes him the administrator. Therefore, both contract and completion should wait until the grant is obtained.

(b)   The Number of Personal Representatives

The grant may be to a single personal representative. If so, it is perfectly safe to deal with him alone. He can on his own give a good receipt for the purchase money (s.27(2) of the Law of Property Act 1925). (Do not confuse a personal representative with a trustee of land. A receipt must be given by at least two trustees, but personal representatives and trustees are different animals.)

The grant may be to two or more personal representatives. The authority of personal representatives to *convey* is joint *only*, i.e. they must *all* execute a conveyance or assent if it is to be valid (s.68 of the Administration of Estates Act 1925).

The authority of personal representatives to enter into an agreement for the sale of freehold land is also only joint (s.16 Law of Property (Miscellaneous Provisions) Act 1994, amending s.2(2) Administration of Estates Act 1925).

(c)   Memoranda Endorsed on the Grant

When looking at the grant, check that no statement has been written on it, to the effect that Blackacre has already been transferred by the personal representative to someone else. If there is such a memorandum, if you have any sense you will realise that the personal representative can no longer transfer Blackacre to you. Completion will not take place, and you will turn hurriedly to Chapter 19 to consider remedies for breach of contract.

If there is *no* such memorandum, this is probably for the simple reason that the personal representative has *not* already disposed of Blackacre to someone else and that is why he now feels free to convey it to you.

However, the interesting thing is that if the personal representative *has* already disposed of the legal estate to someone else (let us call him Ben), and Ben has failed to put a memorandum warning of this on the grant, then, in some circumstances, when the personal representative later conveys to you, you *will* get the legal estate, and Ben will lose it.

The reason for this is s.36(6) of the Administration of Estates Act 1925. There is now set out a simple, and *so far as it goes*, accurate version of s.36(6) – if a personal representative conveys the legal estate in Blackacre to a purchaser for money, and the conveyance contains a statement that the personal representative has not made any previous conveyance or assent in favour of someone else and the purchaser relies on that statement, then the conveyance will vest the legal estate in the purchaser, despite the fact that the personal representative has already passed the legal estate on to a beneficiary of the will or intestacy, provided that the beneficiary has not by then put a memorandum about the disposition to him on the grant. The disposition to the beneficiary is overridden. The personal representative cannot override any earlier disposition to another purchaser for money, be he a purchaser from the personal representative himself, or from the beneficiary. So the protection given to a purchaser from a personal representative by s.36(6) is really very narrow.

If you think this through slowly, the following points will occur to you:

1. any sensible beneficiary, having had the legal estate vested in him by the personal representative, will immediately insist on a memorandum about it being put on the grant. This makes it impossible for him to lose the legal estate to a later purchaser for money from the personal representative. Section 36 gives the beneficiary the right to insist on this. The memorandum does not have to be in any particular form; it will probably say something like 'By an assent dated . . . , Blackacre was transferred by the personal representatives named in this grant to Ben Brown.'

2. any sensible purchaser who is buying from a personal representative will:

    • when drafting the conveyance to himself, put in a statement (usually a recital) that the seller (i.e. the personal representative) has not made any previous assent or conveyance in respect of the property being conveyed. Without this statement, s.36(6) does not apply.

    • on completion, ask to see the original grant to check there is no memorandum on it. He must see the original, and not allow himself to be fobbed off with an office copy, which for this purpose is useless;

    • after completion, put a memorandum on the grant about the conveyance to himself. This is said to be good conveyancing procedure, in all circumstances. It certainly is in the case of a sale of part of the land owned by the deceased, when the personal representative is retaining the deeds. In this case, a memorandum about the sale should be endorsed either on the conveyance to the deceased, as in any sale of part, or on the grant. However, failure on the part of a purchaser from the personal representative to put a memorandum of the sale on the grant cannot prejudice his title by virtue of s.36(6). Remember that a personal representative cannot override a previous conveyance to a purchaser for money, and if you are still in doubt look at problem 3 at the end of this chapter.

3. s.36(6) is perhaps relevant only to unregistered title. If the title is registered, the problem will be solved by provisions of the Land Registration Act 1925. Again for an explanation, look at problem 3.

10.3   The Use of an Assent

Once the personal representative has the grant, he can convey the legal estate. Nothing further is needed if he intends to convey in the capacity of personal representative. No assent will be needed.

An assent is needed (a) to transfer ownership from the personal representative to a beneficiary, or (b) to change the capacity in which the personal representative holds the estate.

(a)   To Transfer Ownership from the Personal Representative to a Beneficiary

This is an area where it is easy to become confused, and it really may be helpful to look first of all at the pre-1926 law, and then to realise the nature of the changes made by the Administration of Estates Act 1925.

Suppose that Albert died in 1924. His will appointed Edward as his executor, and gave the legal estate in Blackacre to Ben. On Albert's death two titles to Blackacre were created. Ben had a title to Blackacre by virtue of the gift in the will. That is why, if Ben had decided to sell the property, the will would have appeared on the abstract. However, the death also gave the executor a title to Blackacre, for the purpose of administering the estate. This meant that if, for instance, money had to be raised to pay the deceased's debts, Edward could have sold Blackacre, and so defeated Ben's title. The title of the executor was the better or 'paramount' title. If it had become clear that the executor would not need to sell Blackacre, he could have allowed the gift to the beneficiary to take effect. In other words he could have 'assented' to the gift. The use of the word 'assent' for what the executor was doing made sense before 1926 as it means 'consent'. The executor consented to the gift, and so released his own superior title to the property. As the assent was not in any way a conveyance to the beneficiary, it could be informal, and the mere fact that a beneficiary was allowed to take possession could indicate assent to the gift. When you consider the nature of a pre-1926 assent, it becomes clear why an administrator could not assent when the deceased died intestate. There was no gift to which to assent, so the administrator would convey the legal estate to the beneficiary by deed.

In 1925, the Administration of Estates Act made considerable changes. An assent made after 1925 is quite different from an assent made pre-1926, and it is a pity that this was not made quite clear by giving a different name to the thing.

On a death after 1925, no title is conferred by the will on the beneficiary. This is why a will of a person who dies after 1925 no longer appears on the abstract of title to prove change of ownership of the legal estate. The title belongs only to the personal representative. If he conveys the legal estate to a purchaser, he will use a deed of conveyance or a land registry transfer. If a sale is not necessary, the personal representative will wish to vest the legal estate in the person entitled to it under the terms of the will or under the intestacy rules. The document that he will use is what is now called an assent. You can see now how an assent has changed its character. It is now actually a document of transfer, passing ownership from the personal representative to the person in whose favour the assent is made. As it does transfer ownership, it can no longer be allowed to be informal; and it can be used by administrators as well as executors, because it no longer depends upon there being a gift in a will.

Form of a post-1925 assent Section 36(4) demands that an assent that relates to a *legal estate* in land be in writing, be signed by the personal representatives (i.e. it need not be executed as a deed) and name the person in whose favour it is made.

An assent of an unregistered title says something like 'I Alice Grace as the personal representative of May East as personal representative assent to the vesting in fee simple of Blackacre in Ann Hyde and I acknowledge the right of Ann Hyde to production of the probate of the will of May East and to delivery of copies thereof. Signed this 4 day of July 1989.'

The assent is by deed if the beneficiary gives a covenant to the personal representative, e.g. an indemnity covenant.

So an abstract of title tracing a change of ownership of the legal estate by virtue of death would now, for example, give details of the following deeds and events:

1 January 1960 Conveyance of Blackacre by W to X.
1 January 1980 Statement that X died on this date.
1 July 1980 Grant of probate to Y + Z.
   [If you were buying from Y + Z as personal representatives, the abstract would end here.]
1 January 1981 Assent signed by Y + Z, saying that they assent to the vesting of Blackacre in Ben.
1 January 1981 A memorandum of the assent endorsed on the grant of probate.

On this basis would we be happy to buy from Ben? Yes, because on the evidence we have here, Ben could convey to us. If there were no memorandum on the grant, we would have cause for concern (see problem 3). [However, remember Chapter 3, para. 2: if an assent is dated on or after 1 April 1998, Ben must apply for first registration of title.]

Points which Might Occur to You

(i) Do we need to see X's death certificate? Realistically, the answer is 'no'. A grant of probate of his will, or a grant of letters of administration to his estate is usually taken as being satisfactory evidence that X really is dead.

(ii) How do we know that Ben was the right person to be given the legal estate? We do not know, and we will not usually enquire. The reason for this is s.36(7) of the Administration of Estates Act 1925, which says that the assent itself is 'sufficient evidence' that the assent has been made to the correct person, and has been made upon the correct trusts, if any. So we can take an assent at face value. That is why we are safe in buying from Ben, and why we will assume he is a beneficial owner, as the assent makes no mention of the legal estate being transferred to him on any sort of trust. If we did have reason to suspect that Ben were not the person entitled to have the legal estate passed to him, or that he ought to be holding it on some sort of trust, *then* we could no longer take the assent at its face value, and we would have to enquire about its correctness. If we did not do this, we would risk being fixed with constructive notice of other beneficiaries' rights. This is because s.36 says that the assent is 'sufficient' evidence, but it does not say it is 'conclusive' evidence. So no enquiry is made *unless* we have cause for suspicion (see Re *Duce* and *Boots Cash Chemists (Southern) Ltd's* Contract [1937]).

(iii) What if the title were registered? The use of the assent is exactly the same. The events would be, for example:

(aa) X is registered proprietor.

(bb) X dies. There is a grant of representation to Y + Z. They have a choice, so,

(cc) *either* Y + Z register themselves as the new proprietors, by producing an office or certified copy of the grant to the Chief Land Registrar. Y + Z could then sign the assent in favour of Ben.

or Y + Z could choose not to be registered. Indeed, there is little point in the personal representatives registering themselves as proprietors if they intend to assent to a beneficiary, or convey to a purchaser, within a reasonable time. Y + Z could sign an assent to a beneficiary, who could register himself by producing a copy of the grant, and the assent, and the land certificate.

An assent of registered title should be made using Land Registry form AS1.

(b) To Change the Capacity in which the Personal Representative Holds the Legal Estate to that of Trustee, or Beneficial Owner

Suppose that Albert's will says 'I appoint X and Y as the executors and trustees of this my will. I give Blackacre to X and Y to hold on trust for my widow for life, and after her death for my daughter Sara absolutely.'

On Albert's death, Blackacre vests in X and Y as *personal representatives*.

If they have to sell it, that is the capacity in which they will convey. When X and Y have administered the estate, they will be ready to change their capacity to that of trustees. They must change their capacity as the final step in the administration of that asset, as there can be difficulties if a personal representative dies with property still vested in him as such (see section 10.4). Re *King's Will Trusts* [1964] decided that s.36(4) of the Administration of Estates Act 1925 (which demands a written assent) applies not only when a personal representative is actually going to transfer ownership of the legal estate, but also when he is going to retain it but wishes to change the capacity in which he holds it. So in order to become trustees, X and Y must sign a written assent in their own favour, e.g. 'We X and Y hereby assent to the vesting of Blackacre in ourselves, upon trust.' Until this written assent is made, there is no change of capacity, and X and Y continue to hold the legal estate as personal representatives.

A similar case would arise if Albert's will said 'I give all my property to X, and appoint him the executor of my will.' X holds the legal estate in Blackacre as personal representative. He does not hold it as beneficial owner until he signs a written assent in his own favour. It is important that this is done if he intends to keep Blackacre, as if he died with the legal estate still vested in him as personal representative, his own personal representatives may not be able to deal with Blackacre at his death (see problem 2).

10.4   The Death of a Personal Representative

A personal representative is himself mortal. If he dies before he has finished administering the estate, there may be difficulties if he is the sole personal representative.

Suppose that Albert dies, and X and Y are his personal representatives. Albert's assets are vested in X and Y jointly, so that if X dies, Y will have the whole of Albert's property vested in him alone, and he can happily continue administering Albert's assets as the sole surviving personal representative. So X's death, although a serious blow to his many admirers, has not caused any difficulty in the administration of Albert's estate.

Suppose now that Y dies, while still in the course of administering the estate, so that on his death there are still assets vested in him as personal representative.

The difficulty now is that Albert has run out of personal representatives. The estate can only be administered by new personal representatives *of Albert*. Where will these new personal representatives come from? There are two possibilities:

1. That there exists what is known as a 'chain of representation' under s.7 of the Administration of Estates Act 1925. It may save you from error if you think of it as a chain of *executorship*. Section 7 provides that on the death of a sole, or last surviving proving executor, *his* proving ex-

ecutor takes over his unfinished executorship. The chain only forms through *proving executors* (i.e. who obtain probate. It is a general rule that executors who are appointed by the will but who do not obtain probate can be ignored.) It only forms through the death of the last proving executor to die. It is best explained through an example. Suppose Albert dies, and Betty and Carol obtain probate of his will. If Betty dies before all of Albert's assets are administered, you do not consider the chain of executorship at all. Albert still has an executor, and Carol will simply carry on alone. Betty's personal representatives do not come into the picture at all. On Carol's death, as she is the last surviving executor of Albert, you will look to see if any of her executors obtain probate of her will. Suppose she has appointed David as her executor, and he obtains probate. The effect of s.7 is that when David becomes Carol's executor, he automatically becomes Albert's executor as well, with power to dispose of his assets. He does not need a further grant to Albert's estate.

If Carol had died without appointing an executor, so that David had been her administrator, having applied for a grant of letters of administration, then David would not acquire any power over Albert's assets. Remember, it has to be a chain of *executorship*.

2.   If a chain of executorship does not exist (for instance, as in the last example, if either Betty and Carol, or David, were administrators) the only way that Albert could acquire a new personal representative is by a new grant of representation to his estate. This would be a grant of letters of administration (if relevant, with will annexed) *'de bonis non administratis'* – that is, it gives the person who obtains the grant the power to deal only with the unadministered part of Albert's estate. Who will be entitled to this grant? It depends on the Non-contentious Probate Rules 1987. Their effect can be summed up very briefly by saying that the grant will be to a person who is in some way entitled to the assets. The grant must be made to create the new personal representative. Without it, no one has power to pass title to the assets.

Workshop

Attempt these problems yourself, then read specimen solutions at the end of the book.

Problem 1

You have contracted to buy an unregistered title from Eric. He has contracted to trace title from a conveyance on sale dated 1 April 1970. The abstract gives details of the following documents:

1 April 1970 Alan conveys as beneficial owner to Bertha.
1 April 1982 Bertha dies.
1 April 1983 Grant of probate to Charles and David, the executors of Bertha's will.

1 April 1985 Conveyance on sale by David to Eric.
Is Eric's title acceptable?

Problem 2

We have contracted to buy Blackacre from Fred. The abstract gives details of the following transactions:

1 April 1975 Alice conveys Blackacre as beneficial owner to Bill.
1 April 1980 Edward conveys it as personal representative to Fred.

The recitals in the 1980 conveyance make the following statements to explain why Edward is the seller:

(i) that Bill died in 1977, and a grant of letters of administration was made to his wife Carol;
(ii) that Carol died in 1978, and a grant of probate of her will was made to Edward.

Was Edward able to convey Blackacre to Fred in 1980?

Problem 3

Consider the following abstract of title:

1970 Albert conveys Blackacre to Bryn as beneficial owner.
1972 Bryn dies.
1973 Grant of probate of his will to Cathy and Drew.
1974 An assent, signed by Cathy and Drew, in favour of Elaine.
1980 Elaine conveys to Fred.

Should we raise a requisition on Fred's title?

11 A Sale by Trustees of Land

11.1 Introduction

Sometimes one feels that the foundations of the earth are trembling. The Trusts of Land and Appointment of Trustees Act 1996 came into force on 1 January 1997.

Before that date, a person who wished to create a trust of land could do it either by creating a strict settlement, governed by the Settled Land Act 1925, or by creating a trust for sale, governed by the Law of Property Act 1925. Strict settlements were not common, and invariably a person who wished to create a trust of land did so by creating a trust for sale. In other words, he conveyed the land to the trustees, and the conveyance expressly declared that they were to hold the land 'on trust to sell it and to hold the proceeds of sale, and pending sale, the income of the land, on trust for . . .'.

Why would he create a trust at all? A trust is needed if, for example, the benefit of ownership is to be given to a minor. Trustees have legal ownership and control of the land, but hold on trust for the minor, who receives the benefit of ownership either by occupying the land or benefiting from the income it produces. A trust is also necessary if the benefits of ownership are to be shared other than by creation of a lease. For example, a trust is needed if the benefits are to be enjoyed in succession (e.g. Robert having the enjoyment of the land for his life, but on his death the land going to Sandra), or if they are to be enjoyed concurrently (e.g. by husband and wife owning the property as joint tenants or as tenants in common).

Why was a trust for *sale* created rather than just a trust? This was because in some circumstances, if the trust of the land was not declared to be a trust for sale, the Settled Land Act would apply. (See the definition of settled land in s.1 Settled Land Act 1925.) For conveyancers who preferred a simple life this would have been a grave misfortune, for Settled Land Act conveyancing was complex and really only suitable for landed families with large estates.

After 1996, it is impossible to create new strict settlements. It is no longer necessary to create a trust of land as a trust *for sale*. What you create is simply what the 1996 Act calls 'a trust of land'. This term includes trusts created expressly, trusts arising by implication of law, trusts created as trusts for sale and bare trusts. So a trust created as a trust for sale, whether before or after the Act, is a trust of land.

11.2 How Do You Know the Sellers are Trustees of Land?

Suppose you are buying an unregistered title. You are buying it from Abel and Bertha. You read a copy of the conveyance to them. A clause in it says 'the purchasers declare that they hold the property hereby conveyed on trust for . . .'. It does not require a great mental effort to deduce from this that Abel and Bertha hold the legal estate as trustees. The trust is expressly declared.

Suppose instead that you read the conveyance and it says 'the seller . . . hereby conveys . . . Blackacre to hold unto Abel and Bertha in equal shares'. This also tells you that Abel and Bertha hold the legal estate on a trust of land. Why? It is because they co-own the beneficial interest. When two or more purchasers co-own the equitable interest, then if no express trust is declared, the legal estate vests in them on an implied trust of land (ss.34–36 of the Law of Property Act 1925 as amended by the 1996 Act). They will always hold the legal estate as joint tenants, whether they hold the equitable interest as joint tenants or tenants in common.

If the conveyance had been to Abel, Bertha, Charles, Deirdre and Edna in equal shares, the difficulty would have arisen that although the equitable interest is owned by five people, a legal estate can only be held by four. The legal estate would vest in the first four adult co-owners named in the conveyance (s.34 of the Law of Property Act 1925). So although the conveyance simply says that the land is conveyed to the five people, it has the same effect as if it read 'to A B C and D on trust for A B C D and E equally'. You can see from this that if you were buying the legal estate, you would need a conveyance signed only by A B C and D. E does not own the legal estate. He is sacrificed in the interests of limiting the number of estate owners, but he has not lost his share of the beneficial interest, which is what really matters.

Now suppose that the title is registered. When Abel and Bertha bought from the then registered proprietor, the transfer would either have declared an express trust, or have disclosed the circumstances which gave rise to an implied trust, e.g. the co-ownership of the beneficial interest by the two of them. Abel and Bertha, as the trustees, are entitled to apply to the Registrar to have themselves registered as proprietors. As they are trustees they are under a duty to apply for a restriction to be entered on the register. (The one exception to this is where they hold on trust for themselves as beneficial joint tenants – see later). The restriction will read 'No disposition by a sole proprietor of the land (not being a trust corporation) under which capital arises is to be registered except under an order of the Registrar or of the court' (Land Registration Rules 1989).

If they do not apply for the entry of the restriction, the Registrar is nevertheless under a duty to enter it whenever it is clear to him that a trust exists (s.58(3) of the Land Registration Act 1925).

The restriction reflects the fact that a sale by a sole trustee of land has no overreaching effect, so should not be accepted by the purchaser.

If Abel and Bertha hold on trust for themselves as beneficial joint tenants, there will be no restriction at all on the register. This reflects the fact that the sole survivor of Abel and Bertha will be able to sell by herself/himself, without any need to appoint another trustee.

Note that a trust of land can be created by will, and is implied on an intestacy. The vesting of the legal estate in the personal representatives, and later in the trustees, is dealt with in Chapter 10.

11.3 Who Are the Current Trustees?

If you are buying a legal estate that is held by trustees, the first obvious question to ask yourself is 'who are the current trustees?' In unregistered conveyancing, the original trustees are identified by reading the conveyance which created the trust. In registered conveyancing, the original trustees will have been registered as the registered proprietors. Of course, trustees, like all mortal things, are transient. They come and go. The important thing is to check that when a trustee goes, he parts with all his interest in the legal estate, and that when a new trustee arrives, the estate is vested in him.

11.4 Changes of Trustees

(a) Death of a Trustee Leaving At Least One Trustee Behind

Suppose that Alice, Beryl and Catherine are the three trustees when the trust first arises. The legal estate is vested in them jointly, no matter how they, or anyone else, might share the equitable interest. If Alice dies, the legal estate remains vested in the surviving trustees. (Remember that it is a characteristic of a *joint* tenancy, as opposed to a tenancy in common, that when a joint tenant dies, the surviving joint tenant(s) continue to own the entire interest.) Beryl and Catherine, therefore, can convey the legal estate. As there are two trustees, the effect of the conveyance will be to overreach the equitable interests, so that they become claims against the purchase price. The only thing that the purchaser has to check is that Alice really is dead. (If she is still alive, a conveyance or transfer by Beryl and Catherine alone will be void; see later.) This is done by seeing a copy of her death certificate.

Note that in registered conveyancing, Beryl and Catherine could have had Alice's name removed from the proprietorship register by sending to the Registrar a copy of the death certificate (Rule 172, Land Registration Rules 1925). They need not do this. They can prove Alice's death to a purchaser from them by a copy of the death certificate, and when registering the transfer the purchaser will send to the Registrar the Land Certificate, the copy of the death certificate, and the transfer signed by Beryl and Catherine.

Appointment of New Trustee   Should Beryl now die, Catherine will be left as sole trustee, owning the legal estate. She cannot sell alone, as a conveyance by a single trustee has no overreaching effect, so another trustee must be appointed to act with her. (As an exception to this general rule, she could sell alone if she and Alice and Beryl had been not only joint tenants of the legal estate, but also the only joint tenants of the beneficial interest; see later.)

Who Can Appoint This New Trustee?   An expressly created trust may give a particular person a power to appoint new trustees. Otherwise, for both express and implied trusts for sale, it is the surviving trustee(s) who can appoint the new one (s.36 of the Trustee Act 1925). In other words the new trustee will be appointed by Catherine.

Method of Appointment   In unregistered title, a trustee can be appointed by writing, but a *deed* of appointment should be used. This is to take advantage of s.40 of the Trustee Act 1925, which provides that if a new trustee is appointed by deed, the deed vests the trust property in the people who become, or are, the trustees after the appointment, without any need for a separate conveyance. For example, Catherine can execute a deed saying that she appoints Deirdre to be the second trustee. The effect of that will be that the legal estate will be vested in Catherine and Deirdre.

If the title is registered, the appointment of Deirdre as a new trustee will not in itself vest the legal estate in her. The legal estate will vest when, after seeing the appointment, the Registrar adds Deirdre's name to the proprietorship register. The appointment can be carried out by Catherine executing a Land Registry transfer to herself and Deirdre. Notice that if Deirdre is appointed solely for the purpose of selling the land, it is not necessary that her name be entered on the register before completion. The purchaser will be registered as proprietor by including in his application for registration copies of the death certificates of Alice and Beryl, the appointment of Deirdre, and the transfer signed by Catherine and Deirdre.

(b)   Death of the Sole, or Last Surviving, Trustee for Sale

Suppose Catherine dies, without having appointed another trustee? There are three ways in which title could now be made to the legal estate:

(i) Section 36 of the Trustee Act 1925 provides that on the death of a sole trustee, her personal representative(s) can appoint new trustees. So suppose Catherine's executor is Dorothy, then Dorothy could appoint Edna and Florence as new trustees of the trust. Edna and Florence could then convey the legal estate to a purchaser.

(ii) Sections 18(2) and (3) of the Trustee Act 1925 provide that on the death of a sole trustee, her personal representatives can actually carry out the trust, i.e. stand in for her and convey the legal estate to a purchaser. However, because the personal representatives, when they do this, are acting in the role of trustees, rather than as personal representatives, there must be at least two of them if the conveyance is to overreach the equitable interests. So, in the above example, Dorothy could not sell the property herself; she could only appoint the new trustees. If Catherine had left two executors, say Dorothy and Deborah, they could themselves exercise the trust by conveying the legal estate under s.18(2).

(iii) If Alice, Bertha and Catherine had been holding on trust for themselves as beneficial joint tenants, then Catherine's personal representative(s) could make title, relying in unregistered conveyancing on the Law of Property (Joint Tenants) Act 1964, or in registered title, on the absence of any restriction on the register (see later).

(c)   Retirement of a Trustee

A trustee might wish to retire from the trust whilst still alive. For example, Alice, Bertha and Catherine might be partners in the running of a grocery business. The shop premises would be owned by them jointly on a trust of land. They would probably own the equitable interest as tenants in common. Alice might wish to retire from the partnership and Bertha and Catherine agree to buy her out. Alice must divest herself of all interest in the legal estate, otherwise, if Bertha and Catherine later wish to sell it, Alice would have to be traced to her retirement home, as her signature to the conveyance or transfer would be needed. If the title to the shop is unregistered, the retirement will be by deed and the effect of s.40 of the Trustee Act 1925 will be that the legal estate will vest in Bertha and Catherine. If the title is registered, the simplest procedure is again for the three registered proprietors to sign a transfer in favour of Bertha and Catherine. On registration of the transfer, the name of Alice will be removed from the register.

11.5   How Many Trustees Are There?

Having identified your current trustees, you must now consider how many there are.

If there are two or more, you must remember that their powers are joint. In other words *all* the trustees must sign the conveyance or transfer. If the legal estate is vested in three trustees, you will not obtain it if only two of these three trustees convey it to you. If there are three registered proprietors of the registered title, all three must sign the Land Registry transfer. Otherwise the conveyance or transfer will not pass ownership of the legal estate.

If the conveyance is by all the trustees, and there are at least two of them, a conveyance (or mortgage) by them will overreach the interests of the beneficiaries, which become claims only against the purchase price (ss.2 and 27 of the Law of Property Act 1925). If there is only one trustee, then generally, as has been said, a second trustee must be appointed. A conveyance by a single trustee will pass the legal estate to the purchaser, but will not overreach the equitable interests.

11.6   Consents

It is possible for the person creating the trust of land to say that the trustees can only sell if they first obtain the consent of some person named by the settlor.

For example, a wealthy testator may in her will give her property to her husband for his lifetime and provide that on his death the capital is to go to the children. As a life interest is being created, the legal estate in any land will have to be held on trust. It is the trustees who have the power to sell the land, but the testator may wish to ensure that her husband will have some control over whether or not the family home is sold. One solution is to appoint the husband as one of the trustees. Alternatively, the will may say that the husband's consent must be obtained to any sale.

If there is a requirement that a consent be obtained, the purchaser from trustees must ensure that the consent is obtained, otherwise he will not get a good title. (In registered conveyancing the need for consent will appear as a restriction on the register.)

However, s.10 Trusts of Land and Appointment of Trustees Act 1966 may make life easier for the purchaser. First, it says that if the person whose consent is necessary is under age, the purchaser need not obtain that consent. Secondly, if that still leaves the purchaser faced with the task of obtaining more than two consents, only two need be obtained. The provision does not exist to make life easier for the trustees. If they sell without obtaining all consents, including the consent of a parent or guardian of a minor, they are breaking their trust.

11.7   Investigating the Equitable Interests

Usually, a purchaser has no need to investigate the equitable interests behind a trust of land, as a conveyance on sale by the trustees will overreach the interests. However, the trustees may not always want to sell. They may wish to end the trust by transferring the legal estate in the land to the adult beneficiary who is absolutely entitled. For example, suppose the trustees hold the land on trust for X for life, and then for Y absolutely. When X dies, the trustees will want to convey the legal estate to Y. The problem is that the transfer will have no overreaching effect, as it is not a *sale* by the trustees. So should a purchaser investigate the equitable interests, to check that no-one other than Y has an interest in the land?

Section 16(4) of the Trusts of Land and Appointment of Trustees Act

1996 solves the problem. If the trustees are transferring the land to an adult or adults who they believe are absolutely entitled to it, they must execute a deed that declares that they, the trustees, are now discharged from the trust. A purchaser of the land from the beneficiary is then entitled to assume that the land is no longer subject to the trusts, unless he has actual notice that the trustees were mistaken in their belief. To return to the example above, the trustees would include the declaration that they are discharged from the trust in the transfer to Y.

11.8   Co-ownership of the Equitable Interest

(a)   The Equitable Interest

If two people are, between them, buying a house, they must decide how they are to own the equitable interest. There are two possibilities. They could own it as beneficial *joint* tenants. If people own property jointly, it is as if they have been fused together to form a single unit. Between them there is what is called the right of survivorship. When one joint tenant dies the entire property belongs to the survivor(s). This is why a joint tenancy is considered apt for a married couple. If H and W own property jointly, say a joint bank account, then on the husband's death, the wife automatically owns the entire property. Her entitlement does not depend on her husband's will. For this reason, she does not need to get probate of her husband's will in order to prove her ownership of the property. She merely has to prove that he is dead, by producing his death certificate.

The other possibility is that the couple could own the equitable interest as tenants in common, i.e. they own shares in the property, although the property has not as yet been physically divided between them. There is no right of survivorship in a tenancy in common, so when one tenant in common dies, his share passes to his personal representative, and from him to the beneficiary named in the will, or to the next-of-kin under the intestacy rules.

(b)   The Legal Estate

They must also decide as to who is to own the legal estate. If X and Y own the equitable interest, whether jointly or in common, and are both adult, it is common sense that they should both own the legal estate. This makes it impossible for either to sell or mortgage the house without the consent of the other, as both signatures will be needed on the transfer or mortgage deed. So the conveyance or transfer to X and Y:

(i) will say that the legal estate is conveyed to them;
(ii) will say how they own the equitable interest, i.e. either jointly or in shares, and if in shares the size of each share;
(iii) may declare an express trust of the legal estate. We have already

seen that if an express trust is not created, a statutory trust will be implied;

(iv) may decrease the statutory powers of dealing with the legal estate.

So, as a tiresome recap, you must appreciate the following matters, otherwise you will always be in a muddle in this area:

1. If you read a conveyance that says the legal estate in Blackacre is conveyed to Ann and Bill as beneficial joint tenants, the result is that Ann and Bill hold the *legal estate jointly* on trust for themselves as *beneficial joint tenants*. So that on Bill's death Ann owns the entire legal estate and, prima facie, the entire equitable interest. The provisions of Bill's will are irrelevant to the ownership of Blackacre.

2. If the conveyance says the legal estate is conveyed to Ann and Bill to hold in equal shares, the result is that they hold the legal estate *jointly* (remember that co-owners always hold the legal estate jointly) on trust, but that they hold the *equitable interest as tenants in common*. The word 'equally' shows that they have *shares* and so cannot hold the equitable interest jointly. On Bill's death, Ann will own the entire legal estate, but only half the beneficial interest. The other half is owned by Bill's personal representatives. The provisions of Bill's will are relevant to the ownership of his share of the equitable interest, but still irrelevant to the ownership of the legal estate.

3. If registered title is transferred to Ann and Bill, they will apply for registration of the transfer. The Registrar will read the transfer. The transfer will say how Ann and Bill own the beneficial interest. If the Registrar believes them to be joint tenants of the beneficial interest he will not put a restriction on the register. Otherwise, he will enter a restriction, preventing a sale by the survivor of Ann and Bill.

Bear this in mind when you read the following section.

11.9 A Conveyance or Transfer by the Sole Surviving Co-owner

The problem is this – Ann and Bill hold the legal estate on trust for themselves. Do you accept a conveyance or transfer from Ann alone after Bill's death?

(a) Ann and Bill Hold on Trust for Themselves as Tenants in Common

You do *not* accept a conveyance from Ann alone. She now holds the legal estate on trust for herself and Bills's personal representative. Again, if the title is registered, there will be a restriction on the register. The solution is for Ann to appoint another trustee.

It may be, of course, that Bill left his share of the beneficial interest in the house to Ann by his will, so that in fact she does now own the entire beneficial interest. However, title should not be proved to a purchaser by tracing ownership of the equitable interest, and the purchaser should not agree to make the investigation. Never mind who now owns Bill's interest, the interest should be overreached. Bill's will is only of relevance to the trustees, when they divide the proceeds of sale. (Note that if the title is registered, and Ann has succeeded to the ownership of Bill's share, she could apply to the Registrar for the removal of Bill's name from the register, and for the removal of the restriction. She would have to provide the Registrar with a copy of Bill's death certificate, and a statutory declaration as to how she became solely and beneficially interested. Once the restriction is removed from the register, a purchaser would accept a conveyance from Ann alone.)

(b) Ann and Bill Hold on Trust for Themselves as Beneficial Joint Tenants

This is the only occasion when the purchaser would consider taking a conveyance from Ann alone. *Prima facie*, on Bill's death, because the right of survivorship applied to both the legal estate and the beneficial interest, Ann became sole beneficial owner. Why only *prima facie*?

The difficulty is that the joint tenancy of the equitable interest can be severed and changed into a tenancy in common. This destroys the right of survivorship. There are various ways in which Bill could have severed the equitable joint tenancy before he died: for example, by selling his equitable interest, by serving written notice on Ann under s.36 of the Law of Property Act 1925, by going bankrupt, or by mutual agreement with Ann. Suppose, for instance, that Bill, before his death, served a notice on Ann, saying that henceforth they were to be tenants in common of the equitable interest. The result would be that Ann and Bill would remain joint tenants of the legal estate, as it is impossible to sever the legal joint tenancy, but they would become tenants in common of the equitable interest. Bill could make sure that the severance came to the notice of any prospective purchaser. In registered title, he could apply to the Registrar for the restriction to go on the register, ensuring that Ann could not transfer the house after his death without appointing another trustee. In unregistered title, he could write a memorandum on the conveyance to himself and Ann, saying that the severance had taken place. This again would prevent Ann from selling the property after his death without appointing a second trustee (see the later discussion of the Law of Property (Joint Tenants) Act 1964).

Bill, however, might do nothing at all, so that on his death Ann would look like a beneficial owner, but would in fact be a trustee holding on trust for herself and for Bill's estate. Traditionally, the answer to the *possibility* of severance of the equitable interest was always to insist that Ann appoint a second trustee, so that if there were a half share of the equitable interest to be overreached, this would be done. It is now usually unnecessary to appoint a second trustee, for the following reason.

Registered Title   When Ann and Bill were first registered as proprietors, there would have been no restriction on the register, because of their *joint* ownership of the beneficial interest. So there is nothing on the register to forbid a transfer by Ann alone after Bill's death. A purchaser from Ann need only see Bill's death certificate, to check that he really is dead, and not just locked away somewhere in a cupboard.

Suppose Bill had severed the joint tenancy of the equitable interest before he died? Suppose when he was alive he sold his equitable interest to Xerxes? Or suppose he served notice of severance on Ann and then left his half-interest to Xerxes in his will. Xerxes could then have applied for the entry of a restriction on the register, or, if Ann would not cooperate in this, he could have lodged a caution. Either would alert the purchaser to the situation and lead to the appointment of a second trustee. Suppose Xerxes does not do this. He is then in the position of having an unprotected minor interest. Remember section 3.13. A transferee for value takes free of an unprotected minor interest. That is why a purchaser is safe in taking a transfer from Ann alone. The absence of a restriction or caution generally ensures that an interest belonging to someone other than Ann will fail to bind the purchaser. However, remember that a transferee for value *does* take subject to overriding interests. If Xerxes has moved in, his interest will be overriding under s.70(1)(g) of the Land Registration Act 1925. So it is the absence of an entry on the register *and* the absence of anyone else in occupation that enables the purchaser to buy from Ann alone in complete safety.

Unregistered Title   If a purchaser buys from Ann alone after Bill's death, he cannot claim that Bill's interest has been overreached. However, there remains the traditional defence of a purchaser against an equitable interest, namely that of being a *bona fide* purchaser for value of the legal estate without notice of the equitable interest. However, no purchaser likes to rely on this defence, because of the difficulty of proving absence of notice, particularly of constructive notice. This is why, before 1965, a purchaser from Ann would have preferred her to appoint another trustee and rely on the defence of overreaching, rather than that of being without notice.

The Law of Property (Joint Tenants) Act 1964 aimed at making this precaution of having a second trustee unnecessary. This Act builds on the defence of being without notice, by providing that if the purchaser takes certain precautions he can assume that the sole survivor of the joint tenants does own all the beneficial interest. The actual wording of the Act (as amended by the Law of Property (Miscellaneous Provisions) Act 1994) is that in favour of the purchaser the sole survivor shall 'be deemed to be solely and beneficially interested if the conveyance includes a statement that he is so interested'.

It is not certain if the assumption that the purchaser can make is irrebuttable. In other words, can the purchaser rely on the Act even if he *knows* that Ann and Bill had become tenants in common before Bill's death? As the doubt exists, it would be unsafe for a purchaser who actually *knows* that Ann is not solely and beneficially entitled, to rely on the Act. Instead, Ann should be asked to appoint a second trustee, so that the equitable interests can be overreached. Indeed, should a purchaser rely on the Act if he merely *suspects* that someone other than Ann might be interested in the house? A purchaser might be suspicious because he finds that Xerxes occupies the house with Ann, although there could be other explanations for Xerxes's presence, apart from his owning an equitable interest. The Act is presumably designed to protect a purchaser against constructive notice of severance, even if not against actual notice. However, as there is doubt on this point, perhaps a purchaser who is merely suspicious should not rely on the Act either, but should insist on a second trustee.

The 1964 Act specifically says that it does not apply if there is a notice of severance endorsed on the conveyance to the joint tenants, nor if there is an entry in the Central Land Charges Registry as to the bankruptcy of Ann or Bill. On both these occasions a second trustee must be used. (The effect of Bill's bankruptcy would have been that the joint tenancy of the beneficial interest would have been severed, and half would belong to Bill's trustee in bankruptcy.)

So, to sum up, if you are buying from Ann after Bill's death, and wish to shelter behind the protection of the 1964 Act, you should take these precautions:

(i)   read the copy conveyance to Ann and Bill, sent to you as part of the abstract of title. Only rely on the Act if the conveyance says they are beneficial joint tenants. Do not use the Act if the conveyance says they are tenants in common, i.e. have shares. If the conveyance does not say whether they are joint tenants or tenants in common, then it is wiser not to rely on the Act;

(ii) look at Bill's death certificate;

(iii) make a land charge search against the names of Bill and Ann, and check there is no registration as to bankruptcy;

(iv) raise a requisition asking for confirmation that there is no memorandum of severance on the conveyance to Ann and Bill, and check the original deed when you see it at completion;

(v)   be sure that the conveyance from Ann says that she is solely and beneficially interested in the land.

You are then entitled to assume that Ann is the sole owner of the equitable interest, and can plead that you took free from Xerxes's claim because you had no notice of it. The Act also applies when it is not Ann who is conveying, but Ann's personal representative. If Bill dies, and then Ann dies, the Act entitles you to assume that Ann at her death owned the legal and all the equitable interest. In this case you must:

  (i) read the copy conveyance to Ann and Bill to check that it was to them as beneficial joint tenants;

 (ii) look at Bill's death certificate;

(iii) look at a copy of the grant of probate or letter of administration to Ann's estate. This is to confirm the identity of her personal representative;

 (iv) make a land charge search as above;

  (v) check for a memorandum of severance as above;

 (vi) be sure that the conveyance by Ann's personal representatives says that Ann was solely and beneficially interested in the land at her death;

(vii) as the sale is by a personal representative, you should also ensure that the conveyance says the personal representative has not made any previous assent or conveyance in respect of this property, that there is no memorandum on the grant of representation about a previous disposition by the personal representative, and that a memorandum about the conveyance to you *is* endorsed on the grant (see Chapter 10).

Do not forget that the Law of Property (Joint Tenants) Act 1964 does *not* apply to registered title. It does apply to a conveyance of unregistered title even before 1965, as the Act is retrospective to the beginning of 1926.

11.10   The Wolf in Sheep's Clothing, or the Problem of the Disguised Trustee

Suppose that X and Y both contribute towards the purchase price of the house. X contributes £30 000 and Y contributes £42 000. As a result, they share the equitable interest. The legal estate, in an ideal world, would have been conveyed or transferred to both of them, and they would hold it on trust for themselves. Any disposition would have to be by the two of them, be it a sale or a mortgage, and the purchaser or mortgagee would be safe from any claim that he took subject to X's and Y's beneficial interests, as these would have been overreached.

Suppose, however, that the legal estate is conveyed into the name of X alone. This could occur because, for example, Y is under 18 so cannot hold a legal estate, or because Y does not have his wits about him and does not realise that he is being put at a disadvantage, or perhaps because Y has not made a direct financial contribution, but a contribution, for example, in the form of considerable works of improvement. In a case such as that, Y may not consider the possibility of his owning part of the house beneficially until he has to defend that ownership against a third party.

X will hold the legal estate on trust for himself and Y, and the trust will be a statutory trust of land arising under ss.34–36 Law of Property Act 1925 as amended by Trusts of Land and Appointment of Trustees Act 1996. (We are assuming that no express trust is created.) X, of course, is a sole trustee. The trouble is that he is a disguised trustee. There is no express trust declared, and there is nothing in the conveyance or transfer to X that reveals the contribution made by Y and his co-ownership of the equitable interest. If X is registered as proprietor, no restriction will appear on the register. To the world at large, X looks like a beneficial owner.

Suppose now that X decides to sell the property or to mortgage it. A purchaser will want to move in. In the case of a mortgage, if X does not keep up the mortgage repayments, the lender will want to sell with vacant possession. Y might go quietly, but it is now that Y might decide to assert this equitable interest and to claim that it binds the purchaser or mortgagee, who as a result can only claim ownership or a mortgage of part of the property, and may not be able to get possession. As X is a sole trustee, the sale or mortgage could not have overreached Y's equitable interest. However, the purchaser or mortgagee may be able to raise the other defence, of having taken free of the interest because he 'had no notice of it'. We now meet 'the dangerous occupier'.

11.11   The Dangerous Occupier

(a)   Unregistered Title

If the title to the house is unregistered, the purchaser or mortgagee will be raising the classic defence that an equitable interest does not bind a *bona fide* purchaser for value of a legal estate without notice of the interest (re-read Chapter 4 and remember that Y's interest, being an interest of a beneficiary behind a trust, is not registrable under the Land Charges Act 1972). If Y is not living on the property and is not X's spouse, the purchaser may well be able to claim that his ignorance of Y's interest means that the purchaser takes free from it. This would leave Y with no claim against the land, but only with the right to pursue X for a share of the purchase price or mortgage loan.

If Y is living on the property, the purchaser will find it difficult to prove lack of notice, as the occupation would give the purchaser constructive notice of the occupier's rights (see section 4.4).

(b)   Registered Title

The doctrine of notice has no place in registered conveyancing. It is s.70(1)(g) of the Land Registration Act 1925 that presents the problem. As we have seen, if Y has an interest in the land, and is in actual occupation, Y's interest is overriding and will bind the purchaser, unless *Y* is asked if he has an equitable interest and he denies it.

(c)   Case Law

Litigation in this area shows a seesaw between the desire to protect Y and the desire to protect the innocent purchaser or lender. There is, at the moment, no way of reconciling their claims. The state of play at the moment seems to be this:

(i) It is now quite clear that the usual overreaching provisions apply, whether or not Y is in occupation. So X could overreach Y's interest by appointing a second trustee to join with X in selling or mortgaging (see *City of London Building Society* v. *Flegg* [1988]).

(ii) If X mortgages the house to the lender as part of the process of buying the house, i.e. the bank provides the purchase price, and Y *knows* of the intention of X to mortgage, the lender takes precedence over Y's interest and is not bound by it. One reason is that Y's equitable interest arises from a trust that is imputed to X and Y, i.e. the courts impute an agreement between them that as each has contributed towards the purchase price, then each will have a share of the beneficial interest. However, when imputing this agreement, the court will, when the balance of the purchase price is to be raised by a mortgage loan, also impute an intention by both X and Y that their interests are to be postponed to the mortgage (see *Bristol and West Building Society* v. *Henning* [1985]). Another way of putting the argument is to say that Y has authorised X to mortgage the house and to give the mortgage priority over Y's interest (see *Abbey National Building Society* v. *Cann and anor* [1990]).* The principle has been extended to the case of a remortgage (see *Equity & Law Home Loans Ltd* v. *Prestridge* [1991] 1 All ER 909).

The principle applies in both registered and unregistered title, and the fact that Y is living there at the time of the mortgage makes no difference. The lender cannot be affected by Y's interest, as the nature of the interest is one that is postponed to the mortgage. The principle seems to offer the lender an excellent defence against Y, because it is unlikely that Y will not know that the balance of the purchase price is being raised by a mortgage loan. However, this has happened, and it has been held (see *Lloyd's Bank plc* v. *Rosset* [1988] in the Court of Appeal) that the courts cannot impute to Y an intention that his interest should be postponed to the mortgage, when Y does not know that the mortgage will exist.

The lender may still not be affected by Y's interest, however, because of the principle stated in the next paragraph.

(iii) When the mortgage loan finances the purchase of the house another reason why Y's interest will not bind the lender is that the conveyance or transfer of the property to X and X's immediate mortgage of it to the lender will be looked on as one indivisible transaction, so that the estate that vests in X is, from the outset, subject to the lender's mortgage, and it is only from that encumbered estate that Y can derive his equitable interest. It follows from this that the mortgage will have priority over Y's equitable interest, whether Y knew of the mortgage or not (*Abbey National Building Society* v. *Cann and anor* [1990]).

(iv) If X already owns the house, and then later mortgages it or sells it, then Y's interest might well bind the lender or purchaser, because of Y's occupation (as already shown).

(d)   What Do We Do about the Dangerous Occupier?

From the Purchaser's Point of View   Not surprisingly the property information form asks the seller if any other person is living on the property, and if that person has any claim of ownership.

If the answer is 'Yes, my Auntie Beryl, and she co-owns the equitable interest', then at least the purchaser knows what to do about it. The seller is disclosed as a single trustee, and must be asked to appoint another trustee. This can be done before contract, so that the two trustees will be the sellers in the contract, or it can be done after the seller has entered into the contract, as the final step in his establishing the soundness of his title. Auntie Beryl would be a good choice as the second trustee, because if she is one of the sellers in the contract, she will be personally promising good title, and vacant possession. If she refuses to leave after completion and makes a nuisance of herself, *she* will be in breach of contract.

If the seller answers 'No, there is no one in occupation but me', or 'Yes, Auntie Beryl is here, but she has no interest in the property', then this is not a satisfactory answer from the purchaser's point of view. If it is a lie, he will have an action against the seller for misrepresentation, but it will not clear Auntie Beryl's interest from the title. It is *Auntie Beryl's* statement that she has no interest that in unregistered conveyancing will save the purchaser from notice, or in registered title, will ensure that her interest is not overriding. So it is still advisable, once Auntie Beryl is discovered, to have her appearing in the contract. However, her role may be different. She is there to put *her* signature to the statement that she has no equitable interest.

From the Seller's Point of View   If the seller knows that there is an equitable interest to be overreached, the mechanism is simple enough. He must appoint another trustee to act with him. The cost of preparing the deed of appointment cannot be thrown onto the purchaser. Any condition in the contract saying that the purchaser must pay the cost is void (s.49 of the Law of Property Act 1925). Nor can the seller say that instead of overreaching the equitable interest, the owner of it will join in the conveyance or transfer to assign it. Any such condition in the contract would also be void (s.49 again). Anyway, a purchaser of the legal estate should never take the trouble and risk of investigating ownership of equitable interests if the equitable interests can be overreached.

The seller should remember that it is not enough to overreach the equitable interest. He is, in the contract, promising vacant possession. So, to revert to our two friends X and Y, X (if he is selling, rather than mortgaging) will be in breach of contract unless Y actually leaves the house before completion. It is true that if Y remains in occupation after his interest has been overreached, the purchaser could successfully sue him for possession, but there will be delay and expense, for which X will have to compensate the purchaser.

If X does not appoint Y as the second trustee so that Y does not become a contracting party, then X is only absolutely safe if Y leaves the property before the date of the contract. If Y is uncooperative, X would have to obtain and enforce a court order for possession. Remember that X holds on trust for himself and Y because Y, through his contribution to the purchase price, owns part of the equitable interest. X and Y may well have bought the property because they intended to live in it together. Y has a right to occupy by virtue of s.12 of Trusts of Land and Appointment of Trustees Act 1996 if 'the purposes of the trust include making the land available for his occupation . . .' The court can remove this right, but may well not do so.

From the Point of View of the Seller's Legal Representative Suppose that you are acting for the seller, and he tells you that his mother owns part of the property. If she is co-owner of the legal estate, it is impossible for your client to sell alone, and instructions to sell are also needed from the mother. You must ask your client to discuss the matter with his mother, and explain to her that her cooperation is needed if the property is to be sold. If, as a result, she also instructs you to act in the sale, you would still be unable to act for her if you have any suspicion that the instructions were not given of her own free will. Otherwise, you can act for your original client and his mother, unless it transpires there is some conflict of interest between them. (These are rules of professional conduct. See the Law Society's Guide to Professional Conduct of Solicitors 7th Edition, Chapters 11 and 15.) You would expect any house bought from the proceeds of the sale also to be put in both their names, and the beneficial interest to be shared in the same way that it was shared in the house just sold.

If you discover that your client is the sole owner of the legal estate, but that his mother owns the entire equitable interest, your client is holding the legal estate on what is called a bare trust. In this case, no sale should take place without the mother's consent. It is her decision, not that of the estate owner, as to whether or not the house is sold.

If you discover that your client is sole owner of the legal estate but that he and his mother share the equitable interest, her interest can be overreached, but as previously said, her consent is needed as your client is promising that the house will be unoccupied at completion. You can approach her to explain that her cooperation is necessary, either as the second trustee, or to join in the contract to promise vacant possession, but you cannot advise her to cooperate, and you should suggest she obtains legal advice. If, in fact, she is quite happy to move, she may instruct you. You can then act for her and her son provided that there is no conflict of interest.

11.12   The Dangerous Spouse

The problem of the concealed trustee and the dangerous occupier is particularly likely to occur in the case of a married couple, and judging from the litigation on the subject, it usually takes the form of the husband holding the legal estate on a concealed trust for himself and his wife, who co-owns the equitable interest. That is why the facts in the next paragraph take that form, but of course everything said is equally applicable where the wife owns the legal estate on trust for herself and her husband.

Let us imagine that Henry and his wife, Winifred, are living together in the matrimonial home, 1 South Avenue. Henry is sole owner of the legal estate. It is true that Winifred may well own an equitable interest in the house. Her interest is overreachable, but as has been said earlier, her consent to any sale by her husband is in fact necessary, because Henry has to promise in the contract that the house will be empty on completion. However, this point about vacant possession would not apply if Henry were mortgaging the house, so that he could, by appointing a second trustee, create a mortgage that would overreach Winifred's interest. This would mean that if the loan were not repaid, the lender could turn Winifred out of the house.

However, an occupying *spouse*, whether or not she (or he) has an equitable interest, has another string to her (his) bow, namely the statutory right to occupy a house that is or has been, or was intended by them to be, the matrimonial home. The right is given to a spouse who does not own the legal interest in it. To put it at its simplest, as Henry owns the legal estate in the home, and Winifred does not, Winifred has this statutory right to remain in occupation until the right is destroyed by an order of the court (ss.30–32 Family Law Act 1996).

Winifred's right is capable of binding any purchaser from Henry, or any mortgagee. So you can see that Winifred has the power to prevent any disposition of the house without her consent. (You can see from this why the Family Law Act 1996 does not apply when both spouses own the legal estate. No disposition is then possible anyway, without both spouses signing the deed.)

However, Winifred's right must be protected if it *is* to bind a purchaser or mortgagee. If the title to the home is registered she *must* put a notice on the register. (The 1996 Act specifically provides that the right of occupation is not overriding under s.70(1)(g) of the Land Registration Act 1925 even though the spouse is living in the home.) If the title to the home is unregistered, Winifred must register a class F land charge against Henry's name. So you can see that if Xerxes is buying from Henry, or lending money to him, Xerxes must be concerned about the possibilities:

(a) that Winifred owns part of the equitable interest;
(b) that Winifred will protect her statutory right of occupation by registering a notice or land charge before completion.

Protecting the Purchaser

If Xerxes is buying, and is worried about the threat of the Family Law Act, he can before contract check whether or not Winifred has already protected her right. If she has, and refuses to join in the agreement for sale, it would be best for both Henry and Xerxes to abandon the idea of sale. Henry will be entering into a contract that he is probably doomed to break. He promises vacant possession and can only give it if Winifred cancels the registration, or if he obtains a court order for the ending of the right of occupation. (By virtue of para. 3 of Schedule 4 of the 1996 Act, a seller who promises vacant possession is also deemed to promise the cancellation of any registration protecting the statutory right of occupation, or that he will on completion give the purchaser an application for its cancellation signed by the spouse.)

However, even if Henry and Xerxes satisfy themselves that Winifred has not registered her right before exchange of the two parts of the agreement, there is nothing to prevent her from registering after contract. The last moment for registration would be the date of Xerxes's pre-completion search. The priority period given by the search would protect Xerxes from any registration after the date of the search. Therefore, both Henry and Xerxes must protect themselves against this registration: Henry, because he faces being liable for breach of contract; Xerxes, because he wants to acquire a house, rather than a right to damages for breach of contract.

The answer is to have Winifred as a party to the contract, in which she will promise not to register the right of occupation, or to cancel any registration that already exists.

To sum up, on the sale of a matrimonial home, you will expect to see both spouses appearing in the contract and signing it, either:

(a) because they both own the legal estate, and are, therefore, joint sellers – this will dispose of their equitable interests, as they will be overreached and no rights of occupation under the Family Law Act 1996 will exist;

(b) because one spouse was originally the sole owner of the legal estate, but has appointed the other spouse as a second trustee;

(c) because one spouse is sole beneficial owner, but the other spouse is joining in to confirm that he/she has no equitable interest, and will be releasing any rights under the Family Law Act 1996.

Protecting the Purchaser's Mortgagee

To recap, you can see that the purchaser's mortgagee faces *two* dangerous spouses, and may be bound by an equitable interest and/or right of occupation belonging to the seller's spouse, and by an equitable interest belonging to the purchaser's spouse.

Any claim by the seller's spouse should be cleared away by the drafting of the contract of sale between seller and purchaser (see above).

It now seems unlikely, following the House of Lord's decision in *Abbey National Building Society* v. *Cann and anor* [1990] (see section 11.10 and case notes) that the mortgagee will be bound by an equitable interest belonging to the borrower's spouse, provided that the money is lent to finance the purchase. If the mortgage is created *after* the house has been acquired, the mortgagee will feel safe if:

1. both the purchase and the mortgage is by both spouses (overreaching); or
2. the purchase and the mortgage is by one spouse, but the other spouse, before completion, gives written confirmation to the lender that he/she knows of the mortgage and agrees that it takes precedence over his/her equitable interest (but see the next section).

11.13   Undue Influence

It has been previously suggested that if the house is in the name of, say, the husband alone, the wife should be made a party to any disposition of it, or at least confirm in signed writing that she does not claim any interest in it. Any person relying on that signature, such as a purchaser or a lender, should be very careful as to how the signature is obtained.

Suppose that a bank is lending money to the husband on the security of a house that he already owns. Perhaps the loan is to provide money for the husband's business. The wife may own a share of the equitable interest, or may be one of the owners of the legal estate. Her signature will be needed to the mortgage papers. The wife thinks that it is imprudent to mortgage the house, but her husband puts pressure on her, and she signs. He fails to meet the mortgage repayments, and the Bank intends to sell the house. Can she escape the consequences of signing the mortgage documents? She might be able to do so.

She would have to establish that she was induced to sign by the undue influence of her husband or by his fraudulent misrepresentation. This would ensure that her signature did not bind her as against her husband. Her signature would not bind her as against the Bank if she could prove either of the two following matters:

(a) that when he persuaded her to sign, her husband was acting as agent or representative of the Bank. (See *Kingsnorth Trust Ltd* v. *Bell** [1986].) For this reason the Bank should approach the wife directly. It should not hand the documents to the husband and ask him to procure his wife's signature on the Bank's behalf
(b) that the Bank had actual or constructive notice of the husband's undue influence.

According to the case of *Barclays Bank plc* v. *O'Brien** [1994], a lender will have constructive notice of undue influence if

1. the transaction is, on the face of it, not to the financial advantage of the co-owner and

2. the lender knows that there is an emotional relationship between the borrower and the co-owner.

To return to our imaginary facts, the close relationship, which will be taken to exist between husband and wife, will not be enough to fix the Bank with constructive notice. The Bank must also be aware that the loan is solely for the benefit of the husband. So, if the Bank were deceived by the husband into thinking that the purpose of the loan was to benefit both himself and his wife; that it was, for example, to pay school fees or to buy a holiday home for them both; the Bank would not have *constructive* notice of undue influence. (See *CIBC Mortgages* v. *Pitt* [1994].) It seems that if the Bank had actual notice of undue influence, then whether or not the transaction is to the disadvantage of the co-owner is immaterial.

What should the Bank do to protect itself against constructive notice? It was said in the O'Brien case that the lender should take reasonable steps to try to ensure that the co-owner understood the nature and effect of the transaction, and that her consent to it was an informed consent. So, the Bank should advise the wife to take separate and independent advice from her own solicitor. This advice should preferably be given at a meeting where the husband is not present, although this is not essential. (See *Banco Exterior Internacional* v. *Mann* [1995].)

Notes

(a) The principles of the O'Brien case apply, as was said in the case, to 'all cases where there is an emotional relationship between the cohabitees'. It covers all cohabitation, whether heterosexual or homosexual. It can apply to other relationships, for example child and parent, if the co-owner 'reposes trust and confidence' in the borrower. (See *Avon Finance Co. Ltd.* v. *Bridger* [1985].)

(b) The lender is protected if a solicitor certifies to him that the co-owner has been advised about the transaction and understands it, even if the solicitor is not only acting for the co-owner, but also acting for the lender and, indeed, for the borrower. (See *Halifax Mortgage Services Ltd.* v. *Stepsky* [1996].) A solicitor who is in this position, however, should clearly consider the possibility of conflict of interest. (See the discussion of this issue in *Clark Boyce* v. *Mouat* [1994].)

Case Notes

Bristol and West Building Society v. *Henning and anor [1985] 2 All ER 606, [1985] 1 WLR 778, 50 P & CR 237*

Mr and Mrs Henning had lived together as man and wife for several years. They decided to buy a house. The title to the house was unregistered. It was bought with the aid of a mortgage loan. The legal estate was conveyed into the name of Mr

Henning alone, and only he created the mortgage. Mrs Henning did not directly provide any of the purchase money, but it was agreed that she should run a self-sufficiency project using the large garden.

The relationship broke down, and Mr Henning left the house and ceased to make the mortgage payments. The Building Society claimed possession. Mrs Henning claimed that she had an equitable interest in the house, and that her interest bound the society, as she was living in the house when the mortgage was executed, and so the Society had notice of it.

It was held that any equitable interest she might have arose from a resulting trust, on the basis of an imputed agreement between herself and Mr Henning that she should have such an interest. If so, it must also be a term of that agreement that her equitable interest should be postponed to the mortgage. She knew and supported the proposal that the purchase price of the house should be raised on mortgage. It was their common intention that the man should have the power to create the mortgage, and it must also have been their intention that the mortgage should have priority over any equitable interests in the house. The mortgagee was, therefore, entitled to possession.

Equity & Law Home Loans Ltd v. *Prestridge and anor [1992] 1 All ER 909*

Mr Prestridge was sole registered proprietor of the house in which he lived with Mrs Brown. She had contributed £10 000 towards the purchase price and the balance had been raised by a mortgage loan of £30 000 taken out by Mr Prestridge with the Britannia Building Society with Mrs Brown's knowledge. Some time after the original purchase, Mr Prestridge applied to Equity & Law to remortgage the house for £43 000. Equity & Law knew that Mrs Brown was living in the house but nevertheless lent the money on the security of a mortgage given by Mr Prestridge alone. He used the money to pay off the money owing to the Britannia, pocketed the balance, left the house and failed to make any payments due on the mortgage. Equity & Law claimed possession.

It was held

- That Mrs Brown owned all the equitable interest in the house. (The reasons for this do not concern us.)
- That her interest had not bound the Britannia Building Society. Applying the reasoning in the *Henning* case led to the conclusion that she had agreed that her interest should be postponed to the Britannia mortgage.
- That her interest did not bind Equity & Law either. This is because the court was prepared to impute to her not only an agreement that her interest should be postponed to the mortgage she knew of, but also to any mortgage that replaced it on no less advantageous financial terms. Note that the imputed agreement only extended to the amount of the original loan, i.e. £30 000. Equity & Law could only enforce the mortgage against the house for that amount, not for the additional £13 000.

Abbey National Building Society v. *Cann and anor [1990] 1 All ER 1085 [1990] 2 WLR 832*

Mr Cann proposed buying a house. He told the Society that he intended to live there by himself, although in fact he was buying the house for his mother to live in. The Society made a formal offer of loan, which was accepted. Contracts for the purchase were then exchanged, and at 12.20 p.m. on 13 August 1984 the purchase and the mortgage were completed. Mrs Cann (the mother) was then abroad on holiday, but at 11.45 a.m. her son started to move the furniture into the house and carpets were laid.

On 13 September 1984 Mr Cann was registered at HM Land Registry as proprietor, and the mortgage was registered as a registered charge. By that date Mrs Cann was living in the house. Mr Cann failed to make the mortgage payments, and the Society sought possession of the house. Mrs Cann claimed an equitable interest in the house (for reasons based on a contribution towards the purchase price and proprietory estoppel) and that this interest was overriding by virtue of s.70(1)(g) of the Land Registration Act 1925 and therefore bound the Society. Her claim failed for the following reasons:

1. That although a purchaser or mortgagee took subject to overriding interests existing at the date of the registration of the dealing, nevertheless if it was claimed that the interest was overriding by virtue of s.70(1)(g), the claimant must prove that she was in occupation not at the date of registration but the earlier date of completion (i.e. in this case, at 12.20 p.m. on 13 August). Mrs Cann was not in occupation at that time (see section 3.17).
2. Alternatively, where the purchase of a property is financed by a mortgage loan, then although in theory there is a tiny gap in time between the completion of the transfer to the purchaser and his subsequent mortgage, so that it might be arguable that an equitable interest could arise after the transfer but before the mortgage and therefore potentially bind the mortgagee, realistically no such gap exists, or certainly not in the case where the loan has been made pursuant to an earlier agreement that it would be secured by a mortgage. It is all one transaction. The only thing ever available to Mr Cann to hold on trust for, or share with, his mother was a *mortgaged* property. For this reason, even if Mrs Cann *had* been in occupation on 13 August, her interest would still not have bound the mortgagee.

Kingsnorth Trust Ltd v. Bell [1986] 1 All ER 423

Mr Bell owned the legal estate in the matrimonial home, but his wife shared the equitable interest. Mr Bell wished to buy a new business, and to raise money to buy it by a mortgage on the home. The solicitors to the Kingsnorth Trust Ltd asked Mr Bell's solicitors to arrange for the execution of the mortgage deeds, and they asked Mr Bell to obtain his wife's signature. He lied to his wife, telling her he needed the money for his existing business. She did not instruct solicitors to act for her, and had no independent advice.

It was held that Kingsnorth Trust, through its solicitors, had instructed the husband to obtain his wife's signature. He had, in effect, been acting as Kingsnorth's agent, and the lenders were bound by his fraudulent misrepresentation.

Barclays Bank Plc v. O'Brien [1994] 1AC 180; [1993] 4 All ER417; [1993] 3WLR 786

Mr. and Mrs. O'Brien owned the matrimonial home. They agreed to execute a second mortgage of it. This was to secure overdraft facilities extended by the Bank to a company in which Mr. O'Brien had an interest, but his wife did not. The Bank did not advise Mrs. O'Brien as to the purport of the mortgage deed nor did it advise her to consult a solicitor before she signed it. She signed the deed without reading it, relying on her husband's false representations that the mortgage only secured a limited amount and would last only three weeks.

It was held that by virtue of her husband's misrepresentation, Mrs. O'Brien had a right as against her husband to have the mortgage deed set aside: that as she was offering to stand surety for her husband's debt in a transaction that was not to her financial advantage the Bank was put on enquiry, unless it took reasonable steps to ensure that her signature has been properly obtained: the Bank had not done this and so had constructive notice of the husband's misrepresentation: that the wife could, therefore, have the mortgage set aside as against the Bank.

Workshop

Attempt these problems yourself, then read the specimen solutions at the end of the book.

Problem 1

The legal freehold estate was conveyed in 1980 to three brothers, Albert Brick, Robert Brick and Sidney Brick. The conveyance declared that they were to hold the legal estate on trust for themselves as tenants in common as part of their partnership assets.

In August 1985 the legal estate was conveyed by Albert and Sidney Brick to Jennifer Cooper. A recital in the 1985 conveyance stated that Robert Brick had retired from the partnership.

You have a copy of a search certificate (the search having been made by Miss Cooper when she bought the land from the two Bricks) which reveals that a C(iv) land charge was registered against the name of Robert Brick and Albert Brick on 3 July 1985, but that there is nothing registered against the name of Sydney Brick.

If you are acting for a purchaser from Miss Cooper, is there anything on this title to cause you concern?

Problem 2

You have been instructed by Mrs Anne Mason to deal with a loan she is obtaining from the County Building Society for the purpose of installing central heating and double glazing in her house. The house was erected thirty years ago and is not in a mining area. She has handed you the land certificate which she explains she and her late husband were given because the title deeds were lost. You have also been instructed to act for the building society, and have obtained office copy entries. There are no entries on the charges register, and the proprietorship register looks like this:

B.   *PROPRIETORSHIP REGISTER*
   Title: Prossessory.
   First registered proprietors
   Alan Mason and Anne Mason
   both of 48 Queens Road, Loamster, Loamshire
   registered on 13 September 1984

She has also handed you her late husband's will which has not been proved. It leaves all his property to her absolutely.

1. Does the will have to be proved in order to complete the mortgage? What steps do you need to take to have the title registered in her sole name?
2. What is the significance of registration with possessory title, and will this fact create any problems in dealing with the mortgage?
3. What searches will you make on behalf of the building society?

12 Easements and Restrictive Covenants

These two incumbrances have been mentioned in nearly all the previous chapters. This chapter discusses them in greater detail.

12.1 Sale of Land that Already has the Benefit of an Easement Over a Neighbour's Land

Simple. Before you draft the particulars in the agreement for sale, re-read Chapter 5. Before you draft the transfer, read Chapters 14 and 15.

12.2 Sale of Land that is Already Burdened with an Easement

Simple. When drafting the agreement for sale, list the easement as an incumbrance on the property (see the topic of disclosure in Chapter 5). When drafting the conveyance of unregistered title, mention the easement (see Chapter 15).

12.3 Sale of Land when the Seller will Continue to Own Land Nearby

Unfortunately, this is not simple. There are two dangers from the seller's point of view:

(a) that he may unintentionally give the purchaser rights over land that he is retaining:
(b) that he may not reserve a right to use the land he is selling, for example as a means of access, even though that use would add considerably to the enjoyment or value of the land he has retained.

Study Figure 12.1.

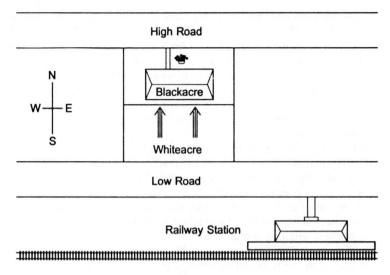

Figure 12.1

Blackacre is a house and surrounding garden. Whiteacre is a field. They are both owned and occupied by O. The house fronts on to the High Road, and if you look carefully you can see the front path, with a tub of flowers beside it. However, O often takes a short cut across Whiteacre to reach the railway station and surrounding shops.

The field is usually reached from Low Road, but O has often driven farm machinery along the edge of Blackacre as a short cut to and from Whiteacre, instead of going the long way round by road.

The arrows indicate light streaming across Whiteacre into the windows of the house on Blackacre.

At the moment there are no easements over either property, as a person cannot have an easement over land which he owns and occupies himself.

Suppose, however, that O now sells Blackacre to P. We will ignore the contract for sale for the moment, and concentrate on the transfer. We will assume that it is a silent transfer, i.e. it makes no express mention of easements. The result of the silent transfer could be this:

(a) Blackacre may acquire an easement of light, and a right of way over Whiteacre.

There are various reasons why a sale of part of the seller's land may contain an implied grant of easements to the purchaser. The reason for the implied grant in these circumstances is what is known as the rule in *Wheeldon* v. *Burrows* [1879]. This says that if at the time O disposes of the land, he is using the land he is retaining to the advantage of the land he is selling, and that use is continuous and apparent, and necessary for the reasonable enjoyment of the land being sold, the purchaser is entitled to continue that use, and the necessary easements are implied into the transfer. Of course, between O and P, whether the short cut was apparent, and whether it is reasonably necessary, are both open to debate. That is why it is unfortunate for P that he has to rely on an *implied* grant, the existence of which O might deny.

It is unfortunate for O that the implied grant might exist. In particular, an easement of light could prevent O building anything on the field that would block off a substantial amount of light to the house's windows.

(b) Whiteacre will not have the benefit of a right of way over Blackacre, so O will be unable to continue to drive across it to reach the field. This is because there is scarcely ever an *implied* reservation of an easement by the seller over the land that he has sold. There is implied an essential means of access, when without the implied right of way the rest of the seller's land could not be reached at all, and probably an easement of support when an owner sells part of his building. Nothing else can be relied on. The short cut across Blackacre is *not* an essential means of access, as the field can be reached from Low Road.

From O's point of view, we can now see that he would have preferred the transfer or conveyance *not* to be silent. He would have liked to see in it:

(a) a clause saying that there was no implied grant of easements to P (*Wheeldon* v. *Burrows* can be ousted by agreement) or at least that there was not an easement of light.
(b) a clause saying that he did reserve a right of way over Blackacre.

From P's point of view, we can see that P would have preferred an express grant of, say, the right of way over Whiteacre. The existence of this right would then be beyond dispute, and could easily be proved when P re-sold. In other words, the transfer or conveyance should not have been silent. Instead, it should have spoken up.

Of course, neither party can insist on anything going into the transfer or conveyance, unless the preceding contract says that it can go in. It is the contract that governs the drafting and contents of the transfer. So O and P, when agreeing the terms of the contract, should have decided on special conditions settling what easements were to be reserved expressly in the transfer, what easements were to be granted expressly, and that the transfer should state that no others were to be granted by implication.

The conditions in the contract are not creating the easements, but merely providing that the easements will be created by the transfer or conveyance. Therefore it is essential to have the necessary grant and reservation in the transfer, together with the statement preventing any implied grant. If through carelessness, the transfer was drafted without any reference to easements, the seller would have no easements over the part sold to the purchaser, and the purchaser could perhaps claim easements other than those that had been intended by the contract.

If O and P forget to put in special conditions to deal with the grant and reservation of easements but the contract incorporates the standard conditions, standard condition 3.4 will govern the drafting of the conveyance or transfer. Condition 3.4.2 states first of all that the buyer will not have any right of light or air over the retained land. This prevents there being any implied grant of such rights by the contract to the purchaser and also entitles the seller to put a clause in the conveyance preventing there being any implied grant by the conveyance.

Subject to this, condition 3.4.2 then provides that the seller as owner of the retained land and buyer as owner of the land being sold will each have the rights over the land of the other which they would have had if they were two separate buyers to whom the seller had made simultaneous transfers of the land being sold and the retained land. Condition 3.4.3 adds that either party can request that the conveyance or transfer contain the necessary express grant or reservation.

At first sight this is incomprehensible, but it is based on this point of law; that if – in the case of Blackacre and Whiteacre – instead of selling Blackacre and retaining Whiteacre O had sold the two properties simultaneously, Blackacre to P and Whiteacre to Q, P would have had an implied grant of easements over Whiteacre and Q would have had an implied grant of easements over Blackacre. So P might well have had a right of light and way over Whiteacre and Q a right of way over Blackacre (not a right of light, as there were no windows on Whiteacre receiving light at the time of the conveyance). Condition 5 is, therefore, saying that you must imagine that O, instead of retaining Whiteacre, is buying it. What easements would have been impliedly granted to O? Answer – *Wheeldon* v. *Burrows* easements and possibly others. Then those are the easements that O can expressly reserve in the conveyance of Blackacre for the benefit of Whiteacre and himself. Similarly, P is entitled to have inserted in the conveyance as express easements those that would have been implied into the conveyance with the exception of easements of light and air. So the condition decreases P's right to easements, but does mean that P can ask for an *express* grant to be written on the face of the conveyance, instead of having to rely on an implied grant. O's right to easements is increased and put on a par with P's. Indeed O's rights are better than P's, because there is nothing in the condition to prevent O expressly reserving rights of light or air, providing that the facts justify it.

There are considerable drawbacks in relying on the standard condition. It may not represent the parties' intentions. The seller, for instance, might not want the purchaser to have any easements at all over his land. Another point is that if one party wants to insist on his rights under it, and have the express grant or reservation written into the transfer, the other party can deny that the easement in question would have been the subject matter of an implied grant, e.g. because it is not continuous and apparent. If it would not have been the subject matter of an implied grant, it cannot, under condition 4.3 be the subject matter of an express grant. So the condition is a breeding ground for dispute.

(*Note:* A grant of easements is not implied only under *Wheeldon* v. *Burrows*. Easements of necessity are implied, and there may be a grant implied into the conveyance or transfer by s.62 of the Law of Property Act 1925. The rules are not dwelt on, as the purpose of this chapter is to urge you to replace an implied grant by an express grant, following a special condition in the contract.)

12.4   Particular Points about Easements and the Land Registration Act 1925

The Land Registration Act seems particularly obscure on the question of easements.

The principles *seem* to be as follows:

(a) If land has the benefit of a legal easement when the title to that land is first registered, then the easement remains legal. It will therefore bind a later purchaser of the servient tenement (the land over which the easement is exercised). If the title to the servient tenement is unregistered, the easement will bind the purchaser of it because the easement is legal. If the title to the servient tenement is registered, the purchaser of it will be bound by the easement, because the easement, being legal, is overriding under s.70(1)(a) of the Land Registration Act 1925.

(b) If an easement is granted out of a registered title, the creation of the easement must be followed by its registration. The principle involved here is one that has been met already in section 3.11. The creation of an easement out of registered title is a registrable dealing. The easement will not be legal until it is registered. (See ss. 19(2) and 22(2) Land Registration Act 1925.) Pending registration, the easement is only equitable, and possibly is only a minor interest (see section 3.15).

If an easement is granted out of registered title, and the servient tenement is also registered land, the registration of the easement has two aspects. The benefit of the easement must be registered on the title to the dominant tenement, and the burden must be registered on the title to the servient tenement.

The Registrar can only register the benefit if he is sure that the grant of the easement is valid. As the title to the servient tenement is registered, it should be quite clear that the servient owner has the power to grant the easement, provided that the servient owner is registered with absolute title. If there is doubt, the registrar may only be able to state in the register to the dominant tenement that the easement is *claimed.*

For the burden to be registered against the servient tenement, the servient owner should be asked to put his land certificate on deposit at the registry. If the land certificate is not put on deposit, a caution will have to be entered on the register to protect the easement.

If this situation – of an easement being granted out of, and for the benefit of, a registered title – occurs on the occasion of a sale of part of the land in the title, registration of the benefit and burden of the easements should present no difficulty. The title is known to the Registrar and the seller's land certificate will have been put on deposit to await the registration of the transfer of part. The Registrar can, therefore, check the validity of the grant, and can register the burden of the easements reserved by the seller on the purchaser's new title, and can register the burden of the easements given to the purchaser on the seller's title.

It is possible, however, that the easement could be granted by a deed of grant, quite independently of any transfer, e.g. by one neighbour to another. In this case it must be remembered that it is insufficient for the benefit to be registered. The burden must also be registered on the title to the servient tenement. If this is not done, there is the possibility that when the servient tenement is sold, the new owner may be able to claim that the easement does not bind him, as it is an unprotected minor interest.

Could this unregistered easement bind the purchaser because it is an overriding interest? There is no certain answer. Remember that the easement is only equitable, because it has not been registered. There is considerable controversy over whether an equitable easement can be overriding under s.70(1)(a) (see 3.15). In view of the uncertainty, it is clearly important that the easement be properly registered.

(c) If an easement is created by a deed of grant, and only the servient tenement is registered, the burden should be registered on that title. If only the dominant tenement is registered, the benefit will be entered on the register, provided that the registrar is satisfied that the grant is valid. He can only be satisfied if the title to the servient tenement is proved to him. Otherwise, at best he can only put a note to the effect that the easement is claimed.

(d) If part of the land in a registered title is sold, the purchaser may acquire easements over the seller's retained land by virtue of an implied grant, e.g. under *Wheeldon* v. *Burrows*, or by virtue of s.62 of the Law of Property Act 1925. These easements take effect as overriding interests, under rule 258 of Land Registration Rules 1925, and do not have to be noted on the register of title to the servient tenement in order to bind a purchaser of it. Nor do they have to be entered on the register of title to the dominant tenement for the dominant owner to enjoy them.

12.5 Covenants

When the seller will continue to own land near the property he is selling, he will also consider whether it is desirable to insist that the purchaser, in the conveyance or transfer to him, give covenants back to the seller.

One purpose of the covenants will be that the seller can control the use of the land he has sold. If he has sold the end of his garden to a developer, he may be prepared to accept the building of a bungalow, but will want a covenant by the developer not to build anything else, for example a block of flats.

Another purpose might be to force the purchaser to carry out work, for example, repairs or fencing. Of course, the covenant might equally well be given by seller to purchaser.

12.6   The Contract

Suppose that Sarah owns both Blackacre and Whiteacre. She contracts to sell Whiteacre to Patricia. The agreement for sale provides that in the conveyance or transfer Patricia will covenant:

(a) to use Whiteacre only as a single dwelling-house;
(b) to fence the boundary between Whiteacre and Blackacre.

Notice that the covenant is going to be given in the conveyance or transfer. The contract is merely giving Sarah the right to insist that the conveyance does contain the covenant. The contract can, and should, prescribe the exact wording to be used in the conveyance, because for example:

(a) The benefit of a covenant can be 'annexed' to the benefited land (in this case, Blackacre) by – amongst other possibilities – saying that it is given 'for the benefit of each and every part of Blackacre'. The result of the covenant being worded in such a way is that the benefit and the land become inseparable, so that a later purchaser of any part of Blackacre that does in fact benefit from the covenant, acquires not only the land but the power to enforce the covenant. There is then no need to show that the benefit of the covenant has been expressly assigned.

   It is true that the benefit of a covenant may be annexed without any express wording, owing to the wording implied into the covenant by s.78 of the Law of Property Act 1925 (as interpreted in the case of *Federated Homes Ltd* v. *Mill Lodge Properties Ltd* [1980]) but as the benefited land should be identified in the conveyance, express words of annexation might as well be used.
(b) A covenant to repair or to fence should define the obligation exactly, so the wording should be settled in the contract.

12.7   The Conveyance or Transfer

In the conveyance, the covenant is actually given by purchaser to seller, or seller to purchaser, using the wording already settled by the preceding contract.

12.8 Protecting the Covenant

We must now distinguish between the two covenants in our imagined contract. The fencing covenant is positive, as it requires labour or the spending of money to perform it. The user covenant is negative. Nothing has to be *done* to observe it, it is rather the case of not doing anything to change the existing use.

The point of the distinction is, of course, that the negative covenant (or, as it is generally called in a conveyancing context, the *restrictive* covenant) is capable of becoming an incumbrance on the land and so may be enforceable not only against Patricia but against whoever claims the land through her (*Tulk* v. *Moxhay* [1848]). However, the incumbrance is an equitable one and so will not automatically bind a purchaser from Patricia.

If the title to Whiteacre is already registered before Sarah sells it, the negative covenant is a minor interest, and will only bind a transferee for value from Patricia if the covenant is protected by an entry on the register, either a notice or a caution. Usually, a covenant is given when part of the seller's land is sold (although this does not have to be so). For this reason a restrictive covenant is usually protected by a notice. Suppose that Sarah, when she sells Whiteacre to Patricia, is selling only part of the land in her registered title, and Patricia covenants in the transfer to use the property only as a dwelling-house. Patricia will lodge the transfer in the Registry, to be registered as proprietor of the part she has bought. The Registrar, when registering the transfer, will also put a notice on the charges register of Patricia's title. If Sarah had given a negative covenant to Patricia, this covenant should be noted on the charges register of Sarah's title. This needs the deposit of Sarah's land certificate but in these circumstances it will already be on deposit to await registration of the transfer of part. If the title to Whiteacre is unregistered, Patricia will have to apply for first registration of title, and, again, the covenant will be protected by an entry on the register of title at HM Land Registry. (It will not be protected by registration as a land charge at the Land Charges Registry – see s.14 Land Charges Act 1972.)

A positive covenant does not create an incumbrance on land, so that when Patricia conveys Whiteacre to Quentin, he will not have to perform the fencing covenant, at least not in the sense that it can be enforced against him directly by Sarah. Sarah could only enforce the user covenant against him.

However, Quentin may be affected by the enforcement against him of an indemnity covenant.

12.9 Indemnity Covenants

Return to Sarah and Patricia. When Patricia gave the two covenants she undertook a perpetual liability. She will have covenanted not only that *she* would perform the covenants but that *anyone* who later succeeded to the land would also perform them (s.79 of the Law of Property Act 1925). Therefore, when Patricia sells Whiteacre to Quentin, if he does not fence or does not observe the user covenant, Sarah can sue *Patricia* for breach of contract.

Sarah may not bother to sue Patricia if it is the negative covenant that is being broken. If the burden of that covenant has run with the land and Quentin has taken subject to it, Sarah's most effective remedy will be to proceed against *him* and obtain an injunction to prevent the breach being continued. However the possibility of being sued remains to haunt Patricia.

As regards the positive covenant, Patricia is the only person who can be sued by Sarah, as Sarah cannot take any action against Quentin.

As she is aware of this possibility of being sued at some time in the future, perhaps long after she has parted with the land, Patricia, when she sells to Quentin, will want a covenant from him to indemnify her against any consequences of a future breach of either covenant. Patricia can only insist on the conveyance or transfer to Quentin containing an indemnity covenant if the contract says that it will.

Conditon 4.5.4 of the standard conditions provides for the insertion of an indemnity covenant into the conveyance or transfer, if despite the sale, the seller will remain liable on any obligation affecting the property. The covenant is given only in respect of future breaches so that Quentin will not be liable for breaches committed before the land was conveyed to him. The condition also requires Quentin to promise to perform the obligation. This means that Patricia would not herself have to be sued before insisting that Quentin fence in accordance with the covenant given by her to Sarah.

A special condition in the contract is therefore not needed unless the standard condition is considered unsatisfactory. Again, remember that the contract does not create the indemnity covenant. The covenant is put in the conveyance or transfer as a result of the condition in the contract.

As Quentin has undertaken a perpetual responsibility to indemnify Patricia, when Quentin sells to Rosemary, he needs an indemnity covenant from Rosemary. He needs an indemnity against his promise to indemnify. The indemnity given by Rosemary should have the same wording as the indemnity given by Quentin. For example, if Quentin promised to *perform* and indemnify, Rosemary should be required to give the same promise to him. If Quentin only promised to indemnify, but not to perform, Rosemary should alter standard condition 4.5.4, so that in the conveyance *she* will only promise to indemnify.

A long chain of indemnity may eventually stretch from Patricia to the current owner of Whiteacre. The older the covenant and the longer the chain, the more ineffective the chain becomes. If Sarah, or Sarah's successor to Blackacre, decides to sue Patricia, Patricia may be untraceable. If Patricia is dead, while it is in theory possible to sue her estate, the expense and difficulty of finding her personal representatives and of tracing her assets into the hands of the beneficiaries will make the remedy impracticable. If Patricia is successfully sued, Patricia may not be able to find Quentin. Remember the only person who can sue Rosemary by virtue of the indemnity chain is Quentin, so if Patricia is unable to sue Quentin, Rosemary will not be called upon for an indemnity, so is unconcerned at the continuance of the breach either by her or her successor. However, if you are acting for a seller who gave an indemnity when he originally bought the land, you make certain that he is indemnified when he sells. You do this, even though it seems very unlikely that your client would ever be sued on the chain.

12.10   Particular Points about Covenants and Registered Title

The restrictive covenants will be set out in the charges register of the burdened land. They may be set out in full or if they are long the register may refer to the document that created them. This document or a copy will be filed at the Registry and a copy bound up in the land certificate.

If positive covenants are created in a transfer of registered title, they will also appear on the register. If in the transfer they were mixed in with negative covenants, the Registrar will not divide them, but will put both the negative and the positive covenants in the charges register. If the transfer contains only positive covenants, their existence will be noted on the proprietorship register. The positive covenants are not really part of the title to the land. They are only noted on the register as a matter of convenience. Without a note on the register their existence could be easily forgotten, as the transfer that created them is filed in the registry. If they were forgotten, the original covenantor or his successors might forget the necessity for an indemnity covenant when retransferring.

Notice that it is not the practice to enter on the register those positive covenants that already exist when the title is first registered. The registry considers this to be unnecessary. The original deeds are returned to the registered proprietor and *these* reveal the existence of the covenants. This is the one reason why the title deeds remain important, despite registration of the title.

Indemnity Covenants

An indemnity covenant given by the applicant for first registration will not be mentioned on the register of title. This is because when he resells, he can recall the fact that he gave, and therefore needs, an indemnity covenant by looking at the title deeds. If an indemnity covenant is given by a later registered proprietor, a note is put on to the proprietorship register, referring to the existence of the indemnity covenant.

Workshop

Attempt these problems yourself, then read the specimen solutions at the end of the book.

Problem 1

Your client is buying a freehold detached house, 21B Landsdown Crescent, from Alice Brown. Alice Brown also owns 21A. She used to own number 21, but this was sold by her to Catherine Douglas in 1986. Figure 12.2 is a plan of the three properties.

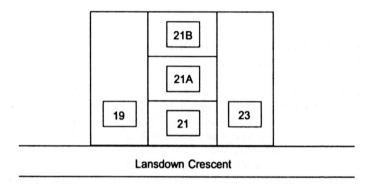

Figure 12.2

Enquiries of the district authority and the property information form reveal that Landsdown Crescent is a public road and that the pipes and wires serving 21A and 21B lead from Landsdown Crescent across number 21.

You are considering the draft contract prepared by Alice Brown's solicitor. You have to decide whether your client will obtain all the easements necessary for his enjoyment of 21B. Do you think he will? What documents should you read?

Problem 2

You are acting for Hebe, the seller of 1 Rosemary Avenue. You are investigating the unregistered title. You have the following title deeds.

- A conveyance dated 1 May 1940, made between the seller A and the purchaser B. This conveyance contains a covenant given by B to A that no buildings whatsoever would be put on the land other than one detached house.
- A conveyance dated 1 June 1980, made between the seller B and the purchaser C. This conveyance contains an indemnity given by C to B against breach of the 1940 covenant.
- A conveyance dated 1 July 1988, made between the seller C and Hebe the purchaser. The conveyance contains an indemnity given by Hebe to C against breach of the 1940 covenant. As soon as Hebe bought the property, she built a large garage.

1. Can the covenant be enforced against Hebe?
2. How do these facts affect your drafting of the agreement for sale?

Problem 3

You are acting for Jacob Green, whose wife, Naomi Green, has just died. He has decided to sell 9 Havelock Street, where he has lived all his married life, and move in with his widowed sister. He has asked you to act for him in the sale.

He has handed you Naomi's will, which divides everything she owns equally between Jacob and their daughter, Dr Ruth Green.

The title to the house is registered. The land certificate is in the possession of the Equine Bank, but you have obtained an office copy of the entries on the register. The property register describes the property as '9 Havelock Street, Spa on Wells, together with the rights granted by but subject to the exceptions and reservations contained in the conveyance dated 1 April 1965, referred to in entry no. 2 of the register.'

The proprietorship register names Jacob and Naomi as proprietors, and contains the restriction that no disposition by the sole survivor under which capital money arises will be registered.

Entry no. 1 on the charges register states that a conveyance of 1922 contains restrictive covenants affecting the land, but that neither the original conveyance, nor a certified copy or an examined abstract of it was produced on first registration. Entry no. 2 says that the conveyance of 1 April 1965 contains restrictive covenants affecting the land, and that a copy of the conveyance is in the certificate. Entries 3 and 4 relate to the registered charge in favour of the Equine Bank.

Jacob tells you that the sale is to include the fitted carpets and all curtains, but is to exclude the garden shed. You now have to draft the agreement for sale. How will the facts set out above affect the drafting of the agreement.

13 Sales of Commercial Properties

So far, this book has been talking primarily about the sale of freehold residential properties. Nevertheless, nearly everything that has been said so far holds true for the sales of freehold shops, offices and other commercial properties. The purpose of this chapter is to explain some differences, and to highlight points peculiar to commercial conveyancing. This chapter is written mainly for students who are studying on a Legal Practice Course at an institution which is introducing elements of commercial conveyancing into its conveyancing course. The chapter will also be useful as an introduction to commercial conveyancing for beginners in the office.

13.1 Procedure

The steps in a conveyancing transaction that are set out in Chapters 1 and 2 will be much the same even though it is shop or office premises that are being sold rather than a house. However the Law Society's Protocol does not apply to a sale of business property, and so the documentation may be different.

As the Protocol does not apply, the seller's solicitor does not have to prepare a pre-contract package. However, when he sends the draft agreement for sale to the purchaser's solicitor, he will also invariably send evidence of the seller's title and any other documents that the purchaser will need to see before he decides to go ahead with the purchase. The Seller's Property Information Form is a Protocol document, and does not contain all the questions that should be asked for a commercial property. There are several forms of pre-contract enquiries that are used for commercial property. A seller who is anxious to save time could complete a standard form of pre-contract enquiries and send this to the purchaser with the draft agreement, but the purchaser might prefer to submit his own form, or to ask further questions.

The Standard Conditions of Sale used in residential conveyancing are also suitable for the sale of commercial property, although there is now in preparation a set of Standard Commercial Property Conditions. These have not yet been published.

In addition to reading the materials sent to him by the seller's solicitor, the purchaser's solicitor will also make the usual pre-contract searches, and any extra searches that are prompted by the nature or locality of the property. As part of his pre-contract investigations, the purchaser's solicitor will pay particular attention to the following matters set out in sections 13.2 to 13.6.

13.2 Planning

When a purchaser buys a residential property, there is not usually any doubt that residential use is the lawful use under the Town & Country Planning Acts. The house was probably built pursuant to a planning permission for residential use, and used as a residence ever since. The only cause for concern would be where a non-residential property had been recently converted for living in. This would be a material change of use, and would require planning permission, but would be safe from enforcement action once four years had passed (see 6.5).

When a purchaser is thinking of acquiring a commercial property, he must check that the present use of the property is also the lawful use under the Planning Acts. It will be the lawful use if either:

- there exists a planning permission for it, or
- it is immune from enforcement action. For example, suppose that when the present use first started it required planning permission but none was obtained. If 10 years have passed from the unauthorised change, and no enforcement notice has been served, the use is now lawful, as no enforcement action can be taken in respect of it (see 6.5 (c)).

In this connection, the buyer must remember the effect of the Use Classes Order 1987. A change of use from a use within one class of use to another use within the same class is not a *material* change of use and does not need planning permission. A change to a use in another class, or to a use not covered by the order may be, and probably is, a material change of use. For example:

Use Class A1 covers use as most sorts of shops.
Use Class A2 covers use for the provision of financial and professional services that are appropriate to provide in a shopping area, where the services are provided principally to visiting members of the public.
Use Class B1 includes use as offices for other than a use within A2.

So, if the buyer is buying a shop for the use of his retail butchery business, he must check the current use and any change of use within the previous 10 years. If throughout the 10 years, the shop has been used as a butcher's and there is no current enforcement notice, all is well. The use the buyer is going to make of the shop is the lawful use. Similarly, if the shop has for the last ten years been used as a greengrocer's, he will not need planning permission to change the use of the shop to a butcher's. Both past and new use are within Class A1. (However, he must remember that he will need planning permission for any building operation that will materially affect the external appearance of the shop.)

On the other hand, if the buyer wants to use the premises as an office, this will be a change of use from Class A1 to Class A2 or B1, and planning permission is needed. Similarly, if the premises are already used as an office, but were changed from a shop less than 10 years ago, the buyer must check that planning permission was obtained for the change. Otherwise, there is a risk that the local planning authority will serve an enforcement notice, preventing any continued use as an office.

After wrestling with the Use Classes Order, the buyer may then need to consult the Town and Country Planning (General Permitted Development) Order 1995 (see 6.5(b)). Some material changes of use that require planning permission are given permission by this order, and express planning permission need not be obtained. For example, a change from A2 (office) to A1 (shop) is authorised by Part 3 of the 1995 Order. Be careful if you intend to rely on this order. Two points to watch are that:

- Frequently, the changes of use are authorised 'one way only'. To return to the previous example, a change *from* Class A1 *to* Class A2 is not authorised by the GPDO and express planning permission must be obtained.
- The Order may not be in full effect for this particular property. The effect of the GPDO may have been cut down by a condition attached to a previous planning permission. For example, a previous permission may say that any future change of use will need express planning permission, even though the change would normally be allowed by the GPDO. (The effect of the Use Classes Order can also be altered in the same way.) In addition, an article 4 direction may exist, by which the local planning authority has directed that all or any of the permissions given by the GPDO shall not apply in the area (see 6.5 (b)).

In his pre-contract enquiries, the purchaser will ask the seller what the present use is of the premises, and if the use is not authorised by an express planning permission, why it is lawful. He will ask for copies of every planning permission and building regulation consent. He will also ask if any building or other work that required planning permission has been carried out on the premises during the past four years.

If there have been any express planning permissions, the purchaser should read them to check:

- that the seller (or his predecessor) has done only what he was authorised to do;
- that if there were conditions attached to the permissions, they have been complied with;
- whether or not a condition attached to an earlier permission has affected the operation of the GPDO or the Use Classes order.

13.3   Restrictive Covenants

The purchaser must check the title to the premises, to see if there are any restrictive covenants that might be broken by his intended use.

13.4 Environmental Law

A buyer of commercial premises should consider the possibility that the land is contaminated by reason of trade or industrial use by previous owners. Why does it matter? Well, apart from concern for the health of the owner and his employees, it is possible that the new owner will incur statutory or common law liability to third parties, even although he is not the person who caused the contamination in the first place and he is not continuing the contaminating process.

The financial risks that might be run by the buyer *include*:

1. The Risk of having to comply with a Remediation Notice served under the Environmental Protection Act 1990 as amended

This Act applies to what it defines as 'contaminated land'. This includes land that the local authority considers to be in such a condition, by reason of substances in, on or under the land, that significant harm is being caused or there is a significant possibility of such harm being caused. The Act defines 'harm' as 'harm to the health of living organisms or other interference with the ecological systems of which they form part, and, in the case of man, includes harm to his property'.

Once the local authority has identified land as being contaminated, it must draw up a 'remediation notice'. This notice specifies what work has to be done by way of remediation and must be served on what the Act calls 'the appropriate person'.

The principle of the Act is that it should be the polluter who pays. So the first person on whom the authority should seek to serve notice is the original polluter. According to the Act, this is the person who caused or knowingly permitted the contaminating substance to be in, on or under the land. If, after reasonable enquiry, the local authority cannot trace the original polluter, then it can serve a remediation notice on the current owner of the contaminated land, and on the occupier.

Suppose we imagine S owning and contaminating land. He then sells it to B. B does not continue the contaminating process. At first sight, it must be S who is served with the remediation notice and S, therefore, who incurs the expense of complying with it. B can only be served if S can not be traced. However, this is not certain. The problem comes from the definition of original polluter who is identified as the person who caused or *knowingly permitted* the contaminating substance to be on the land. It is argued that the definition includes not only S, but also B if when he bought the land he was aware of, or should have been aware of, the contamination and failed to take steps to remedy it. If B is within the definition of an original polluter because of his failure to investigate, then he falls foul of other provisions of the Act which say that if both a seller and a buyer can be identified as original polluter, the primary responsibility as between the two of them is that of the buyer, if the buyer had sufficient information to be aware of the risk of the land being contaminated. It may be, although this is not certain, that a buyer will be treated as having sufficient information simply by virtue of having been given the opportunity to inspect the land.

The cost of complying with a remediation notice could be enormous. The cost of not complying with one could also be high, with fines of up to £20,000 with additional daily fines until the notice is complied with.

2. The risk of having to remedy a statutory nuisance

Land that is a risk to health may be a statutory nuisance if, for example, it is in such a state as to be prejudicial to health. As in the case of any statutory nuisance, the local authority can serve an abatement notice on the person responsible for the nuisance, or if that person cannot be found, on the owner and occupier of the land. Failure to comply with an abatement notice is a criminal offence.

3. The risk of committing the tort of nuisance

If the contamination escapes from the contaminated land onto other land, the person responsible for the contamination may be liable in tort for nuisance. To return to our example, B may be liable, even although he did not cause the contamination, if he knew or ought to have known of the contamination, could reasonably foresee that it could cause harm, and could have taken reasonable steps to prevent it doing so but did not. (NB: if the escape is into, for example, a river, there could be criminal liability under the Water Resources Act 1991.)

To return again to S and B, we have seen that it is extremely important for B to make extensive enquiries before buying land that might be contaminated. If he discovers the contamination before agreeing to buy, he can:

1. Decide not to buy after all. Apart from the financial risks, the owner of contaminated land may find it difficult to obtain planning permission, or to obtain it without onerous 'clean-up' conditions attached. Or
2. Ask for a greatly reduced price. Or
3. Insist that S does remedial work. Or
4. Ask S to indemnify him against any future liability. Of course the value of a promise to indemnify depends on B being able to find S when the time comes, and on S being solvent. Or
5. Ask S to arrange insurance against third party liability for the benefit of B. The insurance company will want to make a thorough assessment of the risk, and may charge a very high premium.

What investigations should a purchaser make? He can, for example:

1. Arrange for a survey. This should be carried out by an expert in environmental investigations. He will inspect the site and may excavate the land to discover what lies below the surface.
2. Investigate past uses of the land. Some industries and trades are known to carry a risk of contaminating land.
3. Obtain details of past planning applications, and planning permissions. If an application failed, why did it fail? If a permission was given, was there any 'clean-up' condition attached to the permission? The purchaser should look particularly at the planning permission which authorised the use by the seller. Does it impose a liability to clean-up the site once the permitted use has ended? If it does, has the seller complied with the condition? If he has not, the purchaser might have to.
4. Ask the Health & Safety Executive or the Environment Agency if they have any records of pollution.
5. Make pre-contract enquiries of the seller as to:

   - past use and current use of the land;
   - any previous environmental surveys and their results;
   - any complaints from owners of neighbouring land or from statutory bodies about pollution;
   - any statutory notices received in connection with the state or use of the land;
   - any polluting incidents known to the seller, such as accidental spillage or leaks.

13.5 Value Added Tax

The sale of land is, for VAT purposes, equivalent to a supply of goods. Just as a seller of goods may have to charge the purchaser with VAT, so may a seller of land.

A seller of land never has to charge a purchaser with VAT unless the seller is registered for VAT, and unless the sale is in the course of his business.

If the seller satisfies these two conditions, then the VAT position depends on whether the seller is making a zero rated supply, a standard rated supply or an exempt supply.

The sale of a freehold of a residential building is a zero rated transaction. This means that the seller cannot charge the buyer with VAT on the purchase price. So the happy young couple buying their first home from the development company will only have to find the purchase price and not VAT as well.

The sale of a new freehold commercial building is a standard rated supply by the seller. (A building is a 'new' freehold building if it was completed in the three years preceding the sale.) This means that the seller must charge the purchaser VAT on the purchase price. The seller will account for the tax he has received to Customs and Excise. Seller and purchaser must decide whether the agreed purchase price is inclusive or exclusive of VAT. Assuming the rate of VAT to be 17.5 per cent, if a purchase price of £100,000 is inclusive of VAT, the buyer will pay £100,000, but the seller will only pocket £85,106, having to send the balance of £14,894 to Customs and Excise. If the purchase price of £100,000 is exclusive of VAT, the buyer has to pay £100,000 plus VAT of £17,500. The seller pockets £100,000 and sends off the balance. The purchase price will be inclusive of VAT unless the agreement for sale says otherwise. If the agreement incorporates the Standard Conditions of Sale it will say otherwise. **Standard condition 1.4.1 states that all monies made payable by the contract are exclusive of VAT.**

The sale of an old commercial building is an exempt supply. This means that the seller cannot charge VAT on the purchase price. However, in the case of an old commercial building, the seller can waive the exemption and turn the exempt supply into a standard rated supply. He can then charge the buyer VAT. There are various reasons why a seller might wish to do this. He might want to recover output tax to set off against his input tax. It might solve cash flow problems. Of course, the waiver of the exemption will be unpopular with the purchaser if the purchase price is exclusive of VAT, as he will have to find the extra money to pay the tax. If the purchaser is in business, registered for VAT and himself making standard rated or zero rated supplies, he will be able to pass the VAT burden on to his own customers or recover VAT from Customs and Excise. Otherwise, he will not, and the extra VAT will be an irrecoverable overhead.

The time that the seller makes the waiver is important. If he makes the waiver before he contracts to sell, the supply is a standard rated supply at the time the contract is made. The seller cannot add VAT to the purchase price if the purchase price is inclusive of VAT but he can if the contract states that the price is exclusive of VAT. If the seller does not waive the exemption until after contract is made, the waiver is treated as an increase in the rate of VAT from 0 per cent to what is then the current rate. So a waiver made at the time of writing would be treated as increasing the rate of tax from 0 per cent to 17.5 per cent. The purchaser may then be caught by s.89 Value Added Tax Act 1994, which provides that where there is a change in the rate of VAT after the making of a contract to supply goods but before the goods are supplied, then, unless the contract states otherwise, the purchase price is increased or decreased by the amount equivalent to the change. Therefore, the amount of the increase can be added to the purchase price despite the general VAT assumption that a purchase price is inclusive of VAT. The result of this is that the buyer cannot be sure whether at completion he will be paying the purchase price alone, or the purchase price + VAT owing to the fact that the seller, after the date of the contract, has decided to waive the exemption. To prevent this uncertainty, the purchaser should ask either:

- for the contract to state expressly that the purchase price is inclusive of VAT (such an express provision prevents s.89 from operating); or

- for the contract to contain a promise by the seller that he will not waive the exemption.

When buying a commercial property, the seller will ask as pre-contract enquiries:

- when the building was completed;
- whether the seller is registered for VAT;
- if the building was completed more than three years ago, whether or not it is the seller's intention to waive the exemption in respect of VAT, and turn the sale into a standard rated supply.

13.6 Insurance

As we saw in 1.8, Standard Condition 5.1 throws the risk of physical damage to the property after agreement for sale but before completion on to the seller. Condition 5 usually remains unchanged in residential conveyancing, but is often changed in an agreement to sell commercial property. The change is to throw the risk of physical damage on to the buyer. This means that if the property is damaged or even destroyed, the buyer must continue with the purchase and the purchase price will not be reduced. In such a case, it is essential for the purchaser to insure the property from the moment of exchange.

Workshop

Attempt this problem yourself and then read the specimen solution at the end of the book.

It is the year 1999. Your client is Holt Development Limited. In July 1998 it bought a piece of land that was then part of the grounds of Malherbe Grange. It demolished the old corn mill that was there and built three blocks of offices called 1, 2 and 3 Old Mill Offices, Malherbe Road, Malherbe, South Humberland, MA21 9MZ. The three blocks stand in a yard and each sale will include part of the yard.

Each office can be reached on foot from the Malherbe Road. There is access for vehicles from the drive to Malherbe Grange. The yard is large enough to provide parking, but as you can see from the sketch map below, the purchaser of, for example, block 3, will only be able to reach his part of the yard by driving across the parts of the yard that belong to blocks 1 and 2. The pipes and wires for the gas, water and electricity reach each block directly from Malherbe Road.

Your client has found its first buyers. They are John Able, Jack Bell, Jill Carter, Joseph David and Jackie Evans. They are partners in a firm of public relations consultants called 'Spindles'. They want to buy the freehold of No. 2 for £125,000. This is the middle block of the three. It will be the new office premises of the partnership. The sketch map below shows what your client will be selling to the partnership. The boundaries between the blocks are not marked on the land in any way.

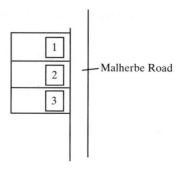

You have obtained from the Land Registry:

- office copy entries and filed plan;
- a copy of the plan attached to the 1998 conveyance that is mentioned in the Property Register and in the Charges Register.

These are reproduced for you at the end of the chapter.

1. You are to consider the drafting of the agreement for sale. (Remember that blocks 1 and 3 have not yet been sold.).

    - How will you describe the Property?
    - How will you describe the Buyers?
    - How will you complete 'Incumbrances'?
    - What Title Guarantee will you promise?
    - What special condition/s will you put in the agreement about access to Block 2?
    - What special conditions will you put in the agreement about continued access to Block 3?
    - Does your client need indemnity covenants in respect of the 1936 covenants and the 1998 covenants on the Charges Register? (To answer this you must read the Proprietorship Register and the covenants themselves very carefully.)
    - Are there any other special conditions that you should put in the agreement?

2. You are to consider the VAT position.

    - What sort of supply is your client making?
    - If the purchase price in the agreement for sale is £125,000, what is the sum that the buyers will have to pay?

OFFICE COPY

Edition date : 9 July 1998   **TITLE NUMBER : SHU 123456**

Entry No.	A. PROPERTY REGISTER containing the description of the registered land and the estate comprised in the Title
	COUNTY **DISTRICT** **SOUTH HUMBERLAND** **MALHERBE**
1	(9 July 1998) The Freehold land shown edged with red on the plan of the above Title filed at the Registry and being the Old Mill, Malherbe Road, Malherbe (MA21 9MZ)

2	(9 July 1998) The land has the benefit of the following rights granted by but is subject to the following rights reserved by the Conveyance dated 26 June 1998 referred to in the Charges Register.
	
	    ``
	
	                       FIRST SCHEDULE
	                            Part 2
	
	The following rights are included in this Conveyance
	1. A right of way for the Buyer its successors in title and the owners and occupiers for the time being of the Property at all times with or without motor vehicles to pass and repass along the part of the driveway which is coloured blue (the 'Blue Land') on the Plan SUBJECT to the Buyer and its successors in title contributing one quarter of the costs of keeping the Blue Land resurfaced and in good repair and condition.
	2. A right of support from the Seller's retained land shown outlined in green (the `Green Land') on the Plan for the Property and all buildings on it.
	
	                          Part 3
	There is reserved from this Conveyance a right of support from the Property for the Green Land and all buildings on it.
	
	Remark: A copy of the Conveyance Plan is sewn up in the Land Certificate

A

OFFICE COPY

This office copy shows the entries subsisting on the register on **6 January 1999**
This date **must be quoted as the `search from date' in any official search** application based on this copy.
Under s.113 of the Land Registration Act 1925 this copy is admissible in evidence to the same extent as the original.
Issued on **7 January 1999** by HM Land Registry. This title is administered by the ODDWAYS District Land Registry.

TITLE NUMBER: SHU 123456

Entry No.	B. PROPRIETORSHIP REGISTER stating nature of the Title, name, address and description of the proprietor of the land and any entries affecting the right of disposing thereof **TITLE ABSOLUTE**
1	(9 July 1998) Proprietor: HOLT DEVELOPMENT LIMITED. Registered Office: Slingsby Business Park, Slingsby, South Humberland (SL24 1RX)

Entry No.	C. CHARGES REGISTER containing charges incumbrances etc. adversely affecting the land and registered dealings therewith
1	(9 July 1998) A Conveyance of the land and other land dated 9 March 1936 made between (1) Henry Butcher (Vendor) and (2) Edward Peters (Purchaser) contains covenants details of which are set out in the schedule of restrictive covenants hereto.
2	(9 July 1998) A Conveyance of the land dated 26 June 1988 made between (1) Dustbourne Estates Limited (Vendor) and (2) Holt Development Limited (Purchaser) contains covenants details of which are set out in the schedule of restrictive covenants hereto.

Entry No	SCHEDULE OF RESTRICTIVE COVENANTS
1	The following are details of the covenants contained in the Conveyance dated 9 March 1936 referred to in the Charges Register:- "The Purchaser so as to bind the land hereby conveyed does hereby covenant with the Vendor that the Purchaser and his successors in title will not at any time hereafter permit or suffer to be carried on upon any part of the said premises any noisy noisome offensive or noxious trade business or occupation nor anything which may be or become a nuisance."

B

Entry No.	SCHEDULE OF RESTRICTIVE COVENANTS (continued)
2	The following are details of the covenants contained in the Conveyance dated 26 June 1998 referred to in the Charges Register. "The Buyer covenants with the Seller for the benefit of the Green Land and the Blue Land and each and every part of either and with the intention of binding the Property and each and every part of it into whosesoever hands the same may come but so that the Buyer shall not be liable for a breach of this covenant occurring on or in respect of the Property or any part of parts thereof after it shall have parted with all interest therein 1. Not to obstruct or hinder the lawful use by others of the Blue Land 2 Not to park leave or stand any vehicle on any part of the Blue Land 3. Not to make any objections, claims or representations whatsoever in relation to any farming activities carried out by the Seller on the Green Land and not to make any objection to, or claims or comments of any description on any application for planning permission made by the Seller in respect of the Green Land or the Blue Land or on any appeal or public enquiry arising from any such application.

***** END OF REGISTER *****

NOTE: A date at the beginning of an entry is the date on which the entry was made in the Register.

C

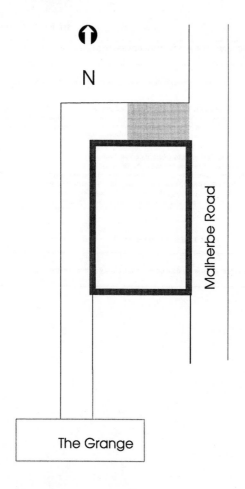

HM LAND REGISTRY
Title No SHU 123456
Copy (liable to distortion in scale)
of plan to Conveyance dated
26 June 1998

Note to readers: 1.   Indicates the land coloured blue on the 1998 plan.

2. The thick black line indicates the land conveyed by the 1998 conveyance, and is the same as the land edged with red on the Filed Plan.

3. The land referred to as the Green Land on the 1998 conveyance includes the Grange, and surrounding grounds.

D

H.M. LAND REGISTRY	TITLE NUMBER	
	SHU 123456	
ORDNANCE SURVEY PLAN REFERENCE	SECTION P	Scale
COUNTY SOUTH HUMBERLAND DISTRICT MALHERBE	© Crown copyright 1998	

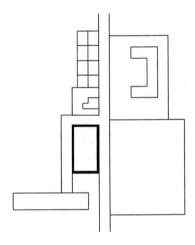

Note:

E   The thick black line indicates the red edging mentioned entry No 1 on the Property Register

14 Drafting a Transfer of Registered Title

14.1 A Transfer of Whole

Imagine you are acting for Ann Holt and Chris Edwards who are buying 1 Smith Avenue. The seller is Bernard Homes Ltd.

The office copy entries of the Seller's title gives you the following information:

Property Register. The property is described as the 'Freehold land shown edged with red on the Plan of the above title filed at the Registry and being 1 Smith Avenue, Hiccup, Kent (DA19 4ZZ)'.

Proprietorship Register. The Registered Proprietor is Bernard Homes Ltd. The company's registered office is at Bernard House, The Mall, Hiccup, Kent DA19 4ZX and its registered number is 0000000001. Below the name of the Registered Proprietor is the following note: 'The transfer to the proprietor contains a covenant to observe and perform and a covenant for indemnity in respect of the covenants referred to in Entry No 1 of the Charges Register'.

Charges Register. Entry No. 1 is a notice of restrictive covenants created in a deed dated 1 July 1991 made between (1) Abel Whyte and (2) Alice Bluegown.

Contracts have been exchanged. There is set out below the agreement for sale signed by the seller. The copy signed by your clients is, of course, in the custody of the seller's solicitor (see Chapter 1, section 1.6.)

As you are the purchaser's solicitor, it is now your right and privilege to draft the purchase deed. In order to draft any purchase deed, it is essential that you begin by re-reading the evidence of title and the agreement for sale. Now look at Appendix D. This is HM Land Registry form TR1, and is the form prescribed by the Land Registration Rules 1925 (as amended by the Land Registration Rules 1997) for use when all the land in a title is being transferred. You must use this form.

Apart from using the correct form, you must draft a transfer that gives effect to the agreement for sale and carries out its promises. It must be stressed that it is the contract that governs the terms of the transfer. Clauses affecting the rights of seller and purchaser against one another, e.g. the grant or reservation of easements, the giving of covenants or the exclusion of implied grant rules, can only be put in the transfer if justified by a provision in the contract. When you draft the transfer, you must ensure that

SPECIMEN AGREEMENT

(Incorporating the Standard Conditions of Sale (Third Edition)

Agreement data	:	
Seller	:	Bernard Homes Ltd. Registered Office – Bernard House, The Mall, Hiccup, Kent DA19 4ZX
Buyer	:	Anne Holt and Chris Edwards of 19 Peaceways, Hiccup, Kent DA19 3YY
Property	:	1 Smith Avenue, Hiccup, Kent DA15 4ZZ
(freehold/leasehold)		Freehold
Root of Title/Title Number	:	KE 1234567
Incumbrances on the Property	:	The restrictive covenants noted in Entry No. 1 on the Charges Register of the title
Title Guarantee (full/limited)	:	Full title guarantee
Completion date	:	
Contract rate	:	
Purchase price	:	£90,000
Deposit	:	9,000
Amount payable for chattels	:	
Balance	:	81,000

The Seller will sell and the Buyer will buy the Property for the Purchase price.
The Agreement continues on the back page.

WARNING	**Signed**
This is a formal document, designed to create legal rights and legal obligations. Take advice before using it.	Seller/Buyer

SPECIAL CONDITIONS

1. (a) This Agreement incorporates the Standard Conditions of Sale (Third Edition). Where there is a conflict between those Conditions and this Agreement, this Agreement prevails.

    (b) Terms used or defined in this Agreement have the same meaning when used in the Conditions.

2. The Property is sold subject to the Incumbrances on the Property and the Buyer will raise no requisitions on them.

3. Subject to the terms of this Agreement and to the Standard Conditions of Sale, the seller is to transfer the property with the title guarantee specified on the front page.

4. The chattels on the Property and set out on any attached list are included in the sale.

5. The Property is sold with vacant possession on completion.

Seller's Solicitors   : XXXXXX

Buyer's Solicitors   : XXXXXXX

the transfer gives the purchaser what the contract promised him. The seller's solicitor must check that the draft transfer tries to give the purchaser nothing more, and that the seller is given any rights which the contract promised him.

Not only the special conditions in the agreement for sale must be checked. Some of the standard conditions affect the drafting of the transfer. These are:

Condition 3.4 possibly justifying the inclusion of an express reservation of easements by the seller and an express grant to the purchaser. It also entitles a seller to put in a declaration negating any implied grant of an easement of light or air to the purchaser. (This condition is discussed in Chapter 12.)

Condition 4.5.2 compelling the seller to transfer with full title guarantee unless there is express provision in the contract to the contrary.

Condition 4.5.4 possibly justifying the inclusion of a covenant by the purchaser to perform and indemnify (see Chapter 12). This could be relevant not only when the title is subject to covenants but also when the property is sold subject to, for example, a mortgage or a rentcharge.

Condition 3.2.2 This is relevant when drafting the transfer of a leasehold estate and is considered in Chapter 16.

So, how should you complete Form TR1?

Panel 1 – stamp duty. The top of the panel is where the stamp office will put any *ad valorem* stamps and any PD stamp that the transfer requires. At the bottom of the panel is the information needed by the Stamp Office to assess the correct amount (if any) of stamp duty payable. As you know (or re-read Chapter 2, section 2.17 if you have forgotten), if the transfer is by way of sale, exemption from stamp duty or a lower rate can be claimed if a certificate can be given that the consideration does not exceed the appropriate statutory figure. In our case, the purchase price is £90,000 so you should certify that the consideration does not exceed £250,000 and therefore claim to pay duty at the rate of 1 per cent rather than the top rate of 3.5 per cent.

If a transfer is not by way of sale, there may be no stamp duty payable at all, if it can be certified that the transfer is within one of the exempt categories of instrument. A transfer by way of gift, for example, is exempt under category L of the Stamp Duty (Exempt Instruments) Regulations 1987, so in that case we would put an 'X' in the top box and put 'L' in the accompanying box.

Panel 2 and 3 – title number and property. These are completed from the office copy entries. When completing 'Property' simply put in the address from the property register. There is no need to repeat the reference to the filed plan. For present purposes you can ignore the printed instructions at the end of the panel.

Panel 4 – the date. This is, of course, not completed in a draft document. The date will be inserted at completion.

Panel 5 – the transferor. This will almost always be the seller in the Agreement for Sale. However it is possible that the transferor will be a different person. This can occur, for example:

- If the seller dies after the contract has been made. The death will have no effect on the validity of the contract, and it will bind the seller's personal representative, who will be the transferor. The purchaser will want to see the grant of representation.
- If the seller becomes bankrupt after the contract. As soon as the bankruptcy petition is presented, any disposition by the seller is invalid except against a purchaser who has no notice of the petition. (See s.284 Insolvency Act 1986.) A buyer of a registered title will have notice if a Bankruptcy Notice is on the Proprietorship Register when he makes his pre-completion search. The transferor will be the seller's trustee in bankruptcy. The trustee, once appointed, can apply to the Land Registry to be registered as proprietor of the property. If he does not, the buyer will want to see a copy of the order declaring the seller to be bankrupt and a copy of the certificate of appointment of the transferor as the trustee in bankruptcy.
- If the seller is a company and goes into liquidation before completion. It is possible, but unusual, for the court to make an order vesting the company's property in the liquidator. In such a case the liquidator will be the transferor, and the purchaser will want to see the court order. More usually, the property will remain vested in the company, which will remain the transferor, although the liquidator will usually join in the execution of the transfer.

In our case the transferor is the seller in the contract, Bernard Homes Ltd. You will insert the name of the company and its Company's Registered Number.

Panel 6 – the transferee. Here you enter the name of the person who is to be registered as the new proprietor of the land. This will usually be the buyer in the contract. In our case, you will insert the names of Anne Holt and Chris Edwards.

Panel 7 – transferee's intended address for service in the UK. What is needed here is the address where your clients will be living when they are registered as the new owners. This is the address that will be put on the register and to where the Land Registry will send any statutory notice. This means that if your clients are buying 1 Smith Avenue to live in, this is the address that you will put in the panel, **not** the address from which they are moving.

If a company is buying, you must give the address of its registered office. If business partners are buying a partnership asset, you must give the partnership's principal place of business.

Panel 8. Here appear the words actually transferring ownership.

Panel 9 – consideration. This is the receipt clause for any consideration paid. On a sale for money, an 'X' will be put in the top box and the purchase price stated in words and figures. This statement has several functions.

- It is on this that the Stamp Office will rely when deciding how much stamp duty is payable.
- It serves the usual function of a receipt. Section 67 of the Law of Property Act 1925 states that if a receipt is contained in the body of a purchase deed, the purchaser cannot ask for any other receipt.
- It authorises the purchaser (or his solicitor), to pay the purchase price not to the seller personally, but to the seller's solicitor. Section 69 of the Law of Property Act 1925 states that where a solicitor (or by virtue of s.34(1)(c) of the Administration of Justice Act 1985, a licensed conveyancer) produces a deed that has in it a receipt for the consideration money, and the deed is executed by the person entitled to give the receipt, (i.e. usually the seller) the deed is sufficient authority to pay the money to the solicitor or licensed conveyancer, without the recipient having otherwise to prove that he has been authorised to receive it. In other words, if the solicitor then decamps with the money, the loss is the seller's, not the purchaser's. It is sometimes argued in textbooks that s.69 authorises the purchaser to pay only the solicitor and not the solicitor's employee. This argument has never impressed conveyancing practitioners, who when attending completion personally, will happily hand over the purchase price to whatever representative of the seller's solicitor's firm materialises in front of them. The point is of less significance nowadays, when completion usually takes place through the post, the purchaser's solicitor wiring the money direct to the client account of the seller's solicitor, and receiving the title documents through the post.

If the consideration is something other than money, for example if the land is transferred in return for company shares, an 'X' will be put in the second box, and details of the consideration given. An 'X' will be put in the third box if, for example, the transfer is a gift or if it is a transfer from retiring trustees into the names of the replacement trustees.

Panel 10 – title guarantee. In the agreement for sale, the seller promised to transfer with a full title guarantee. You will, therefore, put an 'X' in the first box.

Panel 11 – declaration of trust. How this is completed is a matter entirely for the purchaser, and is of no concern to the seller. You should have taken instructions from your clients, Anne and Chris, as to how they wished to hold the equitable interest, during your initial interview with them. If they are a married couple, they probably wish to hold as beneficial joint tenants. When the Land Registrar sees that this is the box with the 'X' in it, he will register Anne and Chris as proprietors in the proprietorship register, and **will not** put under their names any restriction preventing a sale by the sole survivor. If they wish to own the equitable interest in equal shares, you will put your 'X' in the second box. When the Land Registrar sees this, he will know that if, say, Anne dies, although Chris will automatically become sole owner of the legal estate, he will not necessarily become sole owner of the equitable interest as there is no right of survivorship (see Chapter 11). The Registrar will put the restriction under their names preventing a sale by the survivor. This will force Chris to appoint a second trustee to transfer with him, so overreaching the equitable interests. In fact, this restriction will be put on the register in all cases where two or more registered proprietors hold **otherwise** than in trust for themselves as beneficial joint tenants.

Anne and Chris may not wish to hold the equitable interest either as joint tenants or in equal shares. In which case, apart from cursing them for their perversity, you must put an 'X' in the third box, and state how they are to hold the property. Here are some possibilities:

- It may be that they wish to hold on trust for themselves as tenants in common but in unequal shares. In this case the size of the shares must be stated. Perhaps Anne is to have a three quarters share and Chris a one quarter. You could say 'The transferees are to hold the property on trust for themselves in the following shares; namely a three quarters share for Anne Holt and a one quarter share for Chris Edwards'.
- It may be that they are to hold on trust for others. For example, they may be the trustees of a family trust. In such a case, it is inappropriate to set out the trusts in full in the transfer. The trusts will be in a trust deed, which will name the beneficiaries and set out the equitable interests. This trust deed will never be sent to the Registrar, who is uninterested in how the equitable interests are held. So the transfer could say something like 'The transferees are to hold the Property on the trusts declared by a deed dated 1 March 1998 made between (1) Amos Featherstonehaugh (2) Anne Holt and Chris Edwards.' Remember this point. The trust deed may alter the trustees' powers of disposition. Section 6 of the Trusts of Land and Appointment of Trustees Act 1996 gives trustees of land all the powers of disposal that an absolute owner would have. This means that they have full powers of mortgaging and leasing the land as well as selling it. It is possible that the trust deed will cut down these powers, for example by reducing the powers of mortgaging, or by saying that the trustees can only exercise the powers if specified people consent. Any such provision must be reflected by a restriction on the register. A pur-

chaser can assume that registered proprietors have full powers of disposal unless the register says otherwise. Therefore, if a trust deed does alter the trustees' powers, the transfer to the trustees must contain an application for a restriction to be put on the register and the trustees have a duty to make this application. The application will be put in panel 12.

• It may be that Anne and Chris are business partners and are buying the property as a business asset. Partners invariably hold the equitable interest as tenants in common, as the right of survivorship inherent in a joint tenancy would be inappropriate. Panel 11 could then say something like 'The transferees are to hold the property upon trust as an asset of the business carried on by them in partnership under the name of Holt, Edwards & Co.' This would mean that the ownership of the equitable interest would be governed by the terms of the partnership agreement. The partners may wish for a restriction to go on to the register, to prevent the land being disposed of by surviving partners without the consent of the personal representatives of a dead partner. (See below)

Panel 12 – Additional provisions. The panel contains the instruction '*Insert here any required or permitted statement, certificate or application or any agreed covenants, declarations, etc.*' So here are some examples:

• *Applications for restrictions.* As we have seen, applicants for registration who are trustees may have a duty to apply for restrictions that are necessary to protect the position of the beneficiaries. Applicants may also wish to apply for restrictions to achieve a desired result, although the Chief Land Registrar may refuse to accept inappropriate restrictions.

Let us return to the possibility that Anne and Chris are buying as business partners. Under their names on the proprietorship register there will appear the restriction preventing a sale by the sole survivor. The registrar will put this on automatically because they have not declared in the transfer that they hold on trust for themselves as joint tenants. Now, suppose Anne dies. Anne's share in the partnership property may be the most valuable of her assets that will pass on her death to those she held dear. Yet there is nothing to prevent Chris appointing a second trustee and selling the property. Of course, Chris and his fellow trustee will hold the proceeds of sale on trust for Chris and for Anne's personal representatives. However, the personal representatives may wish to control the disposal of the property. Anne and Chris, therefore, when they buy the partnership land and because they wish to protect their respective families, could, in panel 12 insert the following application:

'The transferees apply to the Chief Land Registrar for a restriction to be put on the register to the effect that no disposition is to be registered after the death of any of the proprietors without the consent of the personal representatives of the deceased proprietor.'

- *Indemnity and performance covenants*
- *Restrictive and positive covenants*
- *Grants and reservations of easements*
- *A declaration against an implied grant of easements.*

Does the transfer that you are drafting need any additional provisions? Look again at the office copy entries. The note on the Proprietorship Register tells us that the seller gave indemnity and performance covenants when it bought. Therefore, standard condition 4.5.4 entitles the seller to similar covenants when it sells. These covenants must be put in panel 12. The wording will be something like 'The transferee covenants with the transferor to indemnify the transferor against liability for any future breach of the covenants contained in a deed dated 1 July 1991 made between (1) Abel Whyte (2) Alice Bluegown (Entry No. 1 on the Charges Register of the title) and to perform them from now on'. Remember that the wording of the clause in the transfer is governed by the wording of the standard condition.

Panel 13 – the execution of the transfer. A Land Registry Transfer must be executed as a deed.

Formalities for Execution by an Individual

What is written here applies to deeds executed after the coming into effect of s.1 of the Law of Property (Miscellaneous Provisions) Act 1989 on 31 July 1990. (The formalities for execution of deeds before that date are set out in section 9.2(f).

A conveyance of a legal estate must be by deed. A document will only be a deed if:

- it is signed by its maker;
- if that signature is witnessed and attested;
- if it is clear that the document is intended to be a deed. That intention can be made clear either by describing the document as a deed (e.g. 'This Deed of Conveyance is made 1 September 2000) or because the document is expressed to be executed or signed as a deed (e.g. the attestation clause might say 'signed by the seller as his deed in the presence of _____');
- if the deed is delivered as a deed.

The delivery of a deed may be a matter of intention only. A deed is delivered by a seller when it is signed by him with the intention that he shall be bound by it.

Signature by another The Act makes it possible for an individual to direct another person to sign a deed on his behalf, provided that the signature is made in his presence and there are *two* attesting witnesses.

Delivery by another A deed may be delivered by its maker, or it may be delivered by someone on his behalf.

Escrows A deed may be delivered absolutely, and is then of immediate effect. Alternatively, it may be delivered conditionally, and is then known as an *escrow*.

Until the coming into effect of s.1 of the 1989 Act, conveyancing practice had been that the conveyance was signed and *delivered* by the seller some days before completion. This ensured that every conveyance was delivered conditionally. Had the delivery been absolute, the legal estate would there and then have vested in the purchaser, although he had not yet paid the purchase price. Delivery was conditional upon completion taking place and the purchase price being paid. The conveyance came into full effect when the condition was fulfilled.

So every sale produced an escrow but escrows create difficulties. One is the so-called doctrine of 'relation back', which has the effect that the true date of the conveyance (whatever date it might bear on its face) is the date of the conditional delivery (i.e. some days before completion) rather than the date the condition is fulfilled (i.e. the actual date of completion). Another is that delivery in escrow is binding. It commits the seller; he cannot withdraw from the deed while the time limit for fulfilment of the condition is still running. Only if completion does not take place in due course can he renounce the escrow (see *Glessing* v. *Green* [1975]). One suggested solution to the problem of an escrow is that the seller should sign the conveyance only, and authorise his solicitor to deliver the deed at completion. Up until 1990 the idea was not put into practice as the authority would have had to be given by a power of attorney. This difficulty is now swept aside by s.1 of the 1989 Act, for the section abolishes the rule that the authority to deliver can only be given by deed. It is now, therefore, possible for the deed to be delivered at completion by the seller's solicitor. The purchaser need not check the solicitor's authority to deliver the deed, as the Act provides that where a solicitor or licensed conveyancer (or his agent or employee) delivers an instrument on behalf of a person for whom he is acting, it shall be conclusively presumed in favour of the purchaser that such a person *is* authorised to deliver the instrument. The aim is, therefore, to make it unnecessary for a deed to be delivered by the seller in escrow. What can now happen instead is that before completion the seller will sign the deed, without any intention of being then bound by it. He will then send it to his solicitor. At completion, the solicitor will hand or send it to the purchaser's solicitor, and thereby manifest the seller's intention to be bound. The deed will at the same time be both physically and legally delivered.

Schedule 3 of the Land Registration Rules 1925 (as inserted by the Land Registration Rules 1997) sets out the words of execution that must be used for the execution of Form TR1 and other prescribed forms.

For execution by an individual, these are:

Signed as a deed by (*full name of individual*) in the presence of:

> Sign here

Signature of witness ....
Name (in BLOCK CAPITALS) ....
Address ....
....

Formalities for Execution by a Company Registered under the Companies Acts

What is written here applies to a deed executed by a company after the coming into effect of s.130 of the Companies Act 1989; i.e. again 31 July 1990. For a document to be executed by a company, it is necessary that the document be executed (i.e. sealed or signed) and delivered as a deed.

A company has a choice. It can continue to execute a deed by affixing the company seal to it, and having the fixing authenticated in accordance with the company's articles of association. If that is the company's choice, everything in Chapter 9.4 remains true, and a purchaser from the company will continue to be protected by s.74 Law of Property Act 1925.

Alternatively, a company can execute a deed under the provisions of s.36A Companies Act 1985, inserted by s.130 of the 1989 Act. This provides that the deed can be executed by being signed by a director and the company secretary or by two directors, provided that the document is expressed to be executed by the company. In other words, it must be made clear that the signatures amount to execution by the *company*, rather than execution by the director and secretary *personally*.

If the executed document makes it clear on its face that it is intended to be a deed, it will be a deed when delivered as a deed. It is presumed, unless the contrary appears, to be delivered at the time it is executed

Protection of Third Parties   Section 36A (6) provides that a purchaser for value can presume (a) that the document has been properly executed as a deed by the company if it bears two signatures purporting to be those of a director and the secretary, or those of two directors, and (b) that it has been delivered as a deed, provided it is clear on its face that it is intended by the signatories to be a deed.

The purchaser will be content, therefore, if he sees a statement in the document that it is signed as a deed by the company, and sees accompanying this statement two signatures purporting to be those of directors or director and secretary.

The words of execution prescribed by the Land Registration Rules are as follows:

Execution by a Company under its Common Seal

The common seal of (*name of company*)
was affixed in the presence of:

....
Signature of director

....
Signature of secretary

Common seal of company

Execution by a Company not under its Common Seal

Signed as a deed by (*name of company*) acting by a director and its secretary (*or two directors*)

Sign here

Director

Secretary (or Director)

Who Should Execute the Transfer?

Obviously the transfer must be executed by the person with the power to transfer the title, who will almost always be the seller named in the agreement for sale (see earlier). Otherwise the transfer will be ineffective.

Do the purchaser/s have to execute the transfer. Usually, only if

- the purchaser/s are giving a covenant to the seller;
- the transfer contains a declaration of trust by the purchaser(s);
- the transfer contains any other declaration by the purchaser(s).

If the transfer declares a trust by co-purchasers in favour of themselves, or otherwise states how they are to share the equitable interest, it is vital that the purchasers execute the transfer. The declaration is then binding on them, unless fraud or undue influence can be proved.

Applying this to the transfer you are drafting, you will have to put in an execution clause for the seller, its form depending on whether or not the company will be using its seal, and execution clauses for the buyers, because they are giving an indemnity covenant to the seller and because of the declaration that they are to hold on trust.

14.2   A Transfer of Part of the Land in the Title

Look at Appendix E. This is Land Registry Form TP1, which is used for a transfer of part of the land in a registered title. How should this form be completed?

We have already considered panel 1 when looking at form TR1. In panel 2 we put the title number of the land, part of which we are now transferring. We would complete panel 3 if any covenant or easement to be created by this transfer will affect land in another title.

In panel 4, we must identify the part of the title that is being transferred. We will give a verbal description but that will not be enough. The Land Registration Rules require use of a plan. This will usually be a plan that is attached to the transfer, and may be a copy of the plan that was attached to the agreement for sale. Alternatively, reference may be made to the Land Registry filed plan. But only if the part being transferred is identified on the plan separately from the rest of the land in the title.

Panels 5, 6, 7 and 8 are already familiar to us. These panels provide us with three 'labels' which we can use throughout the rest of the document, namely 'Property', 'Transferor' and 'Transferee'.

Panels 10, 11 and 12 are familiar to us from our study of form TR1.

Panel 13 is for 'Additional Provisions'. The use of this has already been explained. In an agreement for sale of part, there may well be special conditions in which the seller reserves an easement or promises to grant one to the purchaser, in which one party promises to give the other a covenant, or in which it is agreed that a declaration against an implied grant of easements or as to ownership of a boundary fence be put in the transfer. As has been said before, the special conditions in the agreement for sale will govern the wording of the relevant clauses in the transfer, but you will probably find that you have to change the introductory words. For example, the special condition may start by saying 'The Seller shall in the transfer covenant with the Buyer that . . .'. In the transfer this will change to 'The Transferor covenants with the Transferee . . .'.

The panel suggests headings, although these do not have to be used and should be deleted if irrelevant. The first suggested heading is 'Definitions'. Something that you will often wish to identify here is land retained by the Transferor which will be affected by provisions in the transfer. For example, suppose that the registered land is Blackacre. The transfer is of the southern part, and the seller is retaining the northern part. The agreement provides that the seller will reserve a right of light and grant a right of way, and that the buyer will give restrictive covenants to the Seller. Panel 4 will identify the part of Blackacre that is being transferred, both verbally and by reference to a plan attached to the transfer.

When you draft the easements and covenants in panel 13, you must in all the clauses refer to the retained land. The reservation of the right of light and the covenants must name it as the benefited land. The right of way is over the retained land. Therefore you start with something like 'The

Retained Land is the land outlined in blue on the attached plan' or 'is the land remaining in the Registered Title'. Then when you draft the easements and covenants you need only refer to the Retained Land.

Note that in the headings referring to restrictive covenants, you are asked to include words of covenant. The wording should identify the benefited land and include words of annexation (see section 12.6). The headings do refer to restrictive covenants, so separate the positive and indemnity covenants, and include them later in the panel.

Workshop

Attempt this problem yourself, then read the specimen solution at the end of the book.

In the workshop to Chapter 13, you were asked to consider the drafting of an agreement for the sale of No. 2 Old Mill Offices. Set out below is a suggestion of how the agreement could have been drafted. Now imagine that you are acting for the purchasers and complete the blank Form TP1 in Appendix E.

The purchasers intend to own the beneficial interest in unequal shares, according to their partnership agreement dated 9 September 1995.

AGREEMENT
(Incorporating the Standard Conditions of Sale (Third Edition))

Agreement date	:	
Seller	:	Holt Development Ltd, Registered Office: Slingsby Business Park, Slingsby, South Humberland SL24 1RX
Buyer	:	John Able, Jack Bell, Jill Carter, Joseph David and Jackie Evans, carrying on business together in partnership under the name of "Spindles" at ......
Property (freehold/leasehold)	:	No 2 Old Mill Offices, Malherbe Road, Malherbe, South Humberland MA21 9MZ. The Property is more particularly described by being outlined in red on the plan attached to this Agreement ('the Plan')
Root of Title/Title Number	:	SHU 123456
Incumbrances on the Property	:	1. The reservation noted in the Property Register of the title
		2. The covenants noted in entries 1 and 2 of the Charges Register
Title Guarantee (full/limited)	:	Full
Completion date	:	
Contract rate	:	The Law Society's interest rate from time to time in force
Purchase price	:	£125,000
Deposit	:	£12,500
Amount payable for chattels	:	
Balance	:	£112,500

The Seller will sell and the Buyer will buy the Property for the Purchase price.
The Agreement continues on the back page.

WARNING

This is a formal document, designed to create legal rights and legal obligations. Take advice before using it.

Signed

Seller/Buyer

SPECIAL CONDITIONS

1. (a) This Agreement incorporates the Standard Conditions of Sale (Third Edition). Where there is a conflict between those Conditions and this Agreement, this Agreement prevails.

   (b) Terms used or defined in this Agreement have the same meaning when used in the Conditions.

2. Subject to the terms of this Agreement and to the Standard Conditions of Sale, the Seller is to transfer the property with the title guarantee specified on the front page.

3. The chattels on the Property and set out on any attached list are included in the sale.

4. The Property is sold with vacant possession on completion.

5. The Buyer has been supplied with details of the Seller's title to the Property and will raise no requisitions on it.

6. Standard Conditions 5.1.1 and 5.1.2 shall not apply to this contract.

7. The transfer will for the benefit of No. 3 Old Mill Offices (outlined in green on the Plan) reserve over the part of the Property that is coloured blue on the Plan a right of access on foot and for private motor vehicles and light commercial vehicles only in a reasonable manner and so as not to cause any obstruction or undue interference with the rights of any person owning occupying or using the Property.

8. The transfer will for the benefit of the Property grant over the part of No. 1 Old Mill Offices, Malherbe Road, Malherbe, South Humberland MA21 9MZ that is coloured brown on the Plan a right in common with the Seller and all others now or at any future time authorised by the Seller of access on foot and for private motor vehicles and light commercial vehicles only in a reasonable manner and so as not to cause any obstruction or undue interference with the rights of any person owning occupying or using No. 1 Old Mill Offices.

9. The transfer will contain a declaration that the Buyer and their successors in title shall not be entitled to any easements or rights over No. 1 or No. 3 Old Mill Offiices other than those expressly granted in the transfer.

Seller's Solicitors   : XXXX

Boyer's Solicitors   : XXXX

15 Drafting a Conveyance of Unregistered Title

15.1 A Traditional Conveyance

If you are drafting a conveyance of an unregistered title, you can use a traditional form of conveyance, such as the one set out below.

This Conveyance is made the ... day of ... 199 ... between Amy Baker of ... (hereinafter called the Seller) of the one part and Catherine Douglas and Charles Douglas both of ... (hereinafter called the Buyers) of the other part.

Whereas the Seller owns the freehold estate in the property hereinafter conveyed free from incumbrances and has agreed to sell the same to the Buyers at the price of £59 000.

Now This Deed Witnesseth that in consideration of fifty nine thousand pounds now paid by the Seller to the Buyers (receipt whereof the Seller hereby acknowledges) the Seller hereby conveys with full title guarantee all that Property known as 39 Woodbrooke Avenue, Nineoaks, Kent to hold the same to the Buyers in fee simple as beneficial joint tenants.

It is hereby certified that the transaction hereby effected does not form part of a larger transaction or of a series of transactions in respect of which the amount or value or aggregate amount or value does not exceed £60 000.

In witness whereof the parties hereto have hereunto set their hands on the day and year first above written.

**Signed as a deed by
the said Amy Baker
in the presence of**
....

**Signed as a deed by the
said Catherine Douglas
in the presence of**
....

**Signed as a deed by the
said Charles Douglas
in the presence of**
....

Alternatively, if you follow a more modish precedent, the conveyance could take a simpler form, using more modern language.

You will see that in some essentials, the contents of this conveyance are similar to the contents of the Land Registry transfer we considered in the previous chapter. There are the parties, the statement of the purchase price, the seller's receipt, the words of conveyance, the title guarantee, the description of the property, the declaration of how the two purchasers co-own in equity, and the execution by the seller and (because of the declaration), by the purchasers and the certificate of value to claim total exemption from stamp duty. There are some differences, however.

(a) The Recitals

The word 'whereas' introduces the part of the conveyance known as the 'recitals.' Recitals are often omitted in modern conveyances, but can be of use. The first recital in our form of conveyance explains that the seller is able to convey the property. It is often pointless to recite how she came to be in this position, as anyone investigating the matter has only to read the earlier title deeds. The second fact recited is the fact that the seller has contracted to sell the property to the purchasers. This explains the reason for the conveyance taking place and what the conveyance is intended to achieve. Recitals, although their main purpose is explanatory, can have a legal effect.

(i) A recital of fact will create an estoppel against the person making it, and against that person's successor in title. This can be important. For instance, Amy Baker cannot now deny that she owned the property at the date of the conveyance. If she did not, in fact, own it then, but acquires it after the date of the conveyance, the legal estate will automatically vest in Catherine and Charles without the need for any further conveyance by Amy. The estoppel is said to have been fed.

(ii) A recital of fact in a document 20 years old at the date of the contract to sell must be taken as sufficient evidence of the truth of that fact (s.45(6) of the Law of Property Act 1925). The assistance of this rule is not often needed in modern conveyancing.

(iii) If the conveyance is made by a personal representative, a recital that he has not made any previous assent or conveyance will give the purchaser the protection of s.36(6) Administration of Estates Act 1925. (See Chapter 10.)

(iv) If the conveyance is by the sole survivor of beneficial joint tenants, a recital that the seller is solely and beneficially interested in the property will give the purchaser the protection of the Law of Property (Joint Tenants) Act 1964. The same statement should be included when the seller is the personal representative of the sole surviving joint tenant. (See Chapter 11.)

(b) The Habendum

The words 'to hold' introduce what is known as the *habendum*. This describes the title that is to be sold, so it describes the estate and any incumbrances to which the estate is subject.

Suppose the property being conveyed by Amy Baker is subject to restrictive covenants contained in a conveyance dated 1 July 1950 made between (1) Samuel Shaw and (2) Paul Persil.

First, any recital as to Amy's ownership should not say that she owns the unencumbered freehold. It should instead say something like 'the Seller owns the freehold estate in the property hereby conveyed subject as hereinafter mentioned but otherwise free from incumbrances . . .'. Secondly, the habendum should be changed. It should read 'to hold unto the Buyers in fee simple, subject to the restrictive covenants contained in a conveyance dated 1 July 1950 made between (1) Samuel Shaw and (2) Paul Persil', In the case of covenants, there are also often added the words 'so far as the same are still valid and subsisting and capable of being enforced'.

There are two reasons for listing incumbrances in the habendum. One is that it alerts anyone investigating title to their existence. Nowadays, this will usually be the Chief Land Registrar, as a conveyance of an unregistered title will trigger first registration. The other is that it modifies the covenants for title given by a seller who conveys with a full title guarantee. (See Chapter 20.)

Do not forget that whether or not the incumbrance is mentioned in the conveyance has no effect on whether or not the incumbrance will bind the purchaser and be enforceable against him. In the case of a 1950 restrictive covenant, its enforceability depends on whether or not it has been registered as a D(ii) land charge. If it is not registered it will not bind a purchaser for money, even though the conveyance says that the property is conveyed subject to it. (However, see *Lyus* v. *Prowsa* for unusual circumstances in which a constructive trust might arise.) Similarly, if the land were subject to a legal easement, the easement would bind a purchaser because the easement is legal, and whether or not the conveyance mentions it is irrelevant to the issue.

(c) The Possible Inclusion of an Acknowledgement and Undertaking in Respect Of Retained Title Deeds

Usually, the seller of an unregistered title will hand all the original title documents to the purchaser at completion. However, the seller may retain the originals if they relate to land he is retaining or to a subsisting trust. (See s.45(a) Law of Property Act 1925.) So a seller will retain the title deeds if he is selling only part of the land in the title. If the seller is a personal representative, he will retain the grant of representation. The purchaser will be given copies of the originals, certified by a solicitor as being accurate copies. The purchaser will have to apply for first registration of the title, and while the Land Registry is usually satisfied with certified copies, the purchaser may need access to the original documents if the Registry raises a query as to the accuracy or completeness of a certified copy. When the seller retains title documents, the purchaser is entitled to a written acknowledgement of his right to have the retained documents produced for inspection and to an undertaking from the seller that he will keep them safe.

This does not depend on any stipulation in the contract. It is a matter of general law.

The seller's acknowledgement, by virtue of s.64 of the Law of Property Act 1925, gives the purchaser the right to ask for the production of the documents covered by the acknowledgement, at the purchaser's expense. This right can be enforced by a decree of specific performance.

The undertaking for safe custody gives the purchaser a right to damages if the documents are lost, destroyed or injured, unless, to quote s.64, this is due 'to fire or other inevitable accident'.

Section 64 demand that the acknowledgement and undertaking be in writing. They are invariably put in the conveyance itself. The usual wording is 'the seller hereby acknowledges the right of the purchaser to the production of the documents specified in the schedule (the possession of which documents is retained by the seller) and to delivery of copies thereof and undertakes with the purchaser for the safe custody of the said documents.' This wording actually extends the statutory rights, which do not include the right to take copies. The documents will be described in the schedule by their nature, date and parties, for example:

1 April 1980	Conveyance	Ian Williams (1)
		Percy Bishop (2)
3 March	Mortgage (with	
	receipt endorsed)	Percy Bishop (1)
		Minster Bank (2)

The importance of the acknowledgement and undertaking has decreased now that the conveyance will be followed by first registration. Once the title is registered, a buyer will usually only need to refer to the register of title and to copies of documents kept in the Registry. However the acknowledgement and undertaking should be obtained if there is any possibility that the Registrar may ask for production of an original document retained by the seller.

15.2   A Conveyance of Unregistered Title Drafted Using Form TR1

Most practitioners no longer draft a traditional conveyance if the conveyance is to be followed by first registration of the title. Instead they adapt Land Registry Form TR1 or TP1. Turn to form TR1 again, and reread the traditional form of conveyance at the start of this chapter. You can see how this conveyance could be recast in the form of TR1. Panel 1 would contain the certificate of value. Panel 2 would be left blank. The title is not yet registered, so there is no title number. Panel 3 will describe the property being conveyed. Often, a verbal description will be sufficient. If it is not, the description may refer to a plan. This may be a new plan, attached to the transfer, or the reference may be to a plan on an earlier conveyance. Panels

4, 5 and 6 will describe the parties. Panel 9 will contain the purchase price and the receipt. Panel 10 will give the title guarantee. Panel 11 will state that Catherine and Charles are to hold the property on trust for themselves as joint tenants. There will be no additional provisions to put in panel 12. Panel 13 will provide for execution by Amy, Catherine and Charles.

Suppose that the title is incumbered. Suppose again that it is subject to covenants contained in a conveyance of 1 July 1950. It is probably sensible to state this fact in panel 12, for the same two reasons that the covenants would have been mentioned in the traditional form of conveyance. (See 15.1 (b).) You will say something like 'The Property is transferred subject to the restrictive covenants contained in a conveyance dated 1 July 1950 made between (1) Samuel Shaw and (2) Paul Persil so far as the same are still valid and subsisting and capable of being enforced'.

15.3   A Conveyance of Part of the Land in the Title

The fact that it is a sale of part may cause the following alterations:

- Particular care must be taken in describing the part that is being conveyed. If a new boundary is to be defined, a plan is probably essential.
- The contract may justify the inclusion of a reservation or grant of an easement.
- The contract may provide for the inclusion of restrictive or positive covenants.
- The contract may justify the inclusion of a clause preventing an implied grant of easements.
- You should decide if it is necessary to include an acknowledgement and undertaking in respect of a retained deed.

A conveyance of part can again be drafted following a traditional precedent, or, far more usually, will be drafted using Land Registry Form TR1 or TP1. You may find it easier to use form TP1 if there are easements or covenants to be created, but there seems to be no reason why you should not use form TR1 in simple cases.

15.4   A Rule 72 Transfer

Rule 72 of the Land Registration Rules 1925 applies when an unregistered title is conveyed, when this conveyance should be followed by an application for first registration, but the land is reconveyed before the application is made. For example, suppose that A conveys to B. B should apply for first registration of the title, but does not have time, as he wishes almost immediately to convey to C. The conveyance between B and C is a rule 72 Transfer. Rule 72 permits the transfer, but states that the B must transfer in the manner that would be applicable if he were in fact the registered proprietor. It seems, therefore, that the document by which B conveys to C must take the form of a Land Registry transfer. Form TRI will be used, completed as explained in 15.2. Following the transfer, C will apply for first registration of title.

16 Buying a Leasehold

16.1 Introduction

The procedure for buying or selling a leasehold property differs little from the procedure for buying freehold premises. This chapter, therefore, serves only to point out those parts of a conveyancing transaction which are peculiar to leaseholds, and which have not yet been mentioned. [Note that this chapter is dealing with the purchase of an *existing* lease. The grant of a *new* lease will be dealt with in Chapter 17.

Three topics will be discussed generally first, and then set in the context of the transaction.

16.2 Title to be Shown

(a)   What the Purchaser May See

Unless the contract says otherwise, s.44 of the Law of Property Act 1925 provides that a person who has agreed to buy an existing leasehold is entitled to two things:

1.   He is entitled to see the document (i.e. the lease) which granted the estate he is buying. The reasons for this are obvious. The lease must be seen to check that the estate was ever granted in the first place. It must also be seen to discover the terms of the grant, e.g. the covenants, forfeiture clause, etc. Although an open contract allows the purchaser to call for production of the lease, it is a point rarely considered in practice, as a copy of the lease will be provided with the draft agreement for sale. No purchaser will contract to buy a leasehold estate without having previously seen the lease.
2.   He is also entitled to evidence that the seller owns the leasehold estate. This is the same as in freehold conveyancing, and the nature of the evidence is the same.

So how will the seller prove his ownership of a lease registered under the Land Registration Act 1925? By providing a copy of the entries on the register, a filed plan, etc., to comply with s.110 of the Act. The fact that the seller is registered as proprietor of the leasehold estate, whether with absolute or with good leasehold title, means that he owns the legal estate. The register may warn us of third-party interests by disclosing a notice, caution, restriction or registered charge. (Remember that the register is not conclusive as to the contents of the lease, so the lease must be seen, as well as the entries on the register.)

Suppose the title is unregistered. Title to an unregistered freehold is proved by producing past conveyances of it. Equally, title to an unregistered leasehold is proved by the production of past conveyances, although for some reason a conveyance of a leasehold estate is usually called an assignment. To take some examples:

(i) Peter is buying a leasehold from Tom. Tom is the person to whom the estate was granted by landlord Len. Peter will see the lease. Tom establishes his ownership of the leasehold simply by the fact that he is the tenant named in the lease.

(ii) Some years later, Quentin is buying the leasehold from Peter. As Peter is not the original tenant he must produce the assignment of the lease into his name. As the assignment was by the original tenant, that is the only document that can be produced.

(iii) Robert is buying from Quentin. Quentin must produce the assignment into his name. If this assignment between Peter and Quentin took place more than fifteen years ago, Quentin need *only* produce this assignment. This is because he has traced title to the lease from a good root at least fifteen years old. So once Robert has seen an assignment that is fifteen years old, he cannot demand to see any earlier ones, as these would be pre-root (s.44 of the Law of Property Act 1925). This will mean that Robert may not know how the leasehold ever came to be vested in Peter.

If the assignment between Peter and Quentin took place less than fifteen years ago, Robert would be entitled to see the preceding assignment, between Tom and Peter. As this is an assignment by the original tenant, investigation would end there.

(b) What the Purchaser May Not See

Section 44 does not permit the purchaser of a leasehold to demand evidence of any reversionary title. This means that Robert cannot investigate Len's title to grant the lease. This carries considerable risks.

(i) Robert does not know if Len owned the freehold estate, or a leasehold estate, or indeed any estate at all.

(ii) Robert does not know if Len's estate was mortgaged when he granted the lease. Section 99 of the Law of Property Act 1925 empowers a mortgagor who is in possession of the mortgaged property to grant a lease which will bind the mortgagee. In other words, the mortgagee will not be able to obtain possession against the tenant, and will only be able to sell subject to his lease. This statutory power is naturally unpopular with mortgagees, and it can usually be, and usually is, excluded by a clause in the mortgage deed. It may either exclude the power altogether, or make it exercisable only with the mortgagee's consent. Either provision ensures that any lease granted by the mortgagor after the date of the mortgage will not bind the mortgagee, unless the mortgagee consents to its grant. A tenant can, therefore, find himself with no security at all should his landlord fail to keep up with the mortgage payments. If the mortgagee wishes to exercise his power of sale he will evict the tenant if a better price could be obtained by selling the property with vacant possession.

So Robert would like to know if Len's estate was mortgaged when he granted the lease to Tom, and if it was, if the mortgagee consented to the grant. Yet s.44 prevents this enquiry.

(iii)   As Robert does not know if Len owned the freehold or a leasehold estate when he granted the lease to Tom, Robert does not know if he is buying a headlease or an underlease. If he is buying an underlease, he would like to see copies of the superior leases. This is because Robert does not want inadvertently to break a covenant – for example, a user covenant – in a superior lease. This is explained in Problem 1 in the Workshop section.

(iv)   Robert does not know if there are third-party rights affecting the superior titles – for example, any restrictive covenant on the freehold, if it is protected by being registered as a land charge D(ii), or by the entry of a notice or caution on the register of title, will bind the tenant or undertenant, as the registration amounts to actual notice (see s.198 of the Law of Property Act 1925, s.50(2) of the Land Registration Act 1925, and *White* v. *Bijou Mansions* [1938]). Yet the registration cannot be discovered, as s.44 prevents investigation of the freehold title.

The risks that s.44 presents do not exist only on the purchase of an unregistered lease. They are the same when buying a registered lease *if* it is registered only with good leasehold title. The title does not guarantee that the landlord had power to grant the lease, nor will it contain details of incumbrances on the superior titles, which may nevertheless bind the purchaser of the lease.

Section 44 has never presented the same risks to a purchaser of a lease registered with absolute title. This class of title follows investigation of all the superior titles by the Registrar. It guarantees that the lease is valid, and incumbrances affecting the superior titles will be noted on the register of title.

N.B. If the landlord's title is registered under the Land Registration Act 1925, the fact that s.44 Law of Property Act 1925 does not compel the seller to give details of the landlord's title to the purchaser is mitigated by the fact that the landlord's register of title is open to public inspection. (Land Registration Act 1988.) The purchaser will be able to obtain office copies of the register for himself. The only effect of s.44 will be that the purchaser, rather than the seller, will have to pay for these copies. Section 44 remains a difficulty if the landlord's title, or, if relevant, any superior title, is not registered. A public index map search will disclose whether or not the titles are registered, and the title numbers. (See section 6.2.)

(c)   A Special Condition in the Contract

A purchaser can oust s.44 by a special condition in the contract which compels the seller to give details of the freehold title and of any superior leasehold titles. The seller, of course, will not accept the inclusion of such a condition if he has no evidence of the superior titles to supply. The lack of such evidence may discourage a purchaser from entering into the contract, and a mortgagee from lending on the security of the leasehold estate.

Do not forget that s.44 only affects a purchaser who has already entered into an agreement to buy. If there is not yet any agreement, the purchaser can ask to see any documents that he likes. If he is refused, he can decide not to buy.

16.3   Consent to Assignment

A lease may contain a prohibition against assignment or subletting. If this prohibition is absolute, i.e. the tenant covenants not to assign at all, then assignment cannot take place unless the landlord agrees to waive the covenant, and permit the particular assignment. An assignment without his consent would be valid, in the sense that ownership of the lease would pass, but the proud new owner would probably face a forfeiture action, as it is most unusual for a fixed-term lease not to contain a clause allowing the landlord to forfeit the leasehold estate for breach of covenant.

A lease usually contains a qualified covenant against assignment. It says that the tenant covenants not to assign or sublet *without the landlord's consent*. As soon as the covenant is qualified in this way, a statutory proviso is automatically added, whether the landlord likes it or not, to the effect that the landlord cannot unreasonably withhold his consent (s.19(1) of the Landlord and Tenant Act 1927).

The proviso still makes it necessary for a tenant proposing to assign or sublet to seek his landlord's consent. An assignment made without asking for the consent is a breach of covenant even if the landlord had no grounds for withholding it. If the landlord refuses his consent when asked for it, the tenant must consider the reasons for the refusal. If the landlord has reasonable grounds for refusing, the tenant can do nothing. Any assignment without the consent would be a breach. If the grounds are unreasonable, the tenant:

(a)   is now free to assign or sublet without the landlord's consent, and there will be no breach of covenant. The risk is that if the landlord then threatens forfeiture of the lease, the court may disagree with the tenant, and consider that the landlord *was* acting reasonably. In order to persuade a purchaser to buy the lease, the tenant may have to go to court, and obtain a declaration that the landlord's grounds for refusal of consent are unreasonable.

It is outside the scope of this book to consider what may or may not be considered reasonable. An instructive case is *International Drilling Fluids Ltd* v. *Louisville Investments (Uxbridge) Ltd* [1986].

(b) may be able to obtain damages from the landlord. The Landlord and Tenant Act 1988 places a statutory duty on a landlord who is asked for consent to an assignment or subletting to give a decision within a reasonable time, and to give his consent, unless there are reasonable grounds for withholding it.

If the tenant can prove a breach of this duty, he will be able to obtain damages, and an injunction that consent be given. This on the face of it still involves a disappointed tenant in litigation but the hope is that the threat of damages will dissuade a reluctant landlord from acting unreasonably in the first place.

Section 19(1A) of the Landlord and Tenant Act 1927 (inserted by Landlord & Tenant (Covenants) Act 1995) provides that in a lease of commercial premises, a covenant against assignment may provide that the landlord can refuse his consent in circumstances specified in the covenant, and unless specified conditions are met. If, when an assignment is proposed, the circumstances apply, or the conditions are not met, the landlord can refuse his consent even although he may acting unreasonably in so doing. For example, the covenant in the lease may say that the landlord will consent to an assignment only to a public limited company. If the proposed assignee is a person, or a private company, the landlord can withhold his consent, however wealthy and respectable the proposed assignee might be.

Section 19(1A) applies only to commercial leases and only to covenants limiting the right to assign, so not, for example, to a covenant against subletting.

Purchaser's Position

A purchaser of a lease (or a prospective subtenant) will not complete the purchase without the consent of the landlord to the assignment. Ideally, the consent should be obtained before exchange of contracts. However the purchaser and the seller may safely enter into the contract *before* the consent is obtained. Under standard condition 8.3, if the consent is not given by the landlord at least three working days before the contractual completion date, either party can rescind the contract. This means that the contract will be wiped out, no damages will be recoverable by either party against the other, and the deposit will be returned to the purchaser. Of course, this is cold comfort to a purchaser who has already contracted to sell his present house, and such a purchaser would have been better advised to have ensured before contract that the landlord's consent would be given.

The condition places an obligation on the seller to use all reasonable efforts to obtain the landlord's consent and he cannot rescind the contract if he fails in this duty. He would face a claim for damages by the purchaser.

16.4   Breach of Covenants

If the seller of the lease has broken a covenant in it, the purchaser can object to the seller's *title* to the lease. A breach of covenant is a matter of title, because the breach will usually give the landlord the right to forfeit the lease. A title liable to forfeiture is not a good title.

Therefore, strictly, on completion a purchaser is entitled to ask for evidence that the covenants in the lease that he is buying and in any superior lease, have been performed and observed (forfeiture of a headlease leading to forfeiture of underleases). However, s.45(2) of the Law of Property Act 1925 provides a rule of great convenience for the seller. It states that if on completion he produces a receipt for the last rent due before completion under the lease that the purchaser is buying, the purchaser must assume, unless the contrary appears, that the rent has been paid, and all the covenants have been performed, both in the lease that he is buying and all superior leases. Therefore, the purchaser *cannot* ask for evidence that the covenants have been performed and observed, unless there are grounds for suspecting that they have not.

One reason for suspecting a breach of covenant by the seller would be the disrepair of the property. However, the purchaser will probably find himself barred from complaining about the seller's breach of the repairing covenants in the lease by the terms of the contract.

Standard condition 3.2.2 states that a leasehold property is sold subject to any subsisting breach of a condition or tenant's obligation relating to the physical state of the property which makes the seller's own lease liable for forfeiture. The effect of this is that the purchaser has no right to complain of a breach of a repairing or decorating covenant in the lease.

16.5   Changes in Procedure

(a)   *The Property Information Form*

The seller will supply the purchaser with the usual property information form used in freehold transactions, and will also supply the additional leasehold information form (part of the protocol documentation) which contains questions peculiar to leasehold sales. They cover areas such as:

(i) *Service charges*   On the purchase of a flat (or indeed a suite of rooms in an office block) the lease may provide for each tenant to contribute towards the cost of the maintenance and repair of the common parts of the building, e.g. the entrance hall, stairs, lift, roof, etc.

The payment of the service charges can be as burdensome as payment of the rent, and the amount to be paid is unpredictable, as it will depend from year to year on the amount of repairs to be done and their cost. A service charge is often expressed to be payable as additional rent, so that non-payment may lead to forfeiture of the lease.

A tenant of a residential flat or dwelling is protected against unjustified and excessive claims for such charges by ss.18–30 of the Landlord and Tenant Act 1985 as amended by the Landlord and Tenant Act 1987. For the purposes of these sections, a service charge is defined as an amount payable by the tenant of a dwelling for services, repairs, maintenance, insurance, or the landlord's costs of management. The landlord can only recover his costs to the extent that they are reasonably incurred, and if the costs relate to the provision of services or to works, only if the services and works are of a reasonable standard. If the cost of the proposed works will exceed an amount prescribed from time to time by statutory regulations, the landlord must obtain at least two estimates of the cost (one of the estimates must be from a person unconnected with the landlord) and copies of the estimates, accompanied by a notice, must be given to the tenants for their comments.

A tenant may require information as to the costs incurred by the landlord. When the information is given, it must be certified by a qualified accountant unconnected with the landlord.

A landlord may ask for service charges to be paid in advance. This enables a fund to be built up in expectation of future repairs. However, a sum can only be requested in advance if there is provision to that effect in the lease, and only to the extent that the sum is reasonable.

The information form will therefore:

(aa) give details of past service charge payments over the previous three years, and copies of all accounts invoices or certificates relating to these payments.
(bb) say if past service charges have been challenged by the seller or his predecessors.
(cc) give details of any substantial expenditure incurred or contemplated by the landlord likely substantially to increase the contribution by the tenants.

On completion, consideration will have to be given to the apportionment between seller and purchaser of the current year's service charge. Apportionment will be difficult, as the amount finally to be charged by the landlord for the current year may not be known on completion. An apportionment may be made on the basis of the figures for the previous period, with an agreement to readjust when the figures for the current period are known. Otherwise, one party may agree to pay the whole amount for the current period, with the other party promising an appropriate reimbursement.

Standard condition 6.3.5 provides for apportionment on the best estimate available, with a later adjustment.

(ii) *complaints by the landlord* of a breach of any of the covenants contained in the lease, or complaints by the seller of a breach of covenant by the landlord or management company.

(iii) *details of insurance* The lease may provide for insurance by the landlord, with the right for him to recover premiums from the tenant, or may require the tenant to insure, possibly with a particular company specified by the landlord. The purchaser's mortgagee will want details of the insurance arrangements to check that they are sufficient to protect his security. If it is a sale of a flat or a suite of offices, the landlord will often have arranged a block policy covering the entire building, on which the interest of each tenant will be noted. The purchaser will ask for a copy of this policy, any current schedule to it, and a copy of the receipt for the last premium.

Note: whereas on the sale of a freehold property the seller is under no duty to insure the property, on the sale of a leasehold property condition 8.1.3 compels the seller to comply with any obligation to insure imposed on him by the lease.

(b)   Drafting the Agreement for Sale

(i) the seller's solicitor must consider the question of deducing title to the freehold and to any superior leases (see section 15.2).

(ii) the seller's solicitor must consider the need for the landlord's consent to assignment. The landlord will ask for references, and the necessary details of referees should be obtained from the purchaser.

(iii) the particulars of sale will refer to the description of the property in the lease, and a copy of this lease will be supplied with the contract. Standard condition 8.1.2 provides that before the contract is made, the seller must provide the purchaser with full details of the lease. The purchaser is then treated as entering into the contract knowing and accepting the terms of the lease.

(c)   Approval of the Draft Agreement by the Purchaser's solicitor

As well as approving the contract, he will also be considering the provisions of the lease, such as the repairing obligations and the outgoings, to check that they will not be too heavy a burden on the purchaser.

The solicitor must consider his client's future plans. If it is a lease of business premises, the solicitor must know what use his client intends to make of the premises. If this will be a change from the existing use, the lease must be checked for any covenant to the effect that the use cannot be changed, or can be changed only with the landlord's consent.

If the user covenant in the lease totally forbids the proposed change of use, the tenant and the proposed assignee are at the landlord's mercy. If the covenant says 'no change of use without the landlord's consent', there is *no* statutory proviso that the landlord cannot unreasonably withhold his consent. Section 19(3) of the Landlord and Tenant Act 1927 provides only that the landlord cannot demand money for his consent. If the user covenant *expressly* states that the landlord cannot unreasonably withhold his consent, an unreasonable refusal will allow the tenant to change the use without the change being a breach of covenant.

In all cases, the landlord's consent should be obtained before the purchaser agrees to buy the lease.

The lease may also contain a covenant by the tenant that he will not make any alterations to the property. If the covenant is qualified, i.e. it does not totally forbid alterations, but says that they can only be made with the landlord's consent, s.19(2) Landlord and Tenant Act 1927 adds a proviso that the landlord cannot unreasonably withhold his consent to an *improvement*. Whether or not an alteration is an improvement is considered from the tenant's point of view, and it is unlikely that the tenant would plan an alteration to the property that he did not consider to be an improvement.

Again, if the purchaser knows that he will want to alter the property, he should ensure that the landlord's consent, and any necessary planning permission and building regulation consent are obtained before he agrees to buy.

(d)   The Drafting of a Transfer of a Registered Leasehold

Form TR1 will again be used and it will be completed in the same way as it was for a freehold transaction. However, there is a point peculiar to the transfer of a leasehold estate.

If the seller transfers a leasehold estate with a full or limited title guarantee, there is implied into the transfer a covenant by the seller that the lease is subsisting at the time it is transferred and that there is no breach of covenant making the lease liable to forfeiture. If the agreement for sale incorporates standard condition 3.2.2 (see section 16.4), the transfer should be drafted so that there is no possibility of the purchaser claiming a remedy by virtue of the covenants implied into the transfer that he was denied by the contract of sale. Therefore, in panel 12, you should put a statement that reproduces the effect of the standard condition. For example, it could say 'The Property is sold subject to any subsisting breach of covenant relating to the physical state of the Property which renders the lease liable to forfeiture'. This will modify the effect of the implied covenants, as they take effect subject to any contrary indication in the transfer. It is better to do this expressly, even though standard condition 4.5.3 may do it for you by implication. This condition says that 'the transfer is to have effect as if the disposition is expressly made subject to all matters to which the property is sold subject under the terms of the contract'. The reason why an express statement is preferable is that the effect of the transfer should be clear on its face, rather than being dependent on the transfer being read in conjunction with the agreement for sale.

(e) The Drafting of an Assignment of an Unregistered Leasehold

This is a traditional form of assignment of an unregistered lease.

> This Assignment is made the __ day of ____ Between AB (hereinafter called the seller) of the one part and CD (hereinafter called the purchaser) of the other part.
>
> Whereas
> (1) By a lease dated 1 September 1986 and made between Mary Short of the one part and the seller of the other part the property known as 1 Shortlands Grove in the City of York was demised to the seller for a term of 50 years from 1 September 1986 at a yearly rent of £104 subject to the performance and observance of the covenants on the part of the tenant therein contained.
> (2) The seller has contracted to sell the said property for all the residue now unexpired of the said term at the price of £75 000.
>
> Now this deed witnesseth
> (1) that in consideration of £75 000 now paid by the purchaser to the seller, (the receipt whereof the seller hereby acknowledges) the seller with full title guarantee hereby assigns to the purchaser all the property comprised in the said lease to hold unto the purchaser for all the residue now unexpired of the term granted by the said lease subject to payment of the rent reserved by the said lease, and to performance and observance of the covenants on the part of the tenant contained in it.
> (2) The covenants implied by the seller assigning with full title guarantee are hereby modified so that it shall not be hereby implied that the covenants contained in the lease and on the part of the tenant to be performed and observed which relate to the physical state of the above mentioned leasehold property have been observed and performed up to the date hereof.
>
> In Witness whereof etc.

You can see that is very similar to a conveyance of an unregistered freehold, except, of course, that the recitals and the habendum change. The effect of clause (2) has already been explained.

Instead of using a traditional precedent, you can complete a Land Registry form TR1, as explained in section 15.2. Panel 12 must be completed as explained in the previous section of this chapter, to modify any implied covenants.

(f) The Pre-Completion Searches

If the lease being transferred is registered with absolute title, the pre-completion search will be made at the District Land Registry, in the same way, and with the same results, as if it were a transfer of a freehold with absolute title.

If the lease being transferred is registered with good leasehold title, then again a land registry search will be made. If the superior titles are unregistered and have not been deduced the purchaser will know the name of at least one superior owner, i.e. the landlord. It is worth making a land charges search against that name. If the landlord is a freeholder, it might reveal a registration of restrictive covenants. It might also reveal a second mortgage, leading to the query as to whether the lease binds that mortgagee. (It will not reveal a first mortgage, as this will be protected by deposit of title deeds, and not registrable as a land charge.) Of course, if the superior titles are unregistered and have been deduced, the land charges search will be made against the names of all the estate owners revealed by the copy documents.

If the lease is unregistered, a land charges search will be made against the name of the landlord, original tenant, seller and any other estate-owners revealed by the abstract of title to the lease. A search will also be made against the names of superior owners if the superior titles are deduced.

(g) Completion

At completion, the purchaser of an unregistered lease will pick up the lease, past assignments of it, and the assignment executed by the seller. He may also, if appropriate, pick up the landlord's written consent to the assignment and a marked abstract of the title to the freehold and superior leases. The purchaser of a registered lease will pick up the lease, the land certificate and the transfer executed by the seller. He may also pick up the landlord's consent to the assignment, and if the title is good leasehold, a marked abstract of the freehold title and superior leases.

If the leasehold estate is mortgaged, the purchaser will want a receipt on the mortgage deed or Land Registry form DS1 as appropriate, or undertakings in respect of them.

The purchaser will also want to see a receipt for the last rent due (see section 16.4).

(h) Post Completion

The purchaser must consider:

(i) Whether the transfer of the assignment needs stamping with *ad valorem* stamps, and a PD stamp (see section 2.17).

(ii) If it is an assignment of an unregistered lease, whether the purchase must be followed by an application for first registration (see section 3.2).

(iii) If it is a transfer of a registered lease, the need to apply for registration of the transfer, before the priority period given by the Land Registry search expires (see section 3.11).

(iv) The assignment of a share in a management company. Where the land-lord has let flats, the upkeep of the common parts and enforcement of the covenants of the leases are often managed through a management company, in which each tenant has a share. The share will be trans-ferred on completion and the transfer must then be registered with the company.

(v) Notice of assignment The lease may provide that any assignment of the lease, or mortgage of it be notified to the landlord's solicitors, and a fee paid. A failure to do this will be a breach of covenant.

Workshop

Attempt these two problems yourself, then read specimen solutions at the end of the book.

Problem 1

You act for Pamela who is considering buying a lease from Vera. The lease was made between Len as landlord and Vera as tenant for a term of eight years. It contains

1. a covenant against assignment without the landlord's consent;
2. a covenant against change of use without the landlord's consent;
3. an option for the tenant to renew the lease for a further term of eight years.

The premises are currently being used as an office, but Pamela would like to use it as a shop for selling her designer knitwear.
Consider:

(a) What consents should be obtained before Pamela contracts to buy the premises?
(b) Whether Pamela will be able to exercise the option for renewal?

Problem 2

A leasehold estate of ninety-nine years was granted in 1965 by Lena to Alice. The title to the lease remains unregistered. In 1969 Alice assigned the lease to Beatrice. In 1971 Beatrice assigned the lease to Carol. In 1973, she assigned it to Deirdre. In 1988 Deirdre assigned it to Enid. It is now 1999 and Enid has just contracted to sell the leasehold to Pamela. What assignments is Pamela entitled to see?

17 The Grant of a Lease

17.1 Procedure

The grant of a lease may be a fairly informal matter, or may follow the same due formalities that are required on the sale of a freehold. Even in the latter case, although the usual pre-contract steps may be taken, and the prospective tenant may carry out pre-contract searches and investigate the landlord's title, the parties may never actually enter into a contract that the leasehold term will be granted but proceed directly to the grant itself. The point is that leasehold terms vary considerably and so the procedure does as well.

Suppose we start by imagining a tenant who intends to take a long term lease of a house or a flat. A tenant who is taking a term of, say, 99 years will usually be asked to pay a lump sum for the grant. This sum, called the 'premium', amounts to a purchase price for the premises. As this lump sum has been paid, the rent will be a low ground rent, and not a full market rent. This type of tenant is making the same sort of financial and, indeed, emotional commitment as if he were buying the freehold. The procedural steps will therefore be the same as if the freehold were being bought. The prospective tenant will make the usual pre-contract searches and enquiries, and will investigate the landlord's title. There is also the important point that the provisions of the lease must be negotiated. The contents of the lease, its description of the premises, its granting of easements, the responsibilities that it imposes on landlord and on tenant, will affect the tenant's quality of life in the house or flat and may affect his ability to sell the leasehold when he wants to move. If the lease is badly drafted, and denies the tenant essential rights and remedies, he will be miserable when he lives in the premises, and will never be able to assign his leasehold term, unless he can find a buyer who is as careless, ignorant or badly advised as he once was himself. This negotiation must be done before any contract for the grant of the lease is made. The contract will be that the landlord will grant, and the tenant will take, a lease, the contents of which have already been decided. As Standard Condition 8.2.3 says, 'the lease is to be in the form of the draft attached to this agreement'. However the parties may not ever enter into a contract. The negotiation of the provisions of the lease may take a considerable time, and is likely to be the matter that causes the greatest delay. Once the terms of the lease have been negotiated, there may be no reason why the parties cannot proceed immediately to the grant. The premises are ready for occupation, the buyer has the money, and is satisfied with the results of his searches and investigation of title. In other words, there may be little point in actually bothering with a contract, when completion itself can take place in a few days. All that remains for the buyer to do is to make his pre-completion search. The seller will engross the lease in duplicate. One part will be executed by the landlord (the lease) and the other part will be executed by the tenant (this part being called the counterpart lease). The leasehold term will come into existence when these two parts are exchanged.

So as we have seen, although the procedure, and the precautions taken by the prospective tenant will be very similar to an outright purchase, there may never be a contract. A contract will, however, be essential if for any reason there will be a delay in completing the grant, even although the provisions of the lease have been negotiated. This could occur if, for example, the premises are still being built or converted by the landlord. The tenant will not pay the premium and complete the grant until the premises are ready for occupation. During the delay both parties may want the reassurance of the contract, so that the hopeful tenant does not lose the premises and the prospective landlord does not lose his tenant.

A tenancy of business premises may be for a periodic term or for a fixed term. Usually the business tenant will be paying a full market rent and will not be paying any lump sum premium. He is not therefore committing his capital, as is the long term residential tenant. Nevertheless, the business tenant has certain needs:

- He needs stability. If he is forced from occupation by, say, the landlord's mortgagee, he will be faced with the expense of finding new premises, disruption to his business and possible loss of custom.
- He needs to be certain that his intended business use will not break a restrictive covenant on the freehold title, nor in any superior lease, as if it does, his use may be prevented and the premises will be useless to him.
- He needs to know that there is not and there will not be any problem with the local authority over planning or any other matter.
- He needs to negotiate the provisions of the lease very carefully. He needs, for example, a sufficiently generous user clause, a power to make necessary alterations to the premises, a rent review clause that operates reasonably, and an alienation clause that allows him a reasonable power to assign the lease if his business fails or the premises become unsuitable for his needs.

In other words, he is in the same position as the long-term tenant, even although he is not paying a premium. He will usually insist on being given details of the landlord's title, and will carry out the usual pre-contract searches and enquiries. Meanwhile, he will agree the provisions of the draft lease with the landlord. Once all this is done, the creation of a contract to grant the term may again be pointless. The draft lease will be engrossed in duplicate, and one copy signed by each party. The prospective tenant will make his pre-completion search, lease and counterpart lease will be exchanged, and the leasehold term will have come into existence.

A tenant who is taking a short term residential lease (often called a tenancy) will be paying a rent, but will not be sinking any other money into the premises. Imagine a student who is taking a shorthold tenancy of a couple of rooms for a year. He will not dream of asking to investigate the landlord's title or of making pre-contract enquiries. He will inspect the rooms, exchange signed tenancy agreements with the landlord and move in.

If the worst comes to the worst, and it transpires that the landlord is not in fact the owner of the property, or the landlord's mortgagee wants to claim possession from the tenants, the student will have to leave, but no real financial harm is done.

17.2   Title

(a)   A Lease to be Granted Out of the Freehold Estate

If the title to the freehold is unregistered s.44 of the Law of Property Act 1925 provides that the prospective tenant is not entitled to any evidence of the freehold title. This is really buying a pig in a poke. The same problems arise as have been discussed in 16.2(b). The purchaser may be sinking a large premium into the purchase of a void lease, an encumbered lease or a lease that does not bind the landlord's mortgagee. However, remember that s.44 implies a term into the *contract*. So if the proposed tenant has not entered into a contract to accept the grant of the lease, he is free to break off negotiations for the lease if the landlord refuses details of his title. If there is to be a contract, the tenant must beware of s.44, and must have a condition in the contract promising deduction of the freehold title (see later).

Section 110(1) Land Registration Act 1925 does not apply to the grant of a lease, so if the title to the freehold is registered, the prospective tenant cannot insist that the landlord supply a copy of the entries on his register of title. However, the register of title is public, and a prospective tenant will be able to obtain office copy entries for himself from the Registry.

(b)   The Grant of an Underlease

1. *Out of an unregistered lease*   If there is a contract for the grant of an underlease s.44 Law of Property Act 1925 provides that the prospective undertenant is entitled to see

(i) the document creating the leasehold term out of which the underlease is to be granted;
(ii) evidence of the prospective landlord's ownership of the leasehold term (in other words his power to grant the underlease).

He is not entitled to see any evidence of superior titles.

So imagine that Len is the freeholder and Tom is the head tenant. Susan is to be granted an underlease by Tom. Susan is entitled to see the headlease and evidence of Tom's ownership of the leasehold estate granted by it. If Susan later contracts to subunderlet to Ursula, and the contract does not alter the effect of s.44, Ursula may see a copy of Susan's underlease and require Susan to prove her ownership of it (in other words, exactly the same evidence as if Ursula were buying Susan's underlease rather than taking a term granted out of it). Ursula could not ask for a copy of the headlease, nor for proof that Tom had power to grant the underlease; nor can she ask for evidence of the freehold title.

2. *Out of a registered lease*   A sensible person would think that the position of a prospective undertenant would be the same, whether his lease was to be granted from an unregistered or a registered lease. A sensible person would be wrong. We have seen that s.110(1) of the Land Registration Act 1925 does not apply on the grant of a lease. It seems that this covers not just the grant of a headlease, but also that of an underlease. So a prospective tenant whose underlease is to be granted from a registered leasehold estate cannot insist on being supplied with either a copy of his landlord's register of title or a copy of his lease. If we look at the previous example, we can see that if Tom's lease were registered and he contracted to grant an underlease to Susan, she could not ask for a copy of the lease Len granted to Tom, nor require Tom to prove his ownership of the leasehold estate. As has been said, she could acquire a copy of the register of Tom's title from the Registry, but not a copy of his lease. The Registry does not always keep a copy of a lease when registering a leasehold title. Even if the Registry has in Tom's case, the lease, unlike the register of title, is not a public document, and the Registry will not supply a copy. A condition in the contract should require Tom to provide an office copy of the entries on his register and a copy of his lease, and possibly to provide evidence of Len's freehold title.

3. *The effect of condition 8.2.4*   This alters the statutory rules, as it provides that the prospective landlord (called 'the seller' by the standard conditions) must deduce a title that will enable the prospective tenant (the purchaser) to register his lease at HM Land Registry with absolute title. The condition only applies if the lease is to be granted for a term of over 21 years. The restrictions of s.44 continue to apply to a short lease. What is the effect of the condition?

   (i) If the lease is to be granted out of the freehold title, the seller must prove he owns the freehold by supplying evidence of his title in accordance with usual conveyancing practice. So if the freehold is registered, the purchaser must be given office copy entries of the title, or if the freehold is unregistered, a marked epitome and copy title deeds starting with a good root of title at least 15 years old. In both cases, if the freehold is mortgaged, the purchaser must be given a copy of the mortgagee's written consent to the grant of the lease.
   (ii) If an underlease is to be granted out of a leasehold estate that is

registered with absolute title, the seller has to prove his ownership of that leasehold estate by supplying office copy entries of his title. He must also supply a copy of his lease and, if necessary, the consents of his mortgagee and of his own landlord to the grant of the underlease. He does not have to supply any evidence of the freehold title nor of any superior leasehold title. Remember that the registration of the seller's leasehold with absolute title guarantees its validity, so this is not something that he has to prove.

(iii) If an underlease is to be granted out of a leasehold estate that is registered only with good leasehold title or that is not registered at all, the purchaser must be given not only evidence of the seller's ownership of his leasehold estate but also evidence that his lease is valid. This will mean that the purchaser is entitled to

- Office copy entries (registered lease) or past assignments (unregistered lease – see section 15.2(a)).
- The seller's lease.
- Consent of the seller's mortgagee to the grant of the underlease.
- Evidence of the freehold title. If this is unregisterd, title must be traced from a good root that was 15 years old *when the headlease was granted*. The purchaser wants to check the title of the person who granted the lease, not the title of the current freeholder.
- Evidence of any leasehold title superior to that of the seller. This means copies of the leases themselves and evidence of the ownership of each superior leasehold when the underlease was granted out of it.
- Evidence of any necessary consents by superior landlords to the grants of underleases.

Let us apply this to a simple example(!) Suppose that Ann in 1940 bought a freehold house. The locality of the house did not become a compulsory area until 1991. In 1960 Ann granted a lease of 300 years to Beryl. In 1962 Beryl assigned the lease to Carol. In 1998 Carol is contracting to grant an underlease of the house to Don. If condition 8.2.4 applies, Carol must

- Deduce title to the freehold in order to prove the validity of the headlease. This means providing an examined copy of the 1940 conveyance.
- Provide a copy of the 1960 headlease.
- Prove her ownership of the headlease by producing a copy of the 1962 assignment to her.

Should Carol's solicitor alter the standard condition?

(i) Definitely, if Carol does not possess these examined copies. If she did not insist on being given evidence of the freehold title in 1962, she cannot obtain any evidence now. The condition must be excluded. She must not promise what she cannot perform. The exclusion of the condition may discourage a purchaser from entering into the contract. Carol suffers now from her carelessness in 1962.

If she did investigate Ann's title, but her copies of the freehold deeds are not marked as having been examined against the originals, she must exclude standard condition 4.2.3 so that she promises only unexamined copies.

(ii) Even if she feels she does have the necessary evidence of title, she might still be unwilling to offer what is in effect a guarantee that if that evidence is sent to the Registry, an absolute title will result. Why should she, rather than the purchaser, have to evaluate the sufficiency of the evidence? If she feels any doubt on the matter, she could replace the standard condition by a special condition which promises deduction of the freehold title from the 1940 conveyance, but does not promise registration with absolute title.

To end with a more difficult example, suppose that Carol granted the sublease to Don in 1970. After a few years Don assigned his sublease to Ed, and Ed now contracts to grant a sublease out of his own subterm. Ed would have to produce copies of

- the 1940 conveyance of the freehold
- the 1960 headlease
- the 1962 assignment
- the 1970 sublease
- the assignment of the 1970 sublease to him.

17.3 Stamping a New Lease

The lease must be stamped with *ad valorem* stamp duty. This is calculated on the amount of the premium and the rent payable.

If the lease is granted for seven years or more, the lease must be impressed with a 'particulars delivered' stamp.

The counterpart lease must be stamped with 50p duty.

17.4 Registration

After the lease has been granted, you must decide if the title to the leasehold should be registered under the Land Registration Act 1925. Do you remember the contents of Chapter 3? If not, the points are made again here.

(a) If the landlord's title is unregistered, a tenant who is granted a lease of over twenty-one years should, within 2 months of the grant apply for first registration of the title to the leasehold estate (s.123 of the Land Registration Act 1925). If he can give details of all the superior titles to the Registrar he will be registered with absolute title. Otherwise, he will be registered with good leasehold title. If the landlord then sells his reversion any purchaser of it will be bound by the lease as a purchaser of an unregistered title is bound by all legal estates.

If the lease is for twenty-one years or less, the title to it cannot be registered.

(b) If the landlord's title is registered, a tenant who is granted a lease of over twenty-one years must apply for registration of his title. This is because it is a registrable dealing with a registered title. If the tenant made a pre-completion search, he should apply for registration before the priority period expires. It is not sufficient that the title to the lease is registered. A notice of the lease should also be entered on the landlord's register, to ensure that if the reversion is sold, the purchaser of it will be subject to the lease. There is no need for the tenant to apply for this entry. It is done automatically by the registry staff, as part of the process of registering the title to the lease.

There is some dispute as to whether the landlord's land certificate must be put on deposit to perfect the tenant's application. It is clear that if the lease is granted at a rent but without a premium, the application does not have to be accompanied by the landlord's land certificate. This is under the authority of s.64(1)(c) of the Land Registration Act 1925. If the land certificate is not deposited, the Registry will put a notice on the landlord's register. This is an example of how there can be a discrepancy between the register of title and the land certificate. If the lease is granted at a premium, the Land Registry takes the view that the tenant's application for registration is incomplete unless the landlord's land certificate is deposited in the Land Registry, despite the criticism of this viewpoint in the judgements in *Strand Securities Ltd* v. *Caswell* [1965]. It should therefore be agreed between the parties before completion that the landlord will put his certificate on deposit.

(c) If there is no entry on the landlord's title as to the existence of the lease, a purchaser will still be bound by the lease if it is an overriding interest. It may be overriding either under s.70(i)(k) or s.70(i)(g) of the Land Registration Act 1925 (see Chapter 3).

17.5 The Contents of the Lease

If there is a contract that a lease will be granted, standard condition 8.2.3 provides that the lease is to be in the form of the draft attached to the contract. The solicitor for the prospective tenant must, therefore, check that the terms of both the contract and the lease are acceptable before contracts are exchanged. After that date, the tenant will be unable to ask that the terms of the draft lease be altered.

It is outside the scope of this book to consider the drafting of the lease in any detail, but the following is an outline of some of the major matters you should consider when acting on behalf of a prospective tenant of a house or flat.

(a) The Parcels Clause

If the lease is of a flat or part of a house, the exact boundaries of the flat should be stated in the lease, even to the joists below the floor and above the ceiling. The vertical division of the flat's walls should be clear. This is important as it may determine where the tenant's repairing responsibilities end, and the landlord's (or another tenant's) begin.

You should check that the tenant is given any necessary rights of access, car parking, use of communal garden, etc.

(b) Repairing Obligations

You must check that the repairing and decorating obligations to be imposed on the tenant are not too onerous. If the lease of a house will contain a covenant by the tenant to do internal and external repairs (or if the tenant of a flat will have to contribute towards the cost of external or structural repairs via a maintenance charge) the tenant should consider having a survey done before he agrees to take a lease on those terms.

If the property is a flat, you must check that the landlord does covenant to repair the exterior and the common parts of the building such as the entrance hall, stairways, lifts, etc. It is true that the cost of doing this will probably be channelled back to the tenant through a service charge, but it is better for a tenant to contribute towards the cost of repairs than face the dilapidation, danger and devaluing of the property if the repairs are not done at all. Check also that the landlord covenants to provide the services for which any service charge will be levied, e.g. central heating.

(c) User

There are likely to be clauses restricting the tenant to residential use, and preventing immoral use. In the case of a flat, it is important that the landlord promises to put the same covenants in all the leases, and to *enforce* them. Then, indirectly, your client will be able to control the use of the neighbouring flats by suing the landlord if the landlord does not insist on residential use. A lease of a flat may also contain rules about the keeping of pets, playing of musical instruments, etc. These may seem restrictive to your client, but on the other hand they will protect him from the thoughtlessness of his neighbours, provided the landlord promises to enforce the rules. Alternatively, the lease may say that the rules (in so far as they are negative – i.e. what *not* to do) can be enforced directly by tenant against tenant, creating a leasehold equivalent of a development scheme.

(d) Restrictions on Assignment and Subletting

In a long lease of a house (e.g. ninety-nine years) you may consider it unreasonable for the landlord to restrict in any way the assignment or subletting of the entire house. Even so, the landlord could justifiably:

- Restrict the assignment or subletting of *part* of the house, either by totally forbidding it, or by making it subject to his consent;
- Say that any assignment, even of the whole, in the last, say, seven years of the term must be with his consent. It is important for the landlord that the person who is tenant at the end of the lease be solvent, as it is against him that the landlord will be enforcing the tenant's covenant to leave the premises in repair.

In the case of a flat, the landlord may wish to make a disposal even of the whole of the flat subject to his consent. The character of any proposed assignee and his intended use of the property is important not only to the landlord, but also to the tenants of the other flats in the building.

(e)   Insurance

If the landlord covenants to insure, he should also covenant to use any insurance monies to reinstate the damaged premises.

If the lease is of a flat, the landlord will probably arrange the insurance of the entire building, each tenant promising to reimburse part of the premium. The tenant should check that his interest in the building is noted on the policy.

(f)   Forfeiture

In a fixed-term lease the tenant will have to accept the inclusion of a clause permitting the landlord to forfeit the lease for non-payment of rent or breach of covenant. You should not permit the inclusion of a right for the landlord to forfeit should the tenant become bankrupt, as lenders will not lend on the security of a lease containing such a clause.

(g)   Management Companies

If a management company has been formed to manage the block of flats, check that the reversions to the leases are vested in the company. If they are, the company is the landlord and there is no difficulty about enforcement of covenants by the tenant against the company nor by the company against fellow tenants. If the company does not own the reversions it is not the landlord. The prospective tenant should ensure that either he becomes a party to a contract with the company or that he will have remedies against whoever is the landlord if the management company does not do its job.

18 Chain Transactions

In domestic conveyancing, the seller and purchaser are likely to be part of a chain. X's purchase depends on his sale as it is the proceeds from the sale of his present house that will be helping to finance the purchase of his new house. The chain presents problems to the conveyancer.

18.1 Drafting the Contract

The following points arise.

(a) The Deposit

We have already seen in section 5.9 that standard condition 2.2.2 allows the deposit paid to the seller to be used by him as a deposit on his own purchase. The seller should resist any attempt by the purchaser to change that condition.

(b) The Rate of Interest

As we have seen (in Chapter 5) the contract will provide a rate of interest to be paid in the event of late completion. The interest is paid on the balance of the purchase price by the person responsible for the delay. (See Chapter 18 for further detail). It is desirable, if *possible*, for the interest rate to be the same in all the contracts in the chain. For example, suppose Q is selling Blackacre to R (Contract 1) and at the same time R is selling Whiteacre to S (Contract 2). Both contracts contain the same completion date. Suppose Q fails to complete on the agreed date, but completes ten days later. As a result R completes the sale to S ten days late as well. R is going to have to pay interest to S under contract 2 but is entitled to interest from Q under contract 1. There is no problem for R if the amount he has to pay is roughly the same as the amount he will receive. If the amount that R has to pay to S is more than the interest he will receive from Q, R suffers a loss, which he will have to recover from Q by way of damages for delayed completion.

The problem is that having the same rates of interest in contracts 1 and 2 will not necessarily safeguard R if the purchase prices are substantially different.

On the assumption that it is Q who causes the delay, R is all right if he is 'trading up', i.e. buying a property that is more expensive than the one he is selling. He will be receiving interest on the higher sum, and paying interest on the lower sum.

If he is trading down, and selling his large house to replace it with a smaller one, he will be receiving interest on a lower sum, and paying it on a higher sum.

If it is S who causes the delay, R faces a problem if he is trading up. S will pay him interest on the smaller price, and R will have to pay Q interest on the higher price. The loss would have to be recovered by R claiming damages for delay from S.

Ideally, the contract with the lower price should contain a higher rate of interest to remove this sort of imbalance, but this may not be possible. Assuming that R is trading up, we would want a higher rate of interest in contract 2 than in contract 1. However, if we raise the interest in contract 2 this may produce a rate too high for S to accept. If we decrease the interest in contract 1, this may produce a rate too low for Q to accept. It will certainly become impossible to juggle the rates of interest in this way if there are other links in the chain, at different prices.

(c) The Time for Completion

The time for completion should also be considered. A special condition can be put in contract 1 that completion takes place before, for example, 11.30 a.m. so that funds can be transferred to finance the purchase in the afternoon. (Remember that standard condition 6.1.2 permits completion at any time up to 2.00 p.m.)

18.2 Synchronisation of Exchange of Contracts

There should be no time-lag between the exchange of the contracts to sell, and the exchange of the contracts to buy, or as little time-lag as is practically possible. Otherwise, the purchaser faces two unpleasant possibilities:

(a) He might exchange contracts on his sale but find that the exchange of contracts on his purchase falls through at the last moment. He then has a choice of temporary homelessness, or delaying completion of his sale beyond the agreed completion date, and so becoming liable for financial penalties (see Chapter 18).

(b) Alternatively, he might exchange contracts on his purchase, and then find that the exchange of the contracts on the sale falls through. This is a worse problem. He might find temporary finance to complete his purchase on time, but bridging loans are expensive. He might attempt to delay completion of the purchase until he has found a new buyer for his own house, but any attempt at delay can be thwarted by the seller serving a completion notice. If completion does not take place by the date specified in the notice the seller can withdraw from the contract, and keep the 10 per cent deposit. So it is probably better for your client to run the risk of having no house than of having two houses, *if* there has to be a risk at all.

A straightforward method of synchronising exchange of contracts is set out in the answer to problem 1 at the end of this chapter, which would be adequate when only two transactions are involved. Undertakings are given in accordance with Law Society formula A (see section 1.6). If the chain had been longer, this method would not have been satisfactory. For chain transactions the Law Society has a formula C. Like formulae A and B it rests on undertakings given by solicitors or licensed conveyancers which, as a matter of professional conduct, they have to fulfil.

Formula C works in two stages, cunningly named by the Law Society as Part 1 and Part 2. Imagine a chain of sales. W is selling his home to X. X is selling his present home to Y. Y is selling *his* present home to Z, a first-time buyer. It is Monday. The order of events is as follows:

1. Z's solicitor telephones Y's solicitor. They agree a latest time that contracts can be exchanged that day, say 5.00 p.m. They agree that formula C Part 1 shall apply. This means that each confirms that he holds a part of the contract signed by his client, and Z's solicitor confirms that if Y's solicitor wishes to exchange contracts by 5.00 p.m., Z's solicitor will exchange. Notice the effect of this. Z's solicitor has undertaken that he will exchange contracts today if Y's solicitor wishes it. Obviously Z's solicitor needs his client's authority to give that undertaking.
2. Y's solicitor now telephones X's solicitor. Again they agree that formula C Part 1 shall apply but that the latest time for exchange shall be, say 4.30 p.m. So now Y's solicitor must exchange contracts on the purchase if X's solicitor asks him to do so, before 4.30 p.m. Y's solicitor can give his undertaking, because he knows that if a contract for the purchase is forced on him, he can force the sale contract on Z.
3. X's solicitor now phones W's solicitor. W is at the top of the chain, as he has no related purchase. So exchange between W and X can take place, using formula B.
4. X's solicitor phones Y's solicitor. Part 2 of formula C now applies. It is agreed that each solicitor holds the part of the contract in his possession to the order of the other (so exchange has taken place) and each promises to despatch it to the other today.

   What if Y's solicitor has gone out when X's solicitor tries to phone him? Within Part 1 of the formula is an undertaking by the purchaser's solicitor that he or a colleague will be available until the agreed time, in this case 4.30 p.m. in order to exchange. So Y's solicitor cannot go out, unless his colleague remains in.
5. Y's solicitor now phones Z's solicitor. Part 2 of the formula applies, and contracts are exchanged.

What about the deposit? Formula C envisages a deposit travelling up the chain, so that any deposit paid by Z helps to fund the deposit to be paid by X to W. This is the way it works.

Each contract will contain the standard condition stating that the deposit shall be paid to the seller's solicitor (or licensed conveyancer) as stakeholder, but that the seller may use it to pay a deposit on his own purchase.

Suppose W is selling to X for £80000, X is selling to Y for £75000. Y is selling to Z for £60000. To go through the events again:

1. When Z's solicitor and Y's solicitor speak to one another on the telephone, Y's solicitor will ask Z's solicitor to pay the deposit of £6000 to X's solicitor (Y's solicitor knowing nothing yet of W). The Part 2 undertakings that will be given on exchange of contracts include an undertaking by the purchaser's solicitor to despatch the deposit to the seller's solicitor, or some other solicitor specified by the seller's solicitor to be held in formula C terms (i.e. according to the standard condition that should be in the contract, discussed above.)
2. X's solicitor will ask Y's solicitor, in the course of their conversation, to pay the deposit of £7500 to W's solicitor on the same terms, or to *procure its payment*. An undertaking to that effect will be given on exchange of contracts, in accordance with Part 2 of the formula.
3. On the exchange of contracts between W and X, X's solicitor will undertake that he will send £500 to W's solicitor and ensure that £7500 is sent by Y's solicitor.
4. Y's solicitor will undertake that he will send £1500 to W's solicitor, and procure payment of the remaining £6000.
5. When contracts are exchanged with Z's solicitor, Y's solicitor will now ask him to send the £6000 not to X's solicitor but to W's solicitor.

All these payments should be despatched on the day of exchange. W's solicitor will receive £500 from X's solicitor, £1500 from Y's and £6000 from X's. If the money is not forthcoming from Y's or Z's solicitors X has broken his undertaking to W's solicitor, which is a serious matter. But then Y and Z's solicitors are in breach of their undertakings to X's solicitors.

If the full 10 per cent deposits are not being paid, or if the deposit guarantee scheme is to be used, the undertakings in respect of the deposits will have to be changed.

The deposit held by W's solicitor will be held by him as stakeholder, as there is no related purchase. (If Z had been paying more for Y's house than Y was paying for his, so that Y was receiving a deposit larger than he needed for his related purchase, the excess would be held by Y's solicitor as stakeholder.) You must realise that if Y delays in completion of the sale, perhaps because there is something wrong with his title, so that Z discharges the contract by a completion notice, Z has no claim against the deposit held by W's solicitor. Z's deposit was paid to Y (no matter how Y may have utilised it) and must be recovered from him.

18.3 The Transfer of Funds

Funds can be transferred from the sale to the purchase by split banker's drafts. (A banker's draft is an order by a bank to itself to pay the stated sum to the payee named in the draft. It is inconceivable that a bank would dishonour its draft.)

Suppose that the solicitors for Q, R and S all have offices in the same town.

Q is selling his house to R for £40000. It is mortgaged to B Building Society, and the redemption money needed is £15000.

R is selling his present house to S for £34000. R's house is mortgaged to C Building Society for £14000. S's solicitor can arrive at R's solicitor's office with banker's drafts, one for £20000 and one for £14000.

R's solicitor sets the £14000 draft aside for C Building Society, and hastens off to the offices of Q's solicitor. He takes with him the draft for £20000 which he will endorse over to Q's solicitor, plus a second draft for £20000.

Exciting manoeuvres such as these are becoming increasingly rare, as completions by post become the normal thing (see section 2.15). Funds are telegraphed from one solicitor's bank account to another solicitor's bank account, through the Clearing House Automated Payments System.

18.4 The Client's Finances Generally

Your client's finances should be checked at an early stage before he is committed to any contract. The object is to contrast what he will have coming in to finance the purchase, with the total cost of the purchase. If the former is less than the latter, the result, as foreseen by Mr Micawber, will be misery. So do this sum.

Coming in

A   *Net* proceeds of sale, i.e. contract price *less*:

    (i) money needed to redeem first mortgage. Obtain an approximate redemption figure now from the lender.

    (ii) money needed to redeem a second or later mortgage. The possibility of a second mortgage should be checked. Your client may forget to tell you about it, or may not have realised the significance of the piece of paper he signed some time ago. A search of HM Land Registry or the Land Charges Registry should be made if there is any doubt.

    (iii) solicitor's fees and disbursements, plus VAT.

    (iv) estate agent's fees, plus VAT.

B   *Net* loan to be secured by mortgage. Check the amount offered, and deduct

- any arrangement fee.
- in the case of an endowment mortgage, the first premium on the life policy, if this is payable on completion.

- any retention money. If the lender wants substantial work done to the property, the practice is for part of the loan to be withheld until the work is done. The borrower cannot usually do the work before completion, for the simple reason that he has not got possession of the house, so he will have to budget without that part of the loan. He should also consider whether he will have the money to do the work after completion. If the work to be done is minor, the lender will not make a retention, but the borrower may have to undertake to do the work fairly soon after completion, and again he should consider whether he will have the money to do it.
- any legal fees.
- any other payment indicated by the lender. Some lenders deduct the first month's payment of interest.

C   Other sources – e.g. client's savings.

Going out

Purchase price, plus:

- solicitors fees and disbursements, including Land Registry fees and search fees;
- stamp duty if the consideration is over £60000;
- money for all the general expenses like removal costs.

Workshop

Attempt these problems yourself, then read the specimen solutions at the end of the book.

Problem 1

(This is based on the 1983 Law Society examination question.)
You have been instructed by Mr John and Mrs Arabella Archer to act for them in connection with their sale for £40000 of 5 King Street, Ledsham. You have also been instructed to act for them in the purchase for £60000 of 'Greenbank', Juniper Close, Ledsham, and you have been instructed by the West Kirby Building Society to act for them in connection with the mortgage advance on 'Greenbank' and the discharge of the mortgage on 5 King Street. The offer of advance from the Building Society states that it is willing to lend £32000, but subject to a retention of £2000 until the house has been rewired, and a new damp course put in.
    The draft contract for the sale of 5 King Street has been approved by the purchaser's solicitors who have just informed you that their client is now ready to exchange contracts. You have obtained the title deeds to 5 King Street from the Building Society, and they include the first mortgage to the Society, and a notice of a second mortgage to Grasping Bank plc. Your clients inform you that approximately £10000 is owing on the first mortgage and that the second mortgage to the Bank is security for various loans made to Mr Archer's business. You have established

that the second mortgage to the Bank has been registered as a Class C(i) land charge.

What advice would you give your clients regarding the financial arrangements? Is it necessary for you or your clients to make any further enquiries or arrangements regarding the financial aspects of either transaction before exchange of contracts?

It is necessary that exchange of contracts on both sale and purchase be as simultaneous as possible. Explain how this can be achieved in view of the fact that all the firms of solicitors involved are some distance from each other.

Problem 2

You are acting for Mr Fawkes who is selling his house called The Plot, and buying a house called The Tower. He has arranged a loan from the Parliamentary Building Society (for which you will also be acting), and that and the net proceeds of sale of The Plot will ultimately finance the purchase of The Tower. However, although the purchaser of The Plot is prepared to exchange contracts now, he will not agree to a completion date earlier than three months away. As Mr Fawkes wishes to buy The Tower immediately, he has arranged a bridging loan from his bank. The bank will require an undertaking from you to pay the proceeds of the sale of The Plot into Mr Fawkes's account to discharge the loan.

You have received the deeds of The Plot, and you have noticed that the house is owned jointly by Mr Fawkes and his wife.

Mr Fawkes tells you that nearly all the proceeds of sale will be needed to pay off the bridging loan, but says that his wife accepts this and wishes you to act for her as well as himself in connection with the sale.

Will you accept the instructions to act for Mrs Fawkes? What advice will you give, either to her or to Mr Fawkes, and to the Building Society concerning the arrangements? How will you word the undertaking to the bank?

Problem 3

(This is based on the 1984 Law Society examination question.)

Samuel Savage and his wife Sara instructed you some days ago that they wished you to act in the sale of their present property, 22 Mount Road, Mixford. Your clients have come to see you again, and on this occasion they are accompanied by Mr and Mrs Coward who are Sara's elderly parents. Mr and Mrs Savage inform you that they have received two firm offers of £80 000 for Mount Road, and Mr and Mrs Savage and Mr and Mrs Coward inform you that they also wish you to act for them in connection with the purchase by them all of 'The Knoll', 2 Little Acre, Southmaster, Loamshire for £190 000.

Mr and Mrs Coward are retired, and have no property to sell. They live mainly on the income from £70 000, their life savings. They had intended to move to a private nursing home and use their savings to pay the fees, but their daughter has offered to look after them if a suitable house can be found to accommodate both families. The Knoll is a large detached house and the two couples intend to convert the property into two separate flats. Mr Coward tells you that he thinks the cost of conversion will be about £5000 and that he and his wife will bear all this cost, and in addition they have agreed to contribute £45 000 towards the purchase price. Both Mr and Mrs Coward have made Sara a beneficiary under their wills. After the purchase of The Knoll they wish Sara to remain the only person who will benefit from their death. Mr and Mrs Savage are to raise the balance of the purchase price of £145 000 and to pay all the legal costs and disbursements, and have agreed to make all payments due under any mortgage which may be required to raise this sum. Mr and Mrs Savage expect to receive approximately £50 000 as the net proceeds of their sale after repayment of the outstanding mortgage and all the expenses of these transactions. Mr and Mrs Savage and Mr and Mrs Coward have received an offer of advance of £95 000 from the Omega Building Society, and the Society have instructed you to act in connection with the mortgage advance.

(a) Explain to Mr and Mrs Savage and Mr and Mrs Coward whether or not you can act for all four of them.
(b) Explain whether the intended financial arrangements are satisfactory and whether any further information is necessary.
(c) Explain whether the interests and wishes of either couple need protection or explanation, and if so, what steps are recommended by you.

19 Remedies for Breach of Contract

19.1 Introduction

Either seller or purchaser may fail to meet his obligations under the contract. The seller may fail to show the good title he has promised; may be found to have wrongly described the land in the contract; may not be ready to complete on the agreed date. The purchaser may fail to find the money in time for completion.

We are assuming, therefore, in this chapter, that completion has not taken place, and that one party has established that the other party has broken a term of the contract. What remedies has the injured party?

As in any contract, the remedies for the breach will depend on the gravity of the breach.

(a) A breach may be so serious, in the sense that it breaks an essential term of the contract, that it gives the right to the innocent party to treat the contract as discharged by the breach. The choice is the innocent party's. He may decide to continue with the contract and confine his claim to damages. If he does decide to treat the breach as discharging the contract, and tells the other party of his decision, the contract is terminated as regards future obligation of both parties. So the purchaser is released from his obligation to buy, and the seller can now sell the house to someone else. It is not discharged as regards responsibilities that have already arisen. This is why a seller who elects to treat a contract as discharged can sue to recover any part of the deposit not paid on exchange of contracts (see *Dewar* v. *Mintoft* [1912] approved in *Damon Cia Naviera SA* v. *Hapag-Lloyd International SA* [1985]). The discharge of the contract can also be accompanied by a claim for damages.

(b) If the breach is not considered by the court to be sufficiently serious to enable the innocent party to treat the contract as discharged, he can only claim damages.

19.2 Assessment of Damages

Damages for breach of contract are designed to put the innocent party in the same position as if the contract had been performed. However some loss suffered may be irrecoverable, as being considered too remote from the breach. The rule governing remoteness of damage for breach of contract is *Hadley* v. *Baxendale* (1854). The innocent party can recover loss that arises naturally from the breach (i.e. that anyone could reasonably have contemplated arising), and loss that was actually in the contemplation of the parties at the time the contract was made.

Let us look at this from the seller's point of view. He may be able to claim loss of bargain. This would arise if the contract price was £80000, but the property was worth only £76000. He would have lost £4000. Remember, however, that he will be entitled to treat the deposit as forfeited. The deposit of £8000 will be set against any loss he suffers. (Note that s.49(2) of the Law of Property Act 1925 empowers the court to order a seller to repay the deposit to the purchaser even although the seller, under the terms of the contract is entitled to forfeit it. The court will order the return of the deposit if that would be the fairest course between the parties – see *Universal Corp* v. *Five Ways Properties Ltd* [1979].)

If the property were worth only £70000 the loss of bargain would be £10000, so he could claim £2000 actual loss, having taken into account the forfeited deposit.

Common-law damages are usually assessed at the date of the breach, so the value of the property at that date will be used in the calculation. However, in *Johnson* v. *Agnew* [1980] this was said not to be an invariable rule, and circumstances may lead the court to consider that a different date would be fairer. In the case, the purchaser obtained a decree of specific performance, which proved to be unenforceable, as the seller's mortgagees sold the property to someone else. The purchaser returned to the court, and asked for an award of common-law damages. Damages were awarded, assessed on the value of the property at the date the decree proved to be unworkable.

It may not be possible for a seller to prove loss of bargain, because the property has been steadily appreciating in value. He can then claim wasted conveyancing expenses, e.g. legal fees incurred both before and after contract. He cannot claim both loss of bargain and wasted conveyancing costs, as the costs would have been necessary to secure the bargain.

Looking at it from the purchaser's point of view, we can see that the purchaser will be entitled to the return of his deposit, and can claim either loss of bargain, or wasted costs. Suppose that the purchaser was a developer, buying the land with a view to building on it, and then reselling land and house at a large profit. Can the developer recover this profit? The profit will not be treated as loss flowing naturally from the breach (*Diamond* v. *Campbell-Jones* [1961]) and so can only be recovered if the seller knew when the contract was made of the purchaser's intention to develop. Damages will be given to compensate the purchaser for the profits that both parties contemplated he would make (*Cottrill* v. *Steyning and Littlehampton Building Society* [1966]).

19.3   The Seller Breaking his Promise as to Title

Damages for this particular breach used to be limited by the rule in *Bain* v. *Fothergill* (1874). This rule was abolished by the Law of Property (Miscellaneous Provisions) Act 1989, and damages are now assessed as they are for any other breach, under the rule in *Hadley* v. *Baxendale* (1854).

19.4 Misdescription

A misdescription occurs when the property is not as described on the face of the contract. There is clearly a breach of contract as the seller will not be able to convey what he has promised to convey. Usually, the misdescription will be as to the physical characteristics of the property, e.g. a misstatement of the area, or land that is not suitable for development because of an underground culvert being described as valuable building land (re *Puckett and Smith's Contract* [1962]). It can, however, also be of title, as when a sublease is wrongly disclosed as a headlease (re *Beyfus and Master's Contract* (1888)).

In an open contract, the purchaser's remedies depend on whether or not the misdescription is considered to be 'substantial'. The classic definition of a substantial misdescription comes from *Flight* v. *Booth* (1834) which defines it as one that so far affects the subject matter of the contract that 'it may reasonably be supposed that, but for such misdescription, the purchaser might never have entered into the contract at all'. (In the case, a lease was described in the contract as prohibiting offensive trades. In fact it prohibited many inoffensive trades as well, including that of vegetable- and fruit-selling, a serious matter, as the shop was in London's main vegetable market. The misdescription was substantial.)

If the misdescription is substantial, the purchaser can escape the contract. He can claim his deposit back, and specific performance will not be awarded against him. If the purchaser wishes to continue with the contract, he can ask for specific performance at a reduced price. If the misdescription is insubstantial and not fraudulent, the purchaser can only claim a reduction in the purchase price by way of damages. He is not released from the contract.

Standard condition 7.1 restricts the remedies available for misdescription. It has been held (see, for example, *Flight* v. *Booth* (1834)) that no exclusion clause can prevent a purchaser escaping from the contract if the misdescription is substantial. The standard condition does not attempt to do this, as it permits the purchaser to rescind the contract if the error is due to fraud or recklessness, or if the property differs substantially in quantity, quality or tenure from what the misdescription led the purchaser to expect and the difference prejudices him. The condition also permits the seller to rescind the contract if there is a substantial difference prejudicial to him, but favouring the purchaser. The seller can thus escape a decree of specific performance, but will not escape liability for damages.

Whether or not the contract is or could be, rescinded, a 'material' difference between the property as described and as it is will entitle the affected party to compensation. The condition differentiates between 'substantial' differences, and 'material' ones, so that some errors will lead to a claim for compensation, because material, but will not justify rescission, because not substantial. 'Material' is not defined. The provision for compensation means that just as the purchaser is entitled to a reduction in the price if the property is worse than as described, the seller is entitled to an increase if the property is better than its description. So a purchaser who finds he is getting more than he expected must either pay compensation, or refuse to accept a conveyance on the ground that the difference is substantial.

19.5 Delayed Completion

(a) Specific Performance

(i) *The nature of the remedy*   A party who wishes to force completion through, despite the reluctance of the other party, can apply to the court for a decree of specific performance. This decree, if obtained, will order a reluctant seller to execute a conveyance to the purchaser, or will order the reluctant purchaser to pay the agreed purchase price. It is particularly a purchaser's remedy. If the seller refuses to complete as agreed, the purchaser may be able to treat the contract as discharged, and recover damages for breach of contract, but this is cold comfort for a purchaser who wanted the house rather than compensation for failure to get it. A decree of specific performance will secure the house itself. If the seller refuses to comply with the order to convey, the court can order someone to execute the necessary conveyance on his behalf, or can make an order automatically vesting the property in the purchaser.

A seller who is faced with a reluctant purchaser may not want a decree of specific performance. He can, instead, after service of a completion notice treat the contract as discharged, and treat the deposit as forfeited. He may then be able to resell at the same or a higher price, or if forced to sell at a lower price, recover compensation from the purchaser. The occasion when a seller would consider specific performance is when he has succeeded in selling a white elephant which he sees little chance of selling to anyone else.

(ii) *A discretionary remedy*   Specific performance is an equitable remedy, and the court has, therefore, a discretion as to whether or not to award it. However, in the case of a contract for the sale of land, the decree will be awarded as a matter of course, unless there are special circumstances. Factors which might lead a court to refuse the decree include:

(aa) impossibility of performance. The court will not order the seller to convey the property if he has already conveyed it to someone else.

(bb) The badness of the seller's title. If the seller is in breach of contract because his title is bad, he cannot obtain specific performance, because he cannot fulfil his own part of the contract. However, it may be that the purchaser agreed in the contract not to raise requisitions on the title. As we have seen, such a condition is valid provided the seller fully disclosed any defect known to him, so the purchaser should complete, notwithstanding the fact that the title is defective. If the title is totally bad, however, equity will not force the purchaser to accept a conveyance. The purchaser does not thereby escape common-law damages. If the title, although defective, seems to offer the right to undisturbed possession the seller will be granted the decree (see Re *Scott and Alvarez's Contract, Scott* v. *Alvarez* [1895]).

(cc) Delay. A plaintiff who is tardy in applying for the decree may be refused it, certainly if the delay has prejudiced the defendant.

(dd) Hardship. The decree may be refused if to grant it would cause undue hardship to the defendant. Usually, the court will only consider hardship that arises from circumstances at the time the contract was made, or from its terms. In *Wroth* v. *Tyler* [1974] for example, the purchaser failed to get the decree, because the seller could only comply with the contractual promise of vacant possession by litigating against his own wife for the discharge of her rights of occupation under Matrimonial Homes Act 1983. The outcome of the litigation would be uncertain and unlikely to have an improving effect on the marriage.

Hardship arising from a change in circumstances after the contract was made is not usually considered – for example, the fact that the purchaser has lost his money. This is not an absolute rule, and was not applied in *Patel* v. *Ali* [1984] where the grave illness of one of the sellers arising after the date of the contract would have had meant great hardship had she been compelled to move from her home, and specific performance was not, therefore, awarded against her.

(iii) *Failure to obtain a decree*   A plaintiff who is refused the decree may still be able to pursue the common-law remedies e.g. common-law damages for breach of contract. Alternatively, if the plaintiff had a proper case to apply for the decree, but the court refuses it – for example, because of hardship to the defendant – the court can order what are often known as 'equitable damages' which are in substitution for the decree (s.50 of the Supreme Court Act 1981.) These damages were awarded in the case of *Wroth* v. *Tyler* [1974]. In that case, the damages were assessed on the value of the house at the date the decree was refused, rather than the date on which the contract was broken; a logical choice as the damages were to compensate for not obtaining the decree. It resulted in a substantial increase in the size of the award, as the value of the house had been increasing throughout the litigation.

(iv) As has been said, enforcement by the purchaser is comparatively easy, as the court can order transfer of ownership to him. It is not so easy for the seller to enforce the decree. He has in some way to obtain the purchase price. The methods available to any judgement creditor are available to him. He may proceed against other property of the purchaser, or may present a petition for the purchaser's bankruptcy.

When the seller realises that the purchaser is not prepared to comply with the decree he may regret his choice of remedy. If so, he can return to court, and ask it to terminate the contract as having been discharged by the purchaser's breach, and to award common-law damages for breach of contract (see *Johnson* v. *Agnew* [1980].)

(b)   Completion Notice

(i) Any delay in completion, even a single day, is a breach of contract. However, delay in itself is not necessarily a breach that is sufficiently grave for the non-delaying party to claim that the contract has been discharged.

Time of the essence   If time is 'of the essence of the contract' any delay is a sufficiently serious breach to lead to termination of the contract. Time will only be of the essence if a special condition in the contract makes it so, or if it is made so by implication. The fact that the sale is of a wasting asset, so that delay affects its value, would lead to such an implication.

Time not of the essence   In such a case, the delay must be unreasonably long if it is to lead to the right to treat the contract as discharged.

The difficulty is in establishing whether or not the delay is unreasonable. The unreasonableness of the delay is traditionally established by the service of a completion notice by the innocent party on the guilty party. Under an open contract, the rule is that the innocent party can serve a notice at any time after the agreed completion date has passed demanding completion on a date that is a reasonable time from service of the notice (*Behzadi* v. *Shaftesbury Hotels Ltd* [1991] 2 All ER 477). The new date is 'of the essence' in the sense that if completion does not take place then, delay has been established as unreasonable, and sufficient to discharge the contract.

In view of the uncertainty as to the calculation of a reasonable period, it is not surprising that the conditions in a contract provide for the service of a contractual completion notice.

Standard condition 6.8 provides that if the sale is not completed on the agreed date, then either party, provided he is himself ready able and willing to complete, can at any time on or after that date give the other party notice to complete. It then becomes a term of the contract that completion will take place within ten working days of the giving of the notice, and that time shall be of the essence in respect of that period.

(ii) *Its validity*

(aa) The notice is only valid if the person serving it is himself ready to complete the transaction. A person is ready to complete if there are only administrative matters to finish, such as the preparation of a completion statement or the execution of a conveyance. He is not able and ready to complete if there are matters of substance still to be dealt with, so a seller who has not shown good title cannot serve a valid notice. (These examples are taken from the case of *Cole* v. *Rose* [1978].)

(bb) A notice to complete must be clear and unambiguous and leave no reasonable doubt as to how and when it is to operate. (*Delta Vale Properties Ltd* v. *Mills and ors* [1990]). It need not, however, specify an exact date for completion. A letter requiring the recipient to 'treat this letter as notice to complete the contract in accordance with its terms' has been held to be sufficient (*Babacomp Ltd* v. *Rightside Properties Ltd*) [1974]. It is probably better not to specify the date on which the period for completion expires, in case the wrong date is specified. If this misleads the recipient of the notice, the notice may be declared void.

(iii) the completion notice makes time 'of the essence' for both parties, not just for the party who served the notice. In *Finkielkraut* v. *Monahan* [1949] the completion notice was served by the seller, but it was the seller who failed to complete on expiry of the notice. It was held that the purchaser could treat the contract as discharged, and recover his deposit.

The recipient of the notice need not wait to complete until the last day of the specified period. He can complete on any day before the period expires, so can choose whatever date is convenient to himself. However, it seems that any date chosen within this period is not of the essence for either party. It is only the final expiry date of the period that is of the essence (*Oakdown Ltd* v. *Bernstein & Co.* (1984)). For example, if the ten-day period under the standard condition expires on 1 April and the notice is served by the seller, the purchaser can say that he intends to complete on 27 March. If completion does not take place on that day, neither party could treat the contract as discharged, as the obligation of both parties remains that of completing on or before 1 April.

(iv) *Remedies for non-compliance with completion notice*

(aa) Non-compliance by purchaser The seller can forfeit the deposit, and is free to sell the property to someone else. Any loss incurred on the resale can be recovered as damages, a point repeated by standard condition 7.5.2.

(bb) Non-compliance by the seller The purchaser can recover his deposit, (and, under standard condition 7.6.2, interest on it) and can also recover any loss caused by the seller's breach of contract.

(v) *Use of the completion notice*   The true function of the completion notice is to establish a ground on which the contract can be treated as discharged by breach. It is not designed to force an unwilling party to complete, although it is often used as such, in the sense that, say, a purchaser serves a completion notice in the hope that the seller will be forced to complete for fear of losing the contract. If the seller is undismayed, and still refuses to complete, the notice has achieved nothing if in fact the purchaser still wants to buy the property.

The remedy to be used against a seller who is unwilling to complete at all is specific performance. Application for a decree may be made as soon as the agreed completion date has passed, whether or not time is of the essence. Indeed, application for a decree can be made before the completion date has arrived, if the seller has already indicated that he does not intend to complete the sale (see *Hasham* v. *Zenab* [1960]).

(c)   Compensation for the Fact that Completion has Taken Place Later Than Agreed

Damages   To repeat, any delay is a breach of contract. So if completion takes place, but later than agreed, the innocent party can claim damages from the guilty party, even though time is not of the essence. This was established in the case of *Raineri* v. *Miles* [1981]. Suppose that Alan has contracted to sell Blackacre to Bill, and that Bill has contracted to sell his existing house, Whiteacre, to Charles. If Alan delays completion, Bill will either have to live in a hotel, or delay in completing the sale to Charles, so becoming liable to Charles for damages (or possibly interest, see later). The expense to which Bill is put can be recovered by him from Alan. If it is Charles who delays completion, Bill will either have to obtain a bridging loan, or delay the purchase from Alan, becoming liable to Alan for damages or possibly interest. Bill can recover this expense from Charles.

Interest   Standard condition 7.3.1 obliges the party responsible for the delay in completion to pay interest at the contract rate on the purchase price (or, if it is the purchaser paying interest, on the price less the deposit). The condition does not remove the right to claim damages for the delay, but any claim must be reduced by the amount of interest paid under this condition.

Workshop

Attempt this problem yourself, then read the specimen solution at the end of the book.

Problem

(This question is based on a question in Law Society Summer 1980 paper.)

You are acting for Green who has contracted to purchase a dwelling-house number 27 Leafy Lane from Black. The contract includes the standard conditions of sale. He has also contracted to sell his present house with completion on the same date, and this contract also incorporates the standard conditions. Black has gone abroad and will not return for another three months. The contract has been signed by his attomey White who is appointed by a power of attorney dated 31 March 1990 in the form set out in the Powers of Attorney Act 1971.

(a) Can White execute the conveyance? What special documents would you require White to hand over on completion?
(b) A few days before completion, your client tells you that he has heard from White that Black has been killed in an accident. He is concerned that there should not be any delay in completing the purchase and asks what will happen now. Advise Green whether White can complete the sale, and if not, what steps will have to be taken to enable completion to take place.
(c) Assuming there is a delay in the completion of either transaction:

   (i) explain the rights which Green's purchaser will have;
   (ii) what will Green's own rights be under his contract to buy number 27 Leafy Lane?

20 Remedies Available to the Parties after Completion

20.1 Remedies for Breach of Contract

(a) Open Contract

The principle is that on completion of the sale, the contract ceases to exist. It is said to 'merge into the conveyance'. It has been discharged through its performance.

If the sale is of registered title, it is not clear whether the merger takes place on completion (at which point the seller has fulfilled his contractual obligations) or when the transfer is later registered, (which is the point at which the legal estate vests in the purchaser).

If the contract has ceased to exist, there cannot be an action brought on it. So, after completion, it is generally speaking impossible for a disappointed purchaser to sue for breach of contract. However, some terms of a contract do survive completion, and do, therefore, continue to offer a purchaser a remedy. The principle is that a condition will survive if that is what the parties intended. Examples are:

(a) *The promise for vacant possession*   This promise must survive completion, as it is only after completion that a purchaser will discover that it has been broken. In *Beard* v. *Porter* [1948] the seller was unable to give vacant possession on completion, because of his inability to evict a tenant. The purchaser nevertheless completed the purchase. He was awarded damages which consisted of:

   (aa) the difference between the purchase price, and the value of the house subject to the tenancy;
   (bb) payment for somewhere to live until a second house was bought;
   (cc) legal fees and stamp duty connected with the purchase of the second house.

(b) *An express condition* giving the right to compensation for misdescription (*Palmer* v. *Johnson* (1884)).
(c) *A promise by the seller* to build a house on the land (*Hancock* v. *B.W. Brazier* (Anerley) Ltd [1996]).
(d) *Possibly, damages for late completion*   This was stated to be the case in *Raineri* v. *Miles* [1981] although in that case the plaintiff had issued his writ for damages before completion took place.

(b)   Standard Condition 7.4

This says that completion will not cancel liability to perform any outstanding obligation under the contract. Clearly this means that if there is any sort of financial obligation or any work to be done on the house, there will be a remedy for breach of contract even after completion, if the obligations are not met. Indeed, as regards compensation for late completion or apportionment of outgoings, these sums are by standard condition 6.4 made part of the amount to be paid on completion, so that if the purchaser does not add these amounts to the purchase price and proffer them on completion, the seller can refuse to complete.

The effect of condition 7.4 does not seem clear if it is a defect in title or an undisclosed incumbrance that is discovered after completion. Are promises as to title that are not satisfied by the conveyance or transfer outstanding contractual obligations? If they are, the condition has completely overturned the open contract position.

20.2   Remedies for Breach of Promises as to Title Implied into the Conveyance

The right to sue on the contract, lost through merger, is said to be replaced by a right to sue on the conveyance.

If a conveyance or transfer is dated before 1 July 1995, any action will be based on covenants for title implied into the conveyance by s.76 Law of Property Act 1925. If it is dated on or after 1 July 1995, an action will be based on a title guarantee implied into the conveyance by Law of Property (Miscellaneous Provisions) Act 1994.

20.2.1   On the Covenants for Title Implied into Pre-1995 Transactions

(a)   The Right to Sue on the Covenants

Much can be written about these covenants, but little is going to be written here, as the main point of the following paragraphs is to show how rarely these covenants will provide an effective remedy for a disappointed purchaser.

(i) *The beneficial owner covenants*   By virtue of s.76 of the Law of Property Act 1925 (now repealed as regards any disposition made on or after 1 July 1995) when a seller 'conveys and is expressed to convey' a freehold estate as beneficial owner, there will be implied into the conveyance covenants by him as to his title. He does not categorically covenant that he has a good title. He promises that he has the power to convey the property, that the purchaser will be able quietly to enjoy the property, for freedom from incumbrances, and to do anything further that is necessary for vesting the property in the purchaser.

If the conveyance is of a leasehold property, there are also implied covenants that the lease is valid and subsisting, and that the seller has not broken any of the covenants in the lease. These 'beneficial owner' covenants are implied only if the conveyance is for value. They are not implied, therefore, into a deed of gift.

So why do these covenants only rarely offer a remedy? It is because they are qualified in two ways:

(aa) the covenants 'relate to the subject matter of the conveyance as it is expressed to be conveyed'. The basis of an action on the covenants, therefore, is a discrepancy between what the conveyance promises by way of title, and what the purchaser actually gets. If the conveyance is expressly said to be subject to a defect or incumbrance there can be no action under the covenants in respect of that matter. Hence the importance in unregistered conveyancing of setting out incumbrances in the habendum, e.g. 'To hold unto the purchaser in fee simple subject to the restrictive covenants continued in a conveyance of 2 February 1954 made between Alice Baynes of the one part and Christine Davis of the other part' (see Chapter 13).

(bb) the seller is not giving absolute covenants as to the soundness of his title. He is covenanting only in respect of defects or incumbrances arising from the acts or omissions of persons for whom he is responsible.

He is responsible for himself; for his predecessors in title, but not if he claims through those predecessors through a conveyance for money or money's worth; for people who derive a title through him, e.g. his tenants and mortgagees; and for people claiming in trust for him.

An example may make this qualification clear. Suppose that Alex owns Blackacre, and incumbers the land by granting a right of way over it. Alex conveys Blackacre for £75000 to Vera, and the conveyance says he conveys it as beneficial owner. Vera later, in 1994, conveys Blackacre for £80000 as beneficial owner to Paul. Neither conveyance says the land is conveyed subject to the easement.

After completion, Paul is irritated to discover a stranger strolling across his backyard.

The first thing for Paul to consider is whether or not he did take subject to the easement. If the title is unregistered, and the easement is legal, Paul is bound by it.

If the title is registered, Paul is bound by the easement if it is overriding under s.70(1)(a) of the Land Registration Act 1925, or if it registered on the title (a fact which surely would not have escaped Paul's attention until now).

If Paul is bound by the easement he will naturally feel a sense of grievance towards Vera. He cannot sue her for breach of contract even if she is guilty of non-disclosure because the contract no longer exists. He must therefore, sue her for breach of her covenants for title. The covenants have been implied because Vera conveyed as beneficial owner and for value. However, Vera did not create the right of way herself and she is not liable for the acts of Alex, because she claims ownership from him through a conveyance for money.

This is why the covenants given by Vera turn out to be worth so little. As she bought the property from Alex, she is not liable for any defect in title at all, unless she created it. (She is liable for her own omissions, as well as acts, so it seems she would be breaking her own covenants for title if she failed to pay off a mortgage created by a predecessor, but only, it seems if she knew of the mortgage when she conveyed (*David* v. *Sabin* [1893]. She is not liable for a failure to get rid of the easement as this is not something she has power to do.)

Although Paul could not sue Vera, he could sue Alex.

Covenants for title were implied into the conveyance between Alex and Vera; the benefit of the covenants has passed to Paul as the benefit of the covenants runs with the covenantee's estate in the land; and Alex has broken the covenant because he is liable for his *own* acts. Of what use, though, is a right of action against a seller's predecessor in title, when the predecessor is probably untraceable?

If Alex had given the property to Vera, Vera would have broken her covenants, as she would have been responsible for anything done by Alex, as no conveyance for money separates her from Alex. This does not necessarily mean that she is also liable for things done by Alex's predecessors. If Alex bought the property for money, she derives title from *them* through that conveyance, and so is not responsible for their acts.

If a borrower mortgages his property to the lender, and the mortgage deed says he does this as beneficial owner, the covenants for title are absolute, not qualified, so the borrower cannot escape liability to the mortgagee by proving that the incumbrance or default was created by another person.

(ii) If the seller conveys and is expressed to convey as *trustee, personal representative* or as *mortgagee*, he impliedly covenants only that he has not himself incumbered the property.

(b) Covenants for Title and Registered Title

The covenants for title would also seem to be implied into a transfer of registered title. Rule 76 of the Land Registration Rules 1925, as it applied pre-1995, recognised this:

For the purposes of introducing the covenants implied under ss.76 and 77 of the Law of Property Act 1925, a person may in a registered disposition, be expressed to execute, transfer or charge as beneficial owner. . . .

Rule 77 stated that the covenants took effect subject to all charges and other interests appearing on the register when the transfer was executed and to all overriding interests of which the purchaser had notice. So no action can be bought on the covenants for title in respect of these matters. Rule 77 therefore seemed to envisage a purchaser being able to bring an action in respect of an overriding interest of which he did not know.

Although that seems clear to the average person it has been the subject of considerable academic controversy. The argument, put briefly, is this. A transfer of registered title transfers 'all the property comprised in the above title' (see Chapter 14). The transfer promises the title as registered. That is what the purchaser obtains, so there is never any discrepancy between what the transfer promises and what the purchaser gets, and there can be no action on the covenants for title.

There has been a successful case on the covenants for title. In *Dunning (AJ) & Sons (Shopfitters) Ltd* v. *Sykes and Son (Poole) Ltd* the defendants had previously sold part of the land comprised in their registered title. This land was described in the case as the 'yellow land'. The defendants then sold another part of the land to the plaintiffs. The transfer contained two descriptions of the land being transferred. One verbal description said it was part of the land comprised in the defendants' title. This description did not include the yellow land, as it was no longer part of that title. The other description was by reference to the plan annexed to the transfer, and the plan clearly purported to include the yellow land. The transfer also said that the defendants conveyed as beneficial owners.

When the plaintiffs realised that they had not acquired the yellow land they sued the defendants for breach of the covenants for title and were successful.

It was held that the description in the plan prevailed over the description by title number. The transfer did, therefore, promise a title to the 'yellow' land, and the defendants could not give that title by virtue of their own act in conveying it elsewhere. If no plan had been used the plaintiffs would have failed. The transfer would have promised the land in the title, and that is what they would have got, albeit less than they expected. Nor does the case destroy the above argument so far as it relates to overriding interests. The transfer is silent as to incumbrances on the property. It promises the title as registered and registration is subject to all overriding interests. Nevertheless, any decision that there is no right of action in respect of an undisclosed overriding interest makes nonsense of rules 76 and 77.

20.2.2   On the Title Guarantee Implied into Post-1995 Transactions

(a)   The Full Title Guarantee   By virtue of Part I of the Law of Property (Miscellaneous Provisions) Act 1994, when a seller in a conveyance or trans-

fer of land is expressed to dispose of the land 'with full title guarantee', then he impliedly gives the buyer the following covenants:

- that the seller has the right to dispose of the land as he purports to. In other words, the seller covenants that he can do what the disposition says he is doing, for example transferring ownership or granting a lease.
- that he will at his own cost do all that he reasonably can to transfer the title he has purported to give. This amounts to a promise that if the disposition does not successfully give title to the buyer, the seller will, at his own expense, assist the buyer to perfect the title. This includes assisting the buyer in an application for registration of title under the Land Registration Act 1925.
- that the property is disposed of free from all incumbrances, other than those the seller does not know about and could not reasonably know about.

If the disposition is of a leasehold property, a further covenant is implied, that the lease is subsisting at the time it is disposed of and that there has been no breach of covenant making the lease liable to forfeiture.

(b)   The Limited Title Guarantee   If a limited title guarantee is given, the following covenants by the seller are implied:

- that the seller has the right to dispose of the land as he purports to do.
- that he will at his own cost do all that he reasonably can to transfer the title that he has purported to give.
- that he has not himself incumbered the property and that he is not aware that anyone else has incumbered the land since the last disposition for value.
- in the case of a disposition of a leasehold property, that the lease is subsisting and that there is no breach of covenant making the lease liable to forfeiture.

You can see that the covenants implied by a limited title guarantee are very similar to those implied by a full title guarantee. The difference is in the covenant relating to incumbrances. A seller who gives a limited guarantee covenants only that he has not himself incumbered the land. He takes no responsibility for incumbrances created by his predecessors. The exception to this is where the seller did not acquire the property for valuable consideration. In such a case he also covenants that he is not aware of any incumbrances created by a predecessor who is not separated from him by a disposition for value. What does this mean? Well, suppose that X buys land from W, and then gives the property to Y. If Y were to convey to Z with limited title guarantee, Y would be covenanting that he had not created any incumbrances and that he was not aware of any incumbrances created by X. X is not separated from Y by a disposition for value. Y is not giving any covenant at all as regards incumbrances created by W. There is a disposition for value separating W from Y, i.e. the sale by W to X. Here is another example. Suppose that Q dies, and that R is his personal representative. If R conveys or transfers to S with a limited title guarantee, a covenant will be implied by R that he has not incumbered the land and that he is not aware of Q having done so.

(c)   Assents and Gifts   The covenants implied by a limited or full guarantee are implied whether or not the purchaser gave value. They are therefore implied into deeds of gift, if the donor gives a title guarantee and into assents if the personal representative gives a guarantee.

(d)   Leases   The covenants are implied if a landlord grants a lease with a title guarantee.

(e)   Mortgages   If the owner of property mortgages it and gives a title guarantee in the mortgage, he will be giving the mortgagee the above covenants. In addition, if it is a leasehold property that is being mortgaged, there is implied a covenant by the mortgagor that he will fully and promptly observe and perform all the obligations under the lease that are imposed on him as tenant.

(e)   Qualification of the Covenants   The person giving the guarantee is not in breach of the implied covenants in respect of any matter

- to which the disposition is expressly made subject. This means that if the disposition expressly says that the property is disposed of subject to, for example, restrictive covenants created by a conveyance dated 1/4/1946, the person giving the guarantee cannot be sued under the guarantee in respect of that incumbrance. *Note that this qualification does not apply in respect of the implied covenant that the person giving the guarantee will do all that he reasonably can to transfer the title he purports to give.*
- that the buyer knows about at the time of the guarantee. This means that a buyer of a registered title cannot sue the seller in respect of an overriding interest that the buyer knew about at the time of transfer.

20.3   Under s.25 of the Law of Property Act 1969

This remedy is only available to a purchaser of an unregistered title. We saw in Chapter 4 that it is possible for a purchaser to take subject to a registered land charge without having an opportunity to discover the fact of registration, as it is against a pre-root name. If the purchaser had discovered the land charge before completion he would have had remedies for breach of contract. When he discovers it after completion he may have no remedy against the seller under the covenants for title or title guarantee, because of their qualified nature.

In recognition of the fact that it is the system of registration that is at fault, a purchaser who is affected by a pre-root land charge can claim compensation from the Chief Land Registrar under s.25 of the Law of Property Act 1969. The conditions are (a) that the purchaser must have completed in ignorance of the existence of the charge and (b) that the charge is not registered against the name of an estate-owner appearing as such in the title which the seller was entitled to investigate under an open contract. If a document in the title that the purchaser is entitled to investigate refers to an incumbrance, the document creating that incumbrance is treated as part of the title open to investigation by the purchaser.

Consider this example: The title deeds are:

- A 1940 conveyance made from A to B. B gave restrictive covenants to A which were duly registered against B's name.
- A 1950 conveyance from B to C. C later gave an option over the property to D, which D registered against C's name.
- A 1952 conveyance from C to E.
- A 1985 conveyance from E to F.

Under a contract made in 1998, F contracts to sell to G, and G agrees to accept a title traced from the 1985 conveyance. The contract does not disclose the covenants or the option. G completes, and then discovers their existence. G cannot claim compensation for the fact that he has bought subject to the option. Had he not accepted the contractual condition cutting short his investigation of title he could have traced title back to a root at least fifteen years old, so back to the 1952 conveyance, and would have been able to search against C's name.

F can claim compensation for the covenants. Even had he traced title back to 1952, he would still not have discovered B's name. However, he cannot claim compensation if either the 1952 or 1985 conveyance says that the property is conveyed subject to the covenants.

No compensation can be claimed in respect of a land charge registered against a name appearing on a superior title which the purchaser or grantee of a lease cannot investigate because of s.44 of the Law of Property Act 1925. The purchaser's loss is caused by s.44, not by the system of registration under the Land Charges Act 1972.

20.4 For Misrepresentation

A representation is a statement of fact made by the seller or his agent before the contract comes into existence, which helps to induce the contract and on which the purchaser relies. (It is possible for a misrepresentation to be made by a purchaser, but this is likely to be rare.)

If the statement is incorrect, the purchaser will have remedies, both before and after completion. He may be able to rescind the contract or claim damages. A question on misrepresentation appears in the workshop section of this chapter.

Workshop

Attempt this problem yourself, then read the specimen solution at the end of the book.

Problem 1

Pauline has contracted to buy Roger's house. The contract incorporates the standard conditions. She is told by Roger's estate agent before contract that the house has the benefit of a planning permission for the ground floor to be used as a shop but in fact the permission had expired the previous year. Pauline has just discovered this, and she asks if she has any remedies against Roger.

Appendix A

AGREEMENT
(Incorporating the Standard Conditions of Sale (Third Edition))

Agreement date :

Seller :

Buyer :

Property
(freehold/leasehold) :

Root of title/Title Number :

Incumbrances on the Property :

Title Guarantee
(full/limited) :

Completion date :

Contract rate :

Purchase price :

Deposit :

Amount payable for chattels :

Balance :

The Seller will sell and the Buyer will buy the Property for the Purchase price.
The Agreement continues on the back page.

WARNING	Signed
This is a formal document, designed to create legal rights and legal obligations. Take advice before using it.	
	Seller/Buyer

SPECIAL CONDITIONS

1. (a) This Agreement incorporates the Standard Conditions of Sale (Third Edition). Where there is a conflict between those Conditions and this Agreement, this Agreement prevails.

   (b) Terms used or defined in this Agreement have the same meaning when used in the Conditions.

2. The Property is sold subject to the Incumbrances on the Property and the Buyer will raise no requisitions on them.

3. Subject to the terms of this Agreement and to the Standard Conditions of Sale, the Seller is to transfer the property with the title guarantee specified on the front page.

4. The chattels on the Property and set out on any attached list are included in the sale.

5. The Property is sold with vacant possession on completion.

(or) 5. The Property is sold subject to the following leases or tenancies:

[Reproduced for educational purposes only by kind permission of The Solicitors' Law Stationery Society Ltd]

Seller's Solicitors   :

Buyer's Solicitors   :

Appendix B

Standard Conditions of Sale

[Reproduced for educational purposes only by kind permission of the Law Society]

STANDARD CONDITIONS OF SALE (THIRD EDITION)
(NATIONAL CONDITIONS OF SALE 23rd EDITION, LAW SOCIETY'S CONDITIONS OF SALE 1995)

1.
1.1
1.1.1

GENERAL
Definitions
In these conditions:

(a) "accrued interest" means:
  (i) if money has been placed on deposit or in a building society share account, the interest actually earned
  (ii) otherwise, the interest which might reasonably have been earned by depositing the money at interest on seven days' notice of withdrawal with a clearing bank

less, in either case, any proper charges for handling the money

(b) "agreement" means the contractual document which incorporates these conditions, with or without amendment

(c) "banker's draft" means a draft drawn by and on a clearing bank

(d) "clearing bank" means a bank which is a member of CHAPS Limited

(e) "completion date", unless defined in the agreement, has the meaning given in condition 6.1.1

(f) "contract" means the bargain between the seller and the buyer of which these conditions, with or without amendment, form part

(g) "contract rate", unless defined in the agreement, is the Law Society's interest rate from time to time in force

(h) "lease" includes sub-lease, tenancy and agreement for a lease or sub-lease

(i) "notice to complete" means a notice requiring completion of the contract in accordance with condition 6

(j) "public requirement" means any notice, order or proposal given or made (whether before or after the date of the contract) by a body acting on statutory authority

(k) "requisition" includes objection

(l) "solicitor" includes barrister, duly certificated notary public, recognised licensed conveyancer and recognised body under sections 9 or 32 of the Administration of Justice Act 1985

(m) "transfer" includes conveyance and assignment

(n) "working day" means any day from Monday to Friday (inclusive) which is not Christmas Day, Good Friday or a statutory Bank Holiday.

1.1.2 When used in these conditions the terms "absolute title" and "office copies" have the special meanings given to them by the Land Registration Act 1925.

1.2 **Joint parties**
If there is more than one seller or more than one buyer, the obligations which they undertake can be enforced against them all jointly or against each individually.

1.3 **Notices and documents**
1.3.1 A notice required or authorised by the contract must be in writing.
1.3.2 Giving a notice or delivering a document to a party's solicitor has the same effect as giving or delivering it to that party.
1.3.3 Transmission by fax is a valid means of giving a notice or delivering a document where delivery of the original document is not essential.
1.3.4 Subject to conditions 1.3.5 to 1.3.7, a notice is given and a document delivered when it is received.
1.3.5 If a notice or document is received after 4.00pm on a working day, or on a day which is not a working day, it is to be treated as having been received on the next working day.
1.3.6 Unless the actual time of receipt is proved, a notice or document sent by the following means is to be treated as having been received before 4.00pm on the day shown below:

(a) by first-class post: two working days after posting
(b) by second-class post   three working days after posting

(c) through a document exchange: on the first working day after the day on which it would normally be available for collection by the addressee.

1.3.7 Where a notice or document is sent through a document exchange, then for the purposes of condition 1.3.6 the actual time of receipt is:
(a) the time when the addressee collects it from the document exchange or, if earlier
(b) 8.00am on the first working day on which it is available for collection at that time.

1.4 **VAT**
1.4.1 An obligation to pay money includes an obligation to pay any value added tax chargeable in respect of that payment.
1.4.2 All sums made payable by the contract are exclusive of value added tax.

2. **FORMATION**
2.1 **Date**
2.1.1 If the parties intend to make a contract by exchanging duplicate copies by post or through a document exchange, the contract is made when the last copy is posted or deposited at the document exchange.
2.1.2 If the parties' solicitors agree to treat exchange as taking place before duplicate copies are actually exchanged, the contract is made as so agreed.

2.2 **Deposit**
2.2.1 The buyer is to pay or send a deposit of 10 per cent of the purchase price no later than the date of the contract. Except on a sale by auction, payment is to be made by banker's draft or by a cheque drawn on a solicitors' clearing bank account.
2.2.2 If before completion date the seller agrees to buy another property in England and Wales for his residence, he may use all or any part of the deposit as a deposit in that transaction to be held on terms to the same effect as this condition and condition 2.2.3.
2.2.3 Any deposit or part of a deposit not being used in accordance with condition 2.2.2 is to be held by the seller's solicitor as stakeholder on terms that on completion it is paid to the seller with accrued interest.
2.2.4 If a cheque tendered in payment of all or part of the deposit is dishonoured when first presented, the seller may, within seven working days of being notified that the cheque has been dishonoured, give notice to the buyer that the contract is discharged by the buyer's breach.

2.3 **Auctions**
2.3.1 On a sale by auction the following conditions apply to the property and, if it is sold in lots, to each lot.
2.3.2 The sale is subject to a reserve price.
2.3.3 The seller, or a person on his behalf, may bid up to the reserve price.
2.3.4 The auctioneer may refuse any bid.
2.3.5 If there is a dispute about a bid, the auctioneer may resolve the dispute or restart the auction at the last undisputed bid.

3. **MATTERS AFFECTING THE PROPERTY**
3.1 **Freedom from incumbrances**
3.1.1 The seller is selling the property free from incumbrances, other than those mentioned in condition 3.1.2.
3.1.2 The incumbrances subject to which the property is sold are:
(a) those mentioned in the agreement
(b) those discoverable by inspection of the property before the contract
(c) those the seller does not and could not know about
(d) entries made before the date of the contract in any public register except those maintained by HM Land Registry or its Land Charges Department or by

3.1.3 After the contract is made, the seller is to give the buyer written details without delay of any new public requirement and of anything in writing which he learns about concerning any incumbrances subject to which the property is sold.

3.1.4 The buyer is to bear the cost of complying with any outstanding public requirement and is to indemnify the seller against any liability resulting from a public requirement.

Physical state

3.2.1 The buyer accepts the property in the physical state it is in at the date of the contract unless the seller is building or converting it.

3.2.2 A leasehold property is sold subject to any subsisting breach of a condition or tenant's obligation relating to the physical state of the property which renders the lease liable to forfeiture.

3.2.3 A sub-lease is granted subject to any subsisting breach of a condition or tenant's obligation relating to the physical state of the property which renders the seller's own lease liable to forfeiture.

Leases affecting the property

3.3.1 The following provisions apply if the agreement states that any part of the property is sold subject to a lease.

3.3.2 (a) The seller having provided the buyer with full details of each lease or copies of the documents embodying the lease terms, the buyer is treated as entering into the contract knowing and fully accepting those terms.

(b) The seller is to inform the buyer without delay if the lease ends or if the seller learns of any application by the tenant in connection with the lease; the seller is then to act as the buyer reasonably directs, and the buyer is to indemnify him against all consequent loss and expense.

(c) The seller is not to agree to any proposal to change the lease terms without the consent of the buyer and is to inform the buyer without delay of any change which may be proposed or agreed.

(d) The buyer is to indemnify the seller against all claims arising from the lease; after actual completion this includes claims which are unenforceable against a buyer for want of registration.

(e) The seller takes no responsibility for what rent is lawfully recoverable, nor for whether or how any legislation affects the lease.

(f) If the let land is not wholly within the property, the seller may apportion the rent.

Retained land

3.4.1 The following provisions apply where after the transfer the seller will be retaining land near the property.

3.4.2 The buyer will have no right of light or air over the retained land, but otherwise the seller and the buyer will each have the rights over the land of the other which they would have had if they were two separate buyers to whom the seller had made simultaneous transfers of the property and the retained land.

3.4.3 Either party may require that the transfer contain appropriate express terms.

4. TITLE AND TRANSFER

4.1 Timetable

4.1.1 The following are the steps for deducing and investigating the title to the property to be taken within the following time limits:

Step	Time Limit
1 The seller is to send the buyer evidence of title in accordance with condition 4.2	Immediately after making the contract
2. The buyer may raise written requisitions	Six working days after either the date of the contract or the date of delivery of the seller's evidence of title on which the requisitions are raised whichever is the later
3. The seller is to reply in writing to any requisitions raised	Four working days after receiving the requisitions
4. The buyer may make written observations on the seller's replies	Three working days after receiving the replies

The time limit on the buyer's right to raise requisitions applies even where the seller supplies incomplete evidence of his title, but the buyer may, within six working days from delivery of any further evidence, raise further requisitions resulting from that evidence. On the expiry of the relevant time limit the buyer loses his right to raise requisitions or make observations.

4.1.2 The parties are to take the following steps to prepare and agree the transfer of the property within the following time limits:

Step	Time Limit
A The buyer is to send the seller a draft transfer	At least twelve working days before completion date
B The seller is to approve or revise that draft and either return it or retain it for use as the actual transfer	Four working days after delivery of the draft transfer
C If the draft is returned the buyer is to send an engrossment to the seller	At least five working days before completion date

4.1.3 Periods of time under conditions 4.1.1 and 4.1.2 may run concurrently.

4.1.4 If the period between the date of the contract and completion date is less than 15 working days, the time limits in conditions 4.1.1 and 4.1.2 are to be reduced by the same proportion as that period bears to the period of 15 working days. Fractions of a working day are to be rounded down except that the time limit to perform any step is not to be less than one working day.

4.2 Proof of title

4.2.1 The evidence of registered title is office copies of the items required to be furnished by section 110(1) of the Land Registration Act 1925 and the copies abstracts and evidence referred to in section 110(2).

4.2.2 The evidence of unregistered title is an abstract of the title, or an epitome of title with photocopies of the relevant documents.

4.2.3 Where the title to the property is unregistered, the seller is to produce to the buyer (without cost to the buyer):
(a) the original of every relevant document, or
(b) an abstract, epitome or copy with an original marking by a solicitor or examination either against the original or against an examined abstract or against an examined copy.

4.3 Defining the property

4.3.1 The seller need not:
(a) prove the exact boundaries of the property
(b) prove who owns fences, ditches, hedges or walls
(c) separately identify parts of the property with different titles
further than he may be able to do from information in his possession.

4.3.2 The buyer may, if it is reasonable, require the seller to make or obtain, pay for and hand over a statutory declaration about facts relevant to the matters mentioned in condition 4.3.1. The form of the declaration is to be agreed by the buyer, who must not unreasonably withhold his agreement.

4.4 Rents and rentcharges

The fact that a rent or rentcharge, whether payable or receivable by the owner of the property, has been or will on completion be, informally apportioned is not to be regarded as a defect in title.

4.5 Transfer

4.5.1 The buyer does not prejudice his right to raise requisitions, or to require replies to any raised, by taking any steps in relation to the preparation or agreement of the transfer.

4.5.2 If the agreement makes no provision as to title guarantee, then subject to condition 4.5.3 the seller is to transfer the property with full title guarantee.

4.5.3 The transfer is to have effect as if the disposition is expressly made subject to all matters to which the property is sold subject under the terms of the contract.

4.5.4 If after completion the seller will remain bound by any obligation affecting the property, but the law does not imply any covenant by the buyer to indemnify the seller against liability for future breaches of it:

(a) the buyer is to covenant in the transfer to indemnify the seller against liability for any future breach of the obligation and to perform it from then on, and

(b) if required by the seller, the buyer is to execute and deliver to the seller on completion a duplicate transfer prepared by the buyer.

4.5.5 The seller is to arrange at his expense that, in relation to every document of title which the buyer does not receive on completion, the buyer is to have the benefit of:

(a) a written acknowledgement of his right to its production, and

(b) a written undertaking for its safe custody (except while it is held by a mortgagee or by someone in a fiduciary capacity).

5. PENDING COMPLETION

5.1.1 Responsibility for property

The seller will transfer the property in the same physical state as it was at the date of the contract (except for fair wear and tear), which means that the seller retains the risk until completion.

5.1.2 If at any time before completion the physical state of the property makes it unusable for its purpose at the date of the contract:

(a) the buyer may rescind the contract

(b) the seller may rescind the contract where the property has become unusable for that purpose as a result of damage against which the seller could not reasonably have insured, or which it is not legally possible for the seller to make good.

5.1.3 The seller is under no obligation to the buyer to insure the property.

5.1.4 Section 47 of the Law of Property Act 1925 does not apply

5.2 Occupation by buyer

5.2.1 If the buyer is not already lawfully in the property, and the seller agrees to let him into occupation, the buyer occupies on the following terms.

5.2.2 The buyer is a licensee and not a tenant. The terms of the licence are that the buyer:

(a) cannot transfer it

(b) may permit members of his household to occupy the property

(c) is to pay or indemnify the seller against all outgoings and other expenses in respect of the property

(d) is to pay the seller a fee calculated at the contract rate on the purchase price (less any deposit paid) for the period of the licence

(e) is entitled to any rents and profits from any part of the property which he does not occupy

(f) is to keep the property in as good a state of repair as it was in when he went into occupation (except for fair wear and tear) and is not to alter it

(g) is to insure the property in a sum which is not less than the purchase price against all risks in respect of which comparable premises are normally insured

(h) is to quit the property when the licence ends.

5.2.3 On the creation of the buyer's licence, condition 5.1 ceases to apply, which means that the buyer then assumes the risk until completion.

5.2.4 The buyer is not in occupation for the purposes of this condition if he merely exercises rights of access given solely to do work agreed by the seller.

5.2.5 The buyer's licence ends on the earliest of: completion date, rescission of the contract or when five working days' notice given by one party to the other takes effect.

5.2.6 If the buyer is in occupation of the property after his licence has come to an end and the contract is subsequently completed he is to pay the seller compensation for his continued occupation calculated at the same rate as the fee mentioned in condition 5.2.2(d).

5.2.7 The buyer's right to raise requisitions is unaffected.

6. COMPLETION

6.1 Date

6.1.1 Completion date is twenty working days after the date of the contract but time is not of the essence of the contract unless a notice to complete has been served.

6.1.2 If the money due on completion is received after 2.00pm, completion is to be treated, for the purposes only of conditions 6.3 and 7.3, as taking place on the next working day.

6.1.3 Condition 6.1.2 does not apply where the sale is with vacant possession of the property or any part and the seller has not vacated the property or that part by 2.00pm on the date of actual completion.

6.2 Place

Completion is to take place in England and Wales, either at the seller's solicitor's office or at some other place which the seller reasonably specifies

6.3 Apportionments

6.3.1 Income and outgoings of the property are to be apportioned between the parties so far as the change of ownership on completion will affect entitlement to receive or liability to pay them

6.3.2 If the whole property is sold with vacant possession or the seller exercises his option in condition 7.3.4, apportionment is to be made with effect from the date of actual completion; otherwise, it is to be made from completion date.

6.3.3 In apportioning any sum, it is to be assumed that the seller owns the property until the end of the day from which apportionment is made and that the sum accrues from day to day at the rate at which it is payable on that day

6.3.4 For the purpose of apportioning income and outgoings, it is to be assumed that they accrue at an equal daily rate throughout the year.

6.3.5 When a sum to be apportioned is not known or easily ascertainable at completion, a provisional apportionment is to be made according to the best estimate available. As soon as the amount is known, a final apportionment is to be made and notified to the other party. Any resulting balance is to be paid no more than ten working days later, and if not then paid the balance is to bear interest at the contract rate from then until payment.

6.3.6 Compensation payable under condition 5.2.6 is not to be apportioned.

6.4 Amount payable

The amount payable by the buyer on completion is the purchase price (less any deposit already paid to the seller or his agent) adjusted to take account of:

(a) apportionments made under condition 6.3

(b) any compensation to be paid or allowed under condition 7.3

6.5 Title deeds

6.5.1 The seller is not to retain the documents of title after the buyer has tendered the amount payable under condition 6.4.

6.5.2 Condition 6.5.1 does not apply to any documents of title relating to land being retained by the seller after completion.

6.6 Rent receipts

The seller is to assume that whoever gave any receipt for a payment of rent or service charge which the seller produces was the person or the agent of the person then entitled to that rent or service charge.

6.7 Means of payment

The buyer is to pay the money due on completion in one or more of the following ways:

(a) legal tender

(b) a banker's draft

(c) a direct credit to a bank account nominated by the seller's solicitor

(d) an unconditional release of a deposit held by a stakeholder.

6.8 Notice to complete

6.8.1 At any time on or after completion date, a party who is ready able and willing to complete may give the other a notice to complete.

6.8.2 A party is ready able and willing:
(a) if he could be, but for the default of the other party, and
(b) in the case of the seller, even though a mortgage remains secured on the property, if the amount to be paid on completion enables the property to be transferred freed of all mortgages (except those to which the sale is expressly subject).

6.8.3 The parties are to complete the contract within ten working days of giving a notice to complete, excluding the day on which the notice is given. For this purpose, time is of the essence of the contract.

6.8.4 On receipt of a notice to complete:
(a) if the buyer paid no deposit, he is forthwith to pay a deposit of 10 per cent
(b) if the buyer paid a deposit of less than 10 per cent, he is forthwith to pay a further deposit equal to the balance of that 10 per cent.

7. REMEDIES

7.1 Errors and omissions

7.1.1 If any plan or statement in the contract, or in the negotiations leading to it, is or was misleading or inaccurate due to an error or omission, the remedies available are as follows.

7.1.2 When there is a material difference between the description or value of the property as represented and as it is, the injured party is entitled to damages.

7.1.3 An error or omission only entitles the injured party to rescind the contract:
(a) where it results from fraud or recklessness, or
(b) where he would be obliged, to his prejudice, to transfer or accept property differing substantially (in quantity, quality or tenure) from what the error or omission had led him to expect.

7.2 Rescission

If either party rescinds the contract:
(a) unless the rescission is a result of the buyer's breach of contract the deposit is to be repaid to the buyer with accrued interest
(b) the buyer is to return any documents he received from the seller and is to cancel any registration of the contract.

7.3 Late completion

7.3.1 If there is default by either or both of the parties in performing their obligations under the contract and completion is delayed, the party whose total period of default is the greater is to pay compensation to the other party.

7.3.2 Compensation is calculated at the contract rate on the purchase price, or (where the buyer is the paying party) the purchase price less any deposit paid, for the period by which the paying party's default exceeds that of the receiving party, or, if shorter, the period between completion date and actual completion.

7.3.3 Any claim for loss resulting from delayed completion is to be reduced by any compensation paid under this contract

7.3.4 Where the buyer holds the property as tenant and completion is delayed, the seller may give notice to the buyer, before the date of actual completion, that he intends to take the net income from the property until completion. If he does so, he cannot claim compensation under condition 7.3.1 as well.

7.4 After completion

Completion does not cancel liability to perform any outstanding obligation under this contract.

7.5 Buyer's failure to comply with notice to complete

7.5.1 If the buyer fails to complete in accordance with a notice to complete, the following terms apply.

7.5.2 The seller may rescind the contract, and if he does so:
(a) he may
(i) forfeit and keep any deposit and accrued interest
(ii) resell the property
(iii) claim damages
(b) the buyer is to return any documents he received from the seller and is to cancel any registration of the contract.

7.5.3 The seller retains his other rights and remedies.

7.6 Seller's failure to comply with notice to complete

7.6.1 If the seller fails to complete in accordance with a notice to complete, the following terms apply.

7.6.2 The buyer may rescind the contract, and if he does so:
(a) the deposit is to be repaid to the buyer with accrued interest
(b) the buyer is to return any documents he received from the seller and is, at the seller's expense, to cancel any registration of the contract.

7.6.3 The buyer retains his other rights and remedies.

8. LEASEHOLD PROPERTY

8.1 Existing leases

8.1.1 The following provisions apply to a sale of leasehold land.

8.1.2 The seller having provided the buyer with copies of the documents embodying the lease terms, the buyer is treated as entering into the contract knowing and fully accepting those terms.

8.1.3 The seller is to comply with any lease obligations requiring the tenant to insure the property.

8.2 New leases

8.2.1 The following provisions apply to a grant of a new lease.

8.2.2 The conditions apply so that:
"seller" means the proposed landlord
"buyer" means the proposed tenant
"purchase price" means the premium to be paid on the grant of a lease.

8.2.3 The lease is to be in the form of the draft attached to the agreement.

8.2.4 If the term of the new lease will exceed 21 years, the seller is to deduce a title which will enable the buyer to register the lease at HM Land Registry with an absolute title.

8.2.5 The buyer is not entitled to transfer the benefit of the contract.

8.2.6 The seller is to engross the lease and a counterpart of it and is to send the counterpart to the buyer at least five working days before completion date.

8.2.7 The buyer is to execute the counterpart and deliver it to the seller on completion.

8.3 Landlord's consent

8.3.1 The following provisions apply if a consent to assign or sub-let is required to complete the contract.

8.3.2 (a) The seller is to apply for the consent at his expense, and to use all reasonable effort to obtain it
(b) The buyer is to provide all information and references reasonably required

8.3.3 Unless he is in breach of his obligation under condition 8.3.2, either party may rescind the contract by notice to the other party if three working days before completion date:
(a) the consent has not been given or
(b) the consent has been given subject to a condition to which the buyer reasonably objects.

8.3.4 In that case, neither party is to be treated as in breach of contract and condition 7.2 applies.

9. CHATTELS

9.1 The following provisions apply to any chattels which are to be sold.

9.2 Whether or not a separate price is to be paid for the chattels, the contract takes effect as a contract for sale of goods.

9.3 Ownership of the chattels passes to the buyer on actual completion.

Appendix C

Seller's Property Information Form

| SELLER'S PROPERTY INFORMATION FORM | SPECIMEN |

Address of the Property: _____

_____

IMPORTANT NOTE TO SELLERS

* **Please complete this form carefully. It will be sent to the buyer's solicitor and may be seen by the buyer.**

* For many of the questions you need only tick the correct answer. Where necessary, please give more detailed answers on a separate sheet of paper. Then send all the replies to your solicitor so that the information can be passed to the buyer's solicitor.

* The answers should be those of the person whose name is on the deeds. If there is more than one of you, you should prepare the answers together.

* It is very important that your answers are correct because the buyer will rely on them in deciding whether to go ahead. Incorrect information given to the buyer through your solicitor, or mentioned to the buyer in conversation between you, may mean that the buyer can claim compensation from you or even refuse to complete the purchase.

* It does not matter if you do not know the answer to any question so long as you say so.

* The buyer will be told by his solicitor that he takes the property as it is. If he wants more information about it, he should get it from his own advisers, not from you.

* If anything changes after you fill in this questionnaire but before the sale is completed, tell your solicitor immediately. This is as important as giving the right answers in the first place.

* Please pass to your solicitor immediately any notices you have received which affect the property. The same goes for notices which arrive at any time before completion.

* If you have a tenant, tell your solicitor immediately there is any change in the arrangements but do nothing without asking your solicitor first.

* You should let your solicitor have any letters, agreements or other documents which help answer the questions. If you know of any which you are not supplying with these answers, please tell your solicitor about them.

* Please complete and return the separate Fixtures, Fittings and Contents Form. It is an important document which will form part of the contract between you and the buyer. Unless you mark clearly on it the items which you wish to remove, they will be included in the sale and you will not be able to take them with you when you move.

Part I - to be completed by the seller

1 Boundaries

"Boundaries" mean any fence, wall, hedge or ditch which marks the edge of your property.

1.1 Looking towards the house from the road, who either owns or accepts responsibility for the boundary:

Please tick the right answer

	WE DO	NEXT DOOR	SHARED	NOT KNOWN
(a) on the left?				

	WE DO	NEXT DOOR	SHARED	NOT KNOWN
(b) on the right?				

	WE DO	NEXT DOOR	SHARED	NOT KNOWN
(c) at the back?				

1.2 If you have answered "not known" which boundaries have you actually repaired or maintained?

(Please give details)

1.3 Do you know of any boundary being moved in the last 20 years?

(Please give details)

2 Disputes

2.1 Do you know of any disputes about this or any neighbouring property?

NO	YES: (PLEASE GIVE DETAILS)

2.2 Have you received any complaints about anything you have, or have not done as owners?

NO	YES: (PLEASE GIVE DETAILS)

2.3 Have you made any such complaints to any neighbour about what the neighbour has

or has not done?

Please tick the right answer

NO	YES: (PLEASE GIVE DETAILS)

---

3 Notices

3.1 Have you either sent or received any letters or notices which affect your property

or the neighbouring property in any way (for example, from or to neighbours, the council or a government department)?

NO	YES	COPY ENCLOSED	TO FOLLOW	LOST

3.2 Have you had any negotiations or discussions with any neighbour or any local

or other authority which affect the property in any way?

NO	YES: (PLEASE GIVE DETAILS)

---

4 Guarantees

4.1 Are there any guarantees or insurance policies of the following types:

(a) NHBC Foundation 15 or Newbuild?

NO	YES	COPIES ARE ENCLOSED	WITH DEEDS	LOST

(b) Damp course?

NO	YES	COPIES ARE ENCLOSED	WITH DEEDS	LOST

(c) Double glazing?

NO	YES	COPIES ARE ENCLOSED	WITH DEEDS	LOST

(d) Electrical work?

NO	YES	COPIES ARE ENCLOSED	WITH DEEDS	LOST

(e) Roofing?

NO	YES	COPIES ARE ENCLOSED	WITH DEEDS	LOST

(f) Rot or infestation

NO	YES	COPIES ARE ENCLOSED	WITH DEEDS	LOST

(g) Central heating?

NO	YES	COPIES ARE ENCLOSED	WITH DEEDS	LOST

(h) Anything similar? (eg cavity wall insulation)

NO	YES	COPIES ARE ENCLOSED	WITH DEEDS	LOST

(i) Do you have written details of the work done to obtain any of these guarantees?

NO	YES	COPIES ARE ENCLOSED	WITH DEEDS	LOST

Note to students: details of work done have not been reproduced

Please tick the right answer

4.2 Have you made or considered making claims under any of these?

NO	YES: (PLEASE GIVE DETAILS)

---

5 Services

(This section applies to gas, electrical and water supplies, sewerage disposal and telephone cables.)

5.1 Please tick which services are connected to the property.

GAS	ELEC	WATER	DRAINS	TEL	CABLE TV

5.2 Do any drains, pipes or wires for these cross any neighbour's property?

NOT KNOWN	YES: (PLEASE GIVE DETAILS)

5.3 Do any drains, pipes or wires leading to any neighbour's property cross your property?

NOT AS FAR AS WE KNOW	YES: (PLEASE GIVE DETAILS)

5.4 Are you aware of any agreement which is not with the deeds about any of these services?

NOT KNOWN	YES: (PLEASE GIVE DETAILS)

---

6 Sharing with the neighbours

6.1 Are you aware of any responsibility to contribute to the cost of anything used jointly, such as the repair of a shared drive, boundary or drain?

YES (PLEASE GIVE DETAILS)	**NO**

Please tick the right answer

6.2 Do you contribute to the cost of repair of anything used by the neighbourhood, such as the maintenance of a private road?

YES	NO

6.3 If so, who is responsible for organising the work and collection of contributions?

6.4 Please give details of all such sums paid or owing, and explain if they are paid on a regular basis or only as and when work is required.

6.5 Do you need to go next door if you have to repair or decorate your building or maintain any of the boundaries?

YES	NO

6.6 If "Yes", have you always been able to do so without objection by the neighbours?

YES	NO: PLEASE GIVE DETAILS OF ANY OBJECTION UNDER THE ANSWER TO QUESTION 2 (DISPUTES)

6.7 Do any of your neighbours need to come onto your land to repair or decorate their building or maintain the boundaries?

YES	NO

6.8 If so, have you ever objected?

NO	YES: PLEASE GIVE DETAILS OF ANY OBJECTION UNDER THE ANSWER TO QUESTION 2 (DISPUTES)

7 Arrangements and rights

Are there any other formal or informal arrangements which give someone else rights over your property?

NO	YES: (PLEASE GIVE DETAILS)

8 Occupiers

8.1 Does anyone other than you live in the property?

If "No" go to question 9.1.
If "Yes" please give their full names and (if under 18) their ages.

YES	NO

8.2(a)(i) Do any of them have any right to stay on the property without your permission?

NO	YES: (PLEASE GIVE DETAILS)

(These rights may have arisen without you realising, eg if they have paid towards the cost of buying the house, paid for improvements or helped you make your mortgage payments.)

_____

_____

_____

8.2(a)(ii) Are any of them tenants or lodgers?

NO	YES: (PLEASE GIVE DETAILS AND A COPY OF ANY TENANCY AGREEMENT)

_____

_____

_____

8.2(b) Have they all agreed to sign the contract for sale agreeing to leave with you (or earlier)?

NO	YES: (PLEASE GIVE DETAILS)

_____

_____

9 Restrictions

If you have changed the use of the property or carried out any building work on it, please read the note below and answer these questions. If you have not, please go on to Question 10.

Note The title deeds of some properties include clauses which are called "restrictive covenants". For example, these may forbid the owner of the house to carry out any building work or to use it for the purpose of a business - unless someone else (often the builder of the house) gives his consent.

9.1 (a) Do you know of any "restrictive covenant" which applies to your house or land?

NO	YES

(b) If "Yes", did you ask for consent for the work or change of use?

NO	YES: (PLEASE GIVE DETAILS AND A COPY OF ANY CONSENT)

_____

_____

9.2 If consent was needed but not obtained, please explain why not.

_____

_____

9.3 If the reply to 9.1(a) is "Yes", please
give the name and address of the person from
whom consent has to be obtained.

_____

_____

10 Planning

Please tick the right answer

10.1 Is the property used only as a private
home?

YES	NO: (PLEASE GIVE DETAILS)

_____

_____

10.2(a) Is the property a listed building or
in a conservation area?

YES	NO	NOT KNOWN

(b) If "Yes", what work has been carried
out since it was listed or the area became a
conservation area?

_____

_____

10.3 (a) Has there been any building work
on the property in the last four years

NO	YES: (PLEASE GIVE DETAILS)

(b) If "Yes", was planning permission,
building regulation approval or listed
building consent obtained

NO	NOT REQ'D	YES	COPIES ENCLOSED	TO FOLLOW	LOST

10.4 Have you applied for planning
permission, building regulation approval or
listed building consent at any time?

NO	YES	COPIES ARE ENCLOSED	TO FOLLOW	LOST

10.5 If "Yes", has any of the work been
carried out?

NO	YES: (PLEASE GIVE DETAILS)

_____

10.6(a) Has there been any change of use
of the property in the last ten years? (eg
dividing into flats, combining flats or using
part for business use)?

NO	YES: (PLEASE GIVE DETAILS)

(b) If "Yes", was planning permission
obtained?

NO	NOT REQ'D	YES	COPIES ENC	TO FOLLOW	LOST

11 Fixtures

Please tick right answer

11.1 If you have sold through an estate agent, are all the items listed in its particulars included in the sale?	YES	NO

If "No" you should instruct the estate agent to write to everyone concerned correcting this error.

11.2 Do you own outright everything included in the sale?	YES	NO: (PLEASE GIVE DETAILS)

(You must give details of anything which may not be yours to sell, for example, anything rented or on HP.)

_____

_____

12 Expenses

Have you ever had to pay anything for the use of the property?	NO	YES: (PLEASE GIVE DETAILS)

(Ignore rates, water rates, community charge and gas, electricity and phone bills. Include anything else: examples are the clearance of cess pool or septic tank, drainage rate, rent charge.)

_____

_____

13 General

Is there any other information which you think the buyer may have a right to know?	NO	YES: (PLEASE GIVE DETAILS)

_____

_____

Signature(s) _____

_____

Date   _[date]_____

_____

THE LAW SOCIETY

_____

This form is part of The Law Society's TransAction scheme. © The Law Society 1994.
The Law Society is the professional body for solicitors in England and Wales.
March 1994

SELLER'S PROPERTY INFORMATION FORM

SPECIMEN

Part II - to be completed by the seller's solicitor and to be sent with Part 1

Address of the Property:

_____

_____

_____

_____

A   Boundaries

Please tick the right answer

Does the information in the deeds agree with the seller's reply to 1.1 in Part I?

YES	NO: (PLEASE GIVE DETAILS)

_____

_____

B   Relevant Documents

(i) Are you aware of any correspondence, notices, consents or other documents other than those disclosed in Questions 3 or 4 of Part I?

YES	NO

C   Guarantees

If appropriate, have guarantees been assigned to the seller and notice of an assignment given?

YES	NO	NOT KNOWN

If "Yes", please supply copies, including copies of all guarantees not enclosed with Part 1 of this Form

D   Services

Please give full details of all legal rights enjoyed to ensure the benefit of uninterrupted services, eg easements, wayleaves, licences, etc.

_____

_____

_____

Prop 2/1

SPECIMEN

E Adverse Interests

Please give full details of all overriding
interests affecting the property as defined
by the Land Registration Act 1925, s70(1). _____

_____

F Restrictions

Who has the benefit of any restrictive
covenants? If known, please provide the
name and address of the person or company
having such benefit or the name and address
of his or its solicitors.

_____

_____

_____

G Mechanics of Sale

Please tick the right answer

(a) Is this sale dependent on the seller
buying another property?

YES	NO

(b) If "Yes", what stage have the
negotiations reached?

_____

_____

(c) Does the seller require a mortgage?

YES	NO

(d) If "Yes", has an offer been received
and/or accepted or a mortgage certificate
obtained?

YES	NO

H Deposit

Will the whole or part of the deposit be used
on a related transaction?

NO	YES: (PLEASE GIVE DETAILS)

If so, please state to whom it will be paid and
in what capacity it will be held by them

_____

_____

Seller's Solicitor _____
Date _____

Reminder
1. The Fixtures, Fittings and Contents Form should be supplied in addition to the information above.
2. Copies of all planning permissions, building regulations consents, guarantees, assignments and notices
    should be supplied with this form.
3. If the property is leasehold, also complete the Seller's Leasehold Information Form.

Prop 2/2

Appendix D

Land
Registry
Form TR1

**Transfer of whole
of registered title(s)**

HM Land Registry

TR1

(if you need more room than is provided for in a panel, use continuation sheet CS and staple to this form)

1. Stamp Duty

Place "X" in the box that applies and complete the box in the appropriate certificate.

☐ I/We hereby certify that this instrument falls within category ☐ in the Schedule to the Stamp Duty (Exempt Instruments) Regulations 1987

☐ It is certified that the transaction effected does not form part of a larger transaction or of a series of transactions in respect of which the amount or value or the aggregate amount or value of the consideration exceeds the sum of

☐ £

2. Title Number(s) of the Property *(leave blank if not yet registered)*

3. Property

If this transfer is made under section 37 of the Land Registration Act 1925 following a not-yet-registered dealing with part only of the land in a title, or is made under rule 72 of the Land Registration Rules 1925, include a reference to the last preceding document of title containing a description of the property.

4. Date

5. Transferor *(give full names and Company's Registered Number if any)*

6. Transferee for entry on the register *(Give full names and Company's Registered Number if any; for Scottish Co. Reg. Nos., use an SC prefix. For foreign companies give territory in which incorporated.)*

Unless otherwise arranged with Land Registry headquarters, a certified copy of the transferee's constitution (in English or Welsh) will be required if it is a body corporate but is not a company registered in England and Wales or Scotland under the Companies Acts.

7. Transferee's intended address(es) for service in the U.K. *(including postcode)* **for entry on the register**

8. The Transferor transfers the property to the Transferee.

9. Consideration *(Place "X" in the box that applies. State clearly the currency unit if other than sterling. If none of the boxes applies, insert an appropriate memorandum in the additional provisions panel.)*

☐ The Transferor has received from the Transferee for the property the sum of *(in words and figures)*

☐ *(insert other receipt as appropriate)*

☐ The Transfer is not for money or anything which has a monetary value

P.T.O.

10. The Transferor transfers with *(place "X" in the box which applies and add any modifications)*

☐ full title guarantee ☐ limited title guarantee

11. Declaration of trust *Where there is more than one transferee, place "X" in the appropriate box.*

☐ The transferees are to hold the property on trust for themselves as joint tenants.

☐ The transferees are to hold the property on trust for themselves as tenants in common in equal shares.

☐ The transferees are to hold the property *(complete as necessary)*

12. Additional Provision(s) *Insert here any required or permitted statement, certificate or application and any agreed covenants, declarations, etc.*

13. *The Transferors and all other necessary parties should execute this transfer as a deed using the space below. Forms of execution are given in Schedule 3 to the Land Registration Rules 1925. If the transfer contains transferees' covenants or declarations or contains an application by them (e.g. for a restriction), it must also be executed by the Transferees.*

[This form has been reproduced for educational purposes only by kind permission of The Solicitors' Law Stationery Society Ltd]

Appendix E

Land Registry Form TP1

Transfer of part
of registered title(s)

HM Land Registry

SPECIMEN DOCUMENT

TP1

(if you need more room than is provided for in a panel, use continuation sheet CS and staple to this form)

1.   Stamp Duty

Place "X" in the box that applies and complete the box in the appropriate certificate

☐ It is certified that this instrument falls within category ☐ in the Schedule to the Stamp Duty (Exempt Instruments) Regulations 1987

☐ It is certified that the transaction effected does not form part of a larger transaction or of a series of transactions in respect of which the amount or value or the aggregate amount or value of the consideration exceeds the sum of

£

2.   Title number(s) out of which the Property is transferred *(leave blank if not yet registered)*

3.   Other title number(s) against which matters contained in this transfer are to be registered *(if any)*

4.   Property **transferred** *(insert address, including postcode, or other description of the property transferred. Any physical exclusions, eg mines and minerals, should be defined. Any attached plan must be signed by the transferor and by or on behalf of the transferee).*

The Property is defined: *(Place "X" in the box that applies and complete the statement)*

☐ on the attached plan and shown *(state reference eg "edged red")*

☐ on the Transferor's filed plan and shown *(state reference eg "edged and numbered 1 in blue")*

5.   Date

6.   Transferor *(give full names and Company's Registered Number if any)*

7.   Transferee **for entry on the register** *(Give full names and Company's Registered Number if any: for Scottish Co Reg Nos. use an SC prefix. For foreign companies give territory in which incorporated)*

Unless otherwise arranged with Land Registry headquarters, a certified copy of the transferee's constitution (in English or Welsh) will be required if it is a body corporate but is not a company registered in England and Wales or Scotland under the Companies Acts.

8.   Transferee's intended address(es) for service in the UK *(including postcode)* for entry on the register

9.   The Transferor transfers the property to the Transferee

10. Consideration (*Place "X" in the box that applies. State clearly the currency unit if other than sterling. If none of the boxes applies, insert an appropriate memorandum in the additional provisions panel*).

☐ The Transferor has received from the Transferee for the Property the sum of (*in words and figures*)

☐ (*insert other receipt as appropriate*)

☐ The transfer is not for money or anything which has a monetary value

11. The Transferor transfers with (*place "X" in the box which applies and add any modifications*)

☐ full title guarantee ☐ limited title guarantee

12. Declaration of trust *Where there is more than one transferee, place "X" in the appropriate box.*

☐ The Transferees are to hold the Property on trust for themselves as joint tenants.

☐ The Transferees are to hold the Property on trust for themselves as tenants in common in equal shares.

☐ The Transferees are to hold the Property (*complete as necessary*)

13. Additional Provisions

1. Use this panel for:
   - definitions of terms not defined above
   - rights granted or reserved
   - restrictive covenants
   - other covenants
   - agreements and declarations
   - other agreed provisions
   - required or permitted statements, certificates or applications.
2. The prescribed subheadings may be added to, amended, repositioned or omitted.

14. **The Transferor and all other necessary parties (including the proprietors of all the titles listed in panel 3) should execute this transfer as a deed using the space below and sign the plan**. *Forms of execution are given in Schedule 3 to the Land Registration Rules 1925. If the transfer contains transferees' covenants or declarations or contains an application by them (eg for a restriction), it must also be executed by the Transferees.*

Signed as a deed by (enter full name of individual) in the presence of:

Sign here

Signature of witness ....

Name (in BLOCK CAPITALS) ....

Address ....

Signed as a deed by (enter full name of individual) in the presence of:

Sign here

Signature of witness ....

Name (in BLOCK CAPITALS) ....

Address ....

Specimen Solutions to Workshop Problems

Chapter 3

Problem 1

1. Re-read section 2.17. The conveyance must be stamped with *ad valorem* stamps and a PD stamp. The stamping must be done within 30 days of completion.

    Re-read section 3.2. You must apply for first registration of your client's title within 2 months of completion.

    Now consider what entries will appear on the proprietorship and charges registers of your clients' title.

    The proprietorship register will presumably say that the title is absolute. Under the names of Bill and Ben as registered proprietors will appear a restriction. If you do not yet know why, you will do so when you have ploughed through Chapter 11.

    A notice of the restrictive covenant will be entered on the charges register and the mortgage will be registered there as a registered charge.

2. It will send a charge certificate to you, as you are acting for the lender, and you will forward this to the Building Society.

Chapter 5

Problem

(i) D(ii). You must first find out what these restrictive covenants are. You do not seem to have a copy of the deed which created them. A copy of the application for registration of the land charge can be obtained from the registry, and the name and address of the person with the benefit of the covenants discovered. They might have been given by Ada to her neighbour when she sold him part of the garden in 1980. Once it is known what the covenants are, they must be listed in the agreement for sale as incumbrances on the land.

(ii) C(i). This is probably a second mortgage. Again, the name of the lender can be discovered, and you can find from him the sum that will be necessary to redeem the mortgage. You must be satisfied that there will be enough money available at completion to discharge both mortgages, before you commit your client to the contract.

(iii) The contract will promise vacant possession yet Ada's husband has protected his rights of occupation under the Family Law Act 1996. The husband must be approached before contract, and asked if he will join in the contract to release his rights of occupation, and if he will cancel the registration of the Class F. He should be warned to obtain independent advice before agreeing to do this. If he will not cooperate, Ada must not enter into the contract, as she will not be able to fulfil her promise, and might be liable to pay heavy damages.

Now that you know that Ada is married, you should also consider the possibility that her husband has an equitable interest in the house. If he says that he does not, he can be joined in the agreement for sale to repeat that statement. If he says he does, he should be joined in the agreement as a second trustee. Again, it should be suggested that he obtain independent advice unless it is clear that there is no conflict between himself and Ada, and that he is prepared to instruct you to act for him in the sale as well.

Chapter 6

Problem 1

It is usually the seller's responsibility to pay off all financial charges before completion, as they are removable defects. However, do not forget the general conditions. Look at standard conditions 3.1.1. and 3.1.2. The sale is subject to all public requirements. Your client has agreed to buy subject to the road charges. Also read 3.1.4. Your client is to bear the cost of complying with any outstanding public requirement.

However, the seller must have known about the adoption of the road and the road charges. The seller's failure to disclose the charge means that he cannot rely on the conditions and he must remove the charge by paying the authority (see the *Rignall* case).

Problem 2

(a) With regard to the side road, re-read section 6.2(c). Will Mr Jones have the right to walk and drive cars along the side road, or will he have to depend on a permission? If this is not made clear by the documents supplied, an additional enquiry must be made of the seller. Is there any possibility of the road being adopted, with consequent expense to your client? What do the local land charge search and enquiries of the local authority reveal? What is the answer to question 6 on the property information form? With regard to the use of the garage, you need to check the title to see if the land is subject to any restrictive covenant prohibiting business use. Such a covenant may have been imposed when the developer sold the houses sixteen years ago. The developer might have created a development scheme, so that the covenants are enforceable not by the developer but by the owners of the other houses in the estate.

(b) Re-read section 6.5(d). Four years have passed since the garage was built, so no enforcement notice can be served requiring the garage to be demolished.

(c) There has been a change of use in the land from residential to business. There is a 10 year time limit for the service of an enforcement notice.

Problem 3

1. The extension will certainly be development, so permission will be needed. What she must check is whether or not the development comes within the General Development Order. If it does, she will not need express planning permission. This is provided that the effect of the Order has not been negatived by an article 4 direction or by a condition attached to an earlier planning permission.

2. She should apply for it before exchange of contracts, so that if her application is

rejected, she is not committed to the purchase of the house. Alternatively, she could enter into a contract that was conditional on her application for permission being successful (see section 5.9).

Chapter 7

Problem

The Finance Company is selling free from incumbrances. Both charges must, therefore, be cleared from the title. As it is the proprietor of the second registered charge that is selling, it cannot overreach the first mortgage, which will have to be redeemed by it from the proceeds of the sale. In respect of the first mortgage, therefore, there will be handed over the first charge certificate, and either Land Registry Form DS1 or undertakings given by the solicitor to the Y Building Society in respect of it.

The second and any later registered charges will be overreached by the sale. All the Finance Company needs to hand over therefore is its own (i.e. the second) charge certificate, and a transfer executed by it.

Within the priority period given by the Land Registry 94A Search and having had the transfer stamped with a PD stamp and *ad valorem* stamps, you must apply for registration to the District Land Registry. The application will be for the discharge of the two registered charges, registration of the transfer to the Thompsons, and of the charge in favour of the Best Building Society. There will, therefore, after some weeks, issue forth from the Registry a charge certificate, containing in it a copy of the mortgage to the Best Building Society.

As it is an endowment mortgage, there must be sent to the society with the charge certificate a copy of the life policy, a deed executed by the Thompsons assigning it to the building society, and a notice of assignment receipted by the assurance company. (Re-read 2.12 and note that the instructions given to you by the Best Building Society may have made it clear that it did not consider an assignment of the policy to be necessary, the Thompsons, as a condition of the mortgage, having promised to execute an assignment if called upon to do so by the Society.)

Chapter 8

Problem 1

(a) You could specify either the 1970 or the 1973 conveyance as the root, since both are at least fifteen years old. If you specify the 1970 conveyance, you will have to abstract the 1970 mortgage, and the receipt endorsed on it. If you specify the 1973 conveyance, these documents can be omitted. The 1973 conveyance, therefore, seems the better choice.

(b) Assuming that the 1973 conveyance is used as the root, you will have to abstract:

   (i) the 1950 deed creating the covenants. (See the exceptions to s.45 of the Law of Property Act.)
   (ii) the 1970 lease. Although this was created pre-root, it did not end until 1975, and so is part of the post-root title.
   (iii) the 1973 conveyance.
   (iv) the 1973 mortgage.

(v) the 1975 surrender. Remember that it is only leases that expire by effluxion of time that do not have to be abstracted. The purchaser is entitled to check on the validity of the surrender.

If you are not following the protocol, you do not have to abstract the 1973 land charge search certificate, as it is not a document of title, but it would be courteous to do so. It will save the purchaser having to repeat the search against B, but not, you realise, against O'Connor.

Chapter 9

Problem 1

Yes. There is no discrepancy in the name of William Faulkner as it appears on the certificate and in the conveyance. But look at the dates. The priority period given by the search had lapsed before the conveyance was completed. Therefore, the search gives no protection against registrations against William's name that were made after the date of the search, and before the completion of the sale by him, i.e. between 1 June and 1 July. We therefore need to repeat the search to see if there is any such entry.

The search certificate against the names of Anthea Grumble is completely useless. It does not cover any part of her period of ownership, as it was made against her when she was buying. The search would have been made on behalf of the person making the mortgage loan to her, and would have been solely to find whether or not there was a bankruptcy entry against her name.

If Anthea is following the protocol, she should supply you with a recent land-charge search certificate against her name. This is of use, because it might give an early warning of trouble ahead, e.g. a class F land charge. However, another search will have to be made against her name just before completion, to cover her full period of ownership. If this reveals a new entry, she will be in breach of her contract.

Problem 2

Alan needs to check his client's title to that part of the land. There are three possibilities:

1. That the 1970 conveyance did not include the site of the water-garden, but that this extra land was bought by Vesta or her predecessor at some other time. Vesta must be asked if this is so, and asked where the title deeds are. If they are found, the transaction will proceed normally, except that two separate titles will be abstracted.
2. That the 1970 conveyance did include the site of the water-garden. Remember that the 1940 plan was said to be 'for identification only' and it might be completely unreliable. Evidence may be obtained from Vesta, neighbours, or large-scale maps of the area, as to what was occupied as 'Rosedene' in 1970. A special condition can be put in the contract that, for example, a statutory declaration will be supplied by Vesta that she has occupied Rosedene, including the water-garden, since 1970 under the authority of the conveyance. This may satisfy Paula.
3. That the 1970 conveyance did not include the site of the water-garden, nor was it ever conveyed to Vesta by some other deed. Over the years Vesta has simply

encroached on her neighbour's land. In this case, it is most unlikely that Vesta can make good title to the piece of land, as she will not be able to deduce the true owner's title. A special condition should be put in the contract saying that the purchaser must be satisfied with a declaration by Vesta that she has occupied the land for however many years it is.

It is lucky for Vesta that this problem came to light before exchange of contracts. Otherwise, she would have promised good title to the water-garden, and then perhaps been unable to establish it.

Problem 3

The only difficulty is the question of revocation of the power. The Powers of Attorney Act 1971 does not entitle the purchaser to assume that Charles did not have any notice of revocation of the power. The conveyance took place more than 12 months from the date of the power, and there seems to be no statutory declaration made by Charles that he did not have notice of the revocation.

Charles can scarcely be asked to make one now. So the Act is useless. You cannot *presume* that Charles did not know of any revocation, and it is not something that can be *proved*, as no one knows what Charles knew, except Charles himself. What you now need is proof that the power was never in fact revoked, and the only person who can give evidence as to that is Bertha. If Bertha cannot be traced, there is a flaw in the paper title. You could take comfort from the fact that the conveyance took place several years ago, and no one has yet challenged its validity. If the conveyance of 1990 is void, because of the prior revocation of the power, Charles has been in adverse possession, and his successors will eventually acquire a title under the Limitation Act 1982.

These facts do show a loophole in the protection given by the Powers of Attorney Act 1971. The problem could have been avoided if Charles had made the statutory declaration as soon as he completed his purchase.

Problem 4

(a) *Requisition 1*   Is this condition valid? Re-read section 9.2(b).
  Requisition 2   The reply is quite correct. Re-read section 9.6(c).
  Requisition 3   The 1960 conveyance is pre-root.
  However, it is arguable that the description in the 1974 deed is not complete without a copy of the 1960 plan.
  You cannot leave these problems until your colleague's return. See standard condition 4.1.1. You have three working days after receiving the replies to the requisitions in which to respond to them.
(b) An opportunity to revise Chapter 2. You will have to draft the conveyance, if you have not already done this, and send it to the seller for approval. When it is approved you must engross it, and send the engrossment to the seller for execution (see standard condition 4.1.2 for the time limits).
  You must report on title to the XY Building Society, and ask them to provide the money in time for completion. You will draft the mortgage deed, and have it executed by your client. You must prepare a completion statement for your client, showing the balance of the purchase price that he must provide for completion.
  Shortly before completion, you will do a search at the Central Land Charges Registry against the names of all the estate-owners revealed by the abstract of title and against which you do not already have a satisfactory search certificate. This will include the seller's name. You will also search against the name of James

Brown, on behalf of the XY Building Society, to check that he is not bankrupt. You will complete within the priority period given by this search.

Chapter 10

Problem 1

You should not consider it acceptable without further explanation from Eric. In 1973 the legal estate was owned by two personal representatives. We would, therefore, expect to find the next conveyance to be by both of them, bearing in mind that the authority of personal representatives to convey is only joint.

The clue may be in the 1985 conveyance. A conveyance made before 1995 (see Chapter 20) usually states the capacity in which the seller conveys. If the 1985 conveyance says that David conveys the estate 'as personal representative', there are two possibilities:

(i) Charles was still alive on 1 April 1985. If this is so, the conveyance is void. The legal estate remains where it was, in Charles and David jointly. The legal estate can only be obtained by a conveyance from them both.

(ii) Charles was dead on 1 April 1985. If so, the conveyance is valid. David, as the sole surviving personal representative, was competent to convey alone. Proof is needed of Charles's death. Strictly speaking, we cannot insist on seeing the death certificate itself, as it is a document of public record, but we can insist on being given the date of death, so that we can obtain a certificate for ourselves. In fact, if the seller has a copy of the certificate, he would be very churlish not to let us see it. We are not, of course, in the slightest bit interested in seeing the grant of representation to Charles's estate. We only want to check his death, not the identity of his personal representatives.

Suppose that the conveyance says that Charles conveys as 'beneficial owner'. How could his capacity have changed from being one of two personal representatives to being the sole beneficial owner?

The probable answer is that David was also the beneficiary, so that when Bertha's estate had been administered, the land was vested in David. If this is so, we must see the document of transfer. It is likely to be an assent, which under s.36(4) of the Administration of Estates Act 1925 must be in writing signed by Charles and David. So our requisition would be 'Provide an abstract of the assent made in favour of David'. (If an assent is produced, we still have to worry about whether or not a memorandum of it was endorsed on the grant – see problem 3.)

If David and Charles had overlooked the necessity for a written assent – not having read chapter 10 carefully enough – the legal estate remained with them, and the 1975 conveyance by David alone is void. (An interesting point is that the equitable interest might have passed to David, and thence to Eric. Section 36(4) applies only to a legal estate. An assent in respect of an equitable interest can still be informal and inferred from circumstances (see Re *Edward's Will Trusts* [1982]). However, a purchaser requires the legal estate, not just the equitable interest.)

Suppose that having requisitioned for the missing assent, we receive instead an abstract of a conveyance whereby Charles and David convey the land on sale to David as purchaser? This would certainly explain why David was later able to convey as beneficial owner: it would be because he had bought the property. It does not, however, increase our confidence in the title. It is a conveyance on sale by two personal representatives to one of themselves. Do you remember the principle of trust law that a purchase of trust property by a trustee can be set aside by the beneficiaries, no matter how fair the purchase price might be? Eric's title is voidable, and as we will be buying with notice, our title will be voidable too. It is possible that the only beneficiaries are David and Charles themselves, or that any other beneficiaries have, after independent advice, consented to the sale. If, however, no solution can be found, the title is bad, we could refuse it, and consider remedies for the seller's breach of contract in failing to make good title to the land.

Problem 2

The first thing that might occur to us is that we should have copies of the two grants, the one to Carol, and the one to Edward. Even with these, the title is unacceptable. Apparently Carol died still owning Blackacre in her capacity of Bill's personal representative. She was an administrator, so there can be no chain of executorship. When Edward became Carol's personal representative, he did not thereby become Bill's. So he had no power to convey any of Bill's unadministered assets, including Blackacre. Blackacre can only be conveyed by the person who obtains a grant *de bonis non administratis* to Bill's estate. The person entitled to the grant might possibly be Edward; this would be due to his status as personal representative to the beneficiary entitled to Blackacre, Carol being entitled under the intestacy rules. The fact remains that Blackacre cannot be dealt with until the fresh grant to Bill's estate is obtained, and only the person who obtains that grant can convey Blackacre to Fred. (Had Carol been an executor, the chain of executorship would have existed. Edward could have conveyed Bill's assets because by becoming Carol's executor and proving her will, he would also have become Bill's executor.)

There is a final possibility. We have assumed that when Carol died, she owned Blackacre as personal representative. This is because the recitals make no mention of any assent. If, before she died, she signed an assent in her own favour, then she held Blackacre as beneficial owner, in which case Edward, as *her* personal representative, would be entitled to deal with it. The assent, however, would have had to be in writing.

Problem 3

What we should ask for is confirmation that a memorandum of the assent was endorsed on the grant in 1974. If it was, no subsequent conveyance by Cathy and Drew could have diverted the legal estate from Elaine in favour of a purchaser from themselves.

If it were not, there is, at least in theory, the possibility that Cathy and Drew, between 1974 and 1980, conveyed Blackacre to a purchaser for money or money's worth, who relied on a statement made under s.36(6) of the Administration of Estates Act 1925 that the personal representatives had not made any previous assent. If this were so, Elaine no longer had the legal estate in 1980. She could not convey it to Fred. (We do not have to worry about the possibility of the personal representatives having conveyed Blackacre after 1980 – remember that s.36(6) cannot remove the legal estate from a purchaser for money – i.e. Fred.)

So a requisition would have to be raised that Cathy and Drew confirm that no conveyance was made. They are, after all, the only people who can confirm it. Of course, they might now be dead or untraceable. In that case, the fact that Fred is living in Blackacre and has the title deeds is reassuring, and we might feel that we could advise our client-purchaser that the risk of the title being bad is very small.

Notice that the absence of a memorandum has been important because we were deriving title through the *beneficiary* who never protected her assent by a memorandum. Contrast the following abstract:

1972   Albert conveys to Bruce
1973   Bruce dies
1974   Grant of probate to Bruce's will to Carl
1975   Carl conveys on sale as personal representative to David
1976   David conveys to Elaine

Again we may query the absence from the grant of any memorandum of the conveyance. However, in this case the absence of a memorandum is not a defect in title. Even if Carl did convey to another purchaser after 1975, David would not lose the legal estate. So although it is important for a *beneficiary* to endorse a memorandum, it is not a matter of title if a *purchaser* from the personal representatives fails to do so. Nevertheless, as has been mentioned earlier, it would be sensible if he did.
NB
1. As you read about s.36(6), you may have been asking yourself, *why* do the personal representatives, having transferred the property to A, then seek to transfer it to B? Does the Act consider personal representatives peculiarly liable to lapses of memory? A double conveyance can occur in the case of badly drawn parcels clauses and maps, so that a border strip is conveyed twice. It can also happen that the deceased has two consecutive and separate personal representatives, e.g. on the making of a grant *de bonis non administratis*. It is possible that the administrator *de bonis non administratis* may not know of an assent made by his predecessor. However, if you feel that s.36(6) is a lot of fuss about nothing much, you have my sympathy. Still, if s.36(6) offers protection to a client who is buying from a personal representative, it is a conveyancer's job to procure it for him by putting the correct recital in the conveyance to him.
2. Another point worth mentioning here is that when reading an assent or a conveyance by a personal representative, check if it contains an acknowledgement for the production of the grant. Although the grant is a public document and copies can be obtained by anyone from the Probate Registry, a later purchaser will want to see the original because of the importance of checking for memoranda. Acknowledgements are discussed in Chapter 15, and you will see that the absence of an acknowledgement is not a defect in title.
3. Section 36(6)is sometimes said to have no relevance to registered title. Suppose you are buying from the personal representative of the dead registered proprietor, and you are considering the possibility of there having been a previous assent to a beneficiary. There are two possibilities:

    (i) the beneficiary has registered himself as the new proprietor. If he does this, your pre-completion search of the register will disclose the new proprietor, and you will not complete the purchase from the personal representatives.
    (ii) if he has not registered himself as the new proprietor, he has an unprotected minor interest, and your defence will be based on the Land Registration Act 1925 (a transferee for value taking free from an unprotected minor interest). However, if the beneficiary is living on the property, his interest is overriding, not minor. So you must realise that the Land Registration Act will not protect you against the earlier assent if the beneficiary is living in the house. So s.36(6) may be of use, and certainly no harm is done by putting the statement in the transfer that the personal representative has not made any previous assent.

Chapter 11

Problem 1

Do you remember the principle that *all* the trustees must execute the conveyance? The fact that Robert retired from the partnership did not of itself divest him of the legal estate. You need to see a conveyance of the legal estate from Albert, Robert and Sidney to Albert and Sidney. This might take the form of a deed of retirement (see section 11.4(c)). Alternatively, you need evidence that Robert died before 1975, in which case the legal estate would have vested automatically in the surviving Bricks. If the legal estate was still vested in all three Bricks in 1975, the conveyance by two of them was void.

The search certificate is, at first sight, puzzling. The contract, or whatever it is that is protected by the C(iv) registration, would have had to be created by all three of them. The power of trustees to enter into a contract is joint only. Even if all of them entered into the contract, registration against only some of the estate-owners is not effective. Re-read section 4.5(c). Do you notice the discrepancy between the name on the deed, 'Sidney', and the name on the certificate, 'Sydney'? The certificate of search is useless, the search having been made against an incorrect version of the name. If we search again we probably shall find a C(iv) registered against Sidney.

If this is so, you must approach Miss Cooper's solicitor, and ask for an assurance that this land charge does not affect the land you are buying. There is a possibility that it does not, as it might be a contract in respect of other land owned by the Bricks. Another possibility is that it is protecting the contract by the Bricks to convey to Jennifer. If this is so, you can ask her solicitor to apply for cancellation of the registration. This should have been done by the solicitor as soon as the purchase by Miss Cooper was completed.

The solicitor may argue that the registration is protecting a void contract or one that was discharged by breach, and that he was satisfied as to this when he bought the land for his client. The answer should be that it is not your task to pass judgement on the validity of the contract; it is the seller's task to have the registration cancelled. (This question is taken from part of the Law Society Summer 1988 paper.)

Problem 2

1. As both the Masons are registered as proprietors, you know that both owned the legal estate. They must have held it as joint tenants. There is no restriction on the register, so you can assume that they owned the beneficial interest jointly, too. Therefore, when her husband died, Mrs Mason became sole owner of the legal estate and the beneficial interest *simply because her husband had died*. She does *not* trace her claim to ownership of even the equitable interest through the will. The will is completely irrelevant, therefore. To have the title registered in her own name, she need only produce her husband's death certificate.
2. The drawbacks of registration with a possessory title are set out in section 3.6(d). You can imagine that the building society will be reluctant to lend on the security of such a title. Notice, though, that the title was registered in 1974. Re-read section 3.7. Mrs Mason can apply to have the title upgraded to absolute.
3. The building society needs to know as much about the property as a purchaser would, so the searches made are the same as if the building society were actually buying the house. So you start by doing what in the context of a purchase would be called 'the pre-contract' searches and enquiries. Re-read Chapter 6, find the answers to the questions in the property information form, and

make the local land-charge search and additional enquiries of the district authority. (For inspection of the property, you will be relying on the building society's surveyor.)

In this case there will be no contract for the grant of a mortgage, but these usual searches and enquiries may reveal things that would affect the value of the property. When the results of the searches are known, you will investigate the title and draft the mortgage deed. Before completion, you will make your pre-completion search at the district land registry, to enquire if there are any adverse entries on the register, either since the date of office copy entires obtained by you, or since the date when the land certificate was last officially compared with the register (re-read section 7.5).

You will complete the mortgage within the priority period given by the search. Completion will consist of your asking Mrs Mason to execute the mortgage and give you custody of the land certificate in return for the advance. It will have been part of the arrangement between herself and the society that you be able to deduct your fees and disbursements from the loan. You will then have to apply for registration of the mortgage as a registered charge, again before the priority period expires.

Note the searches you did *not* make:

(i) the coal board search, for obvious reasons;
(ii) the commons registration search – the house was built 30 years ago;
(iii) the public index map search – the title is registered;
(iv) the 'bankruptcy only' search at the Land Charges Registry. In this case the registered proprietor and the borrower are one and the same person. If Mrs Mason is insolvent, the register of her title will warn us. If the land registry search discloses no bankruptcy entry, you can safely lend money to her.

Suppose there had been a restriction on the register to the effect that no disposition by the sole survivor of the registered proprietors would be registered. You know that Mrs Mason has succeeded to her husband's share of the equitable interest under the terms of the will. Nevertheless, if she were *selling* the house, the simplest thing would be for her to appoint another trustee to act with her, so that the equitable interests are overreached. So again, for the purpose of making title to the house, the will would be irrelevant. It would only be of relevance when it had to be decided by the trustees how the proceeds of the sale were to be accounted for.

However, in this case Mrs Mason is keeping the house. It is probably better, therefore, to have the restriction removed, by proving to the Registrar the fact that she does now own the whole of the equitable interest. Probate of the will must be obtained, an assent in respect of the equitable interest made in her favour (but *not* in respect of the legal estate, as she owns this by virtue of the right of survivorship) and a statutory declaration made to the Registrar of these facts (see section 11.9(a)).

Chapter 12

Problem 1

You can see the problem. 21B has no direct access to the public road. The house can only be reached by crossing others' land. Pipes and wires must cross others' land to reach the public sewers and to obtain electricity, gas, telephone services, etc.

To deal with number 21, the question we have to ask here is 'What easements already exist over number 21 for the benefit of 21A and 21B?' In other words, what easements were reserved by Alice Brown when she conveyed to Catherine, because it is only the benefit of these easements that can be passed on to us. To stress a point that is obvious but can be forgotten in the heat of the moment, Alice can only pass to us the benefit of easements that already exist over number 21. She cannot create *new* easements over land she no longer owns.

If the title to number 21 is unregistered, you need a copy of the conveyance to Catherine. You will be looking in it for an express reservation over number 21 for the benefit of 21A and 21B of rights of way for pedestrians and vehicles, rights of drainage, and rights for all other necessary pipes and wires. You would also expect to see a right for the owners of 21A and 21B to enter number 21 for the purpose of inspecting and repairing the pipes, etc., and you would not be surprised to see a promise by the owners of 21A and 21B to contribute towards the cost of maintenance of the pipes, etc. If these rights were reserved, our client will succeed to the benefit of them. (If the conveyance to Catherine did contain a reservation, a copy of the conveyance – or even perhaps a duplicate – should have been kept with Alice's deeds.)

If the conveyance does not contain an express reservation, there will have been a reservation implied into it, but, as we have seen, possibly only an essential means of access, so the pipes, wires, drains, and sewers would seem only to be there by virtue of Catherine's permission.

If the title to these properties had been registered at the time of the sale of number 21 to Catherine, any reservation of an easement in the transfer of part to Catherine would have been entered on the register of Catherine's title, and the benefit of it would have been entered on the register of Alice's title to 21A and 21B.

The absence of easements over number 21 would be a difficult problem to solve. The only person who can now grant an easement is Catherine, who may be unwilling to encumber her land. *She* may be willing to allow the pipes, etc., to remain where they are, but a purchaser from her may not be. The problem may be serious enough for our client to decide against buying number 21B.

If Alice finds that her failure expressly to reserve the necessary easements is making 21A and 21B unsellable, she should consider the contract that preceded her conveyance of number 21. As has been seen, the conditions in that contract might well have allowed her to put an express reservation of easements in the conveyance or transfer. She might now be able to apply to the court for rectification of the conveyance as it is not carrying out the terms of the contract but this right of rectification, if it exists, will not bind any purchaser of number 21 from Catherine, unless that purchaser has notice of it.

Number 21A presents a quite different problem. This is owned by the seller, so any easements your client needs over 21A can be granted by Alice. It is really a question of settling special conditions in the draft agreement for sale. Alice should promise your client in the contract that the conveyance will contain all the rights needed for access and services. These rights should be specified. She may wish to reserve easements, although from the plan it is difficult to see why she would require any. The contract should also agree shared obligations as to maintenance and rights of entry as previously mentioned.

The special conditions should replace the standard condition. If the standard condition is not expressly excluded, it might 'top up' what the parties have expressly agreed to grant and reserve, contrary to their real intentions.

Problem 2

The enforcement of the covenant against Hebe has two aspects. One possibility is that the covenant could be enforced against her by A, or whoever has succeeded to the benefited land together with the benefit of the covenant. For the burden of the covenant to have passed with the land, it would have been essential for the covenant to have been registered as a D(ii) land charge against the name of the original covenantor, B. You need to make a land charges search against B's name. If a land charge is registered, the person with the benefit of the covenant may take action against Hebe. If no land charge is registered, the covenant is not an incumbrance on the land. The covenant cannot be enforced directly by A against Hebe.

However, the fact remains that A *can* sue B, as B promised that the covenant would *always* be observed. B can sue C, and C can sue Hebe. So despite lack of registration, Hebe should not have ignored the covenant.

The Contract   Clearly, if the covenant is registered, the covenant must be disclosed and the contract must list the covenant as an incumbrance on the property. What must also be disclosed is the *breach* of the covenant. (Even if it is not expressly disclosed in the contract, the seller must give an honest answer to the enquiry on the property information form which asks if the seller has observed all the restrictions affecting the property.)

Usually, Hebe, having promised an indemnity to C, would like an indemnity from her purchaser. However, the purchaser will not be prepared to promise a general indemnity for he knows that the covenant has already been broken. The standard condition promises an indemnity only in respect of breaches committed after the date of the conveyance, and the purchaser will not agree to an alteration to this.

If the covenant is registered, the purchaser may be concerned about the consequences of an action brought by A. He does not want to find himself paying damages or having to dismantle the garage.

If a covenant has been broken, there are various ways to make the title acceptable to the purchaser. The seller might offer to indemnify the purchaser and his successors against the consequence of any breach (i.e. the seller will be promising to indemnify the purchaser against past breaches, and the purchaser will be promising to indemnify the seller against future breaches). This is not really satisfactory for either party if the consequences are likely to be serious, for example, if it had been the house itself, rather than a garage, that had been built in breach of covenant. The value of the indemnity depends on the seller's continued solvency (and traceability). The seller lives under a threat of one day having to find an unknown, but possibly large, sum of money.

Another possibility is taking out insurance against the risk of enforcement. The size of the premium will, of course, depend on the size of the risk.

(The purchaser will also be considering the planning position. Remember that express planning permission would have been needed, unless the garage came within the General Development Order. If the garage was built without planning permission, no enforcement notice can be served after four years have elapsed – see Chapter 6, section 6.5)

Problem 3

1. *The Restriction on the Proprietorship Register*   Jacob must appoint another trustee, so that the transfer can be by two trustees. If the second trustee is appointed now, both will be named in the contract as sellers, and the contract will say that they will convey as trustees.

2. The *Property Register*   The particulars in the contract may say '9 Havelock Street, Spa on Wells, as the same is registered with absolute title under title no KT1111111 at Tunbridge Wells District Land Registry'. An office copy of the entries on the register will accompany the contract, and naturally, the purchaser will want

to know exactly what easements were granted and reserved by the 1965 conveyance. You must, therefore, obtain a copy of it. You could do this by asking the Equine Bank to photocopy the charge certificate. Alternatively, you could obtain an office copy of the deed from the Land Registry. The reservation of the easement certainly must be disclosed.

3. *Entry no. 1 on Charges Register*   If it was known what the 1922 covenants were, the contract could simply have said that the property was sold subject to entries 1 and 2 on the charges register of the title. (Not, notice 'subject to the entries on the charges register' as the sale is *not* subject to entries 3 and 4.) However, as no one knows what the 1922 covenants are, it is best for the contract to say not only that the sale is subject to the 1922 covenants, but also that there is no information about what the covenants are, and that no requisitions about them can be made by the purchaser.
It is unfortunate that while it is quite clear that the covenants will bind the purchaser, as they are entered in the register, nobody knows what they are. This situation is not uncommon. The applicant for first registration produced the recent conveyances, all of which said the property was conveyed subject to the covenants, but the 1922 deed itself had been lost.

4. *Entry no. 2*   The contract will say that the sale is subject to the 1965 covenants. Again, the purchaser will see a copy of these before exchange of contracts.

5. *Entries 3 and 4*   The sale is not subject to the mortgage, but there is no need to say this expressly in the contract because of the effect of standard condition 3 (see section 5.5).

6. *Fixtures and Fittings*   Do not bother to rack your brain as to whether or not the shed is a fixture. Ask your client to fill in the fixtures fittings and contents form (in which all these items are included) and attach it to the contract.

7. *The Will?*   Did you fall into the trap of thinking that the will was in some way relevant to the title to the home? It was not.
After Naomi's death, Jacob was sole owner of the legal estate, by virtue of the right of survivorship. He owned it as sole trustee for sale. He could not however transfer it alone, because of the restriction on the register. The sale by two trustees would overreach the equitable interests.
Naomi's will did affect the ownership of the equitable interests (but not the legal estate) but a purchaser does not have to investigate the interests of the beneficiaries. The will is of interest to the two trustees, as it determines how they should deal with the purchase price. It cannot all be given to Jacob. Some share of it must go to Ruth.
Note: You need to check, when looking at the office copies, whether the Greens were the applicants for first registration. If they were, you will have to ask the bank to let you see the pre-registration deeds to discover if the Greens gave an indemnity covenant in respect of the covenants when they bought. If they did, Jacob will need an indemnity from the purchase. You will not need a special condition to provide for the indemnity, unless you consider the standard condition to be inadequate.
If the Greens were not the applicants for first registration, but were later transferees of the title, they apparently gave no indemnity covenant, as one does not appear on the proprietorship register. If they did not give an indemnity covenant, Jacob will not need one when he resells.

Chapter 13

Problem

Property

As only part of the land in the title is being sold, it is vital to describe exactly *which* part. There are no physical boundaries between the three blocks, so probably the only way of identifying which part of the yard is being sold with Block 2 is to describe the Property by reference to a plan that will be attached to the agreement. The plan must be accurate and drawn precisely to scale. (See chapter 5, section 5.7(b).) It would be a good idea physically to mark out the boundaries between the three properties in some way, e.g. by tape, so that prospective buyers of each block will know exactly what will be transferred to them.

Buyers

The partnership does not exist as a legal entity so the buyer cannot be described as 'Spindles'.

The way partners are often identified in an agreement in which they are buying what is to be a partnership asset is '[*names of partners*] carrying on business together in partnership under the name of [*partnership name*] at [*address of principal place of business*]'.

There is the complication here that there are five partners. Of course, when the contract is carried out and the legal estate is transferred, it cannot be transferred to more than four people. (Have you forgotten Chapter 11 already?) However, there is no reason why all five cannot be buyers in the contract and all of them acquire contractual rights.

Incumbrances

You only list here incumbrances that already exist, not ones that are going to be created in the transfer. At the moment there are three incumbrances:

1. the covenants contained in entry no. 1 on the charges register;
2. the covenants contained in entry no. 2 on the charges register;
3. the right of support reserved in the conveyance dated 26 June 1998 noted in the property register.

Title Guarantee

There is no reason why your client should not give a full title guarantee.

Access to Block 2

The property register makes it clear that there is already a right of way for vehicles over the drive to Malherbe Grange to reach the site of the three office blocks. This was granted in 1998. However, the buyers of Block 2 will need a right of way (i.e. an easement) over Block 1. A special condition in the contract should state that your client will, in the transfer, grant the buyers a right of way for vehicles over the yard of Block 1. Such a grant might well be implied, but having read Chapter 12 you realise that a special condition in the contract followed by an express grant in the transfer is to be preferred.

Access for Block 3

Your client will need a right of way over the yard of Block 2 in order to reach Block 3. The agreement must, therefore, contain a special condition stating that the transfer to the buyers shall reserve a right of way for the seller over the yard of Block 2.

Any later buyer of Block 3 will acquire the benefit of this easement. If your client sells Block 3 before it sells Block 1, the buyer of Block 3 will also be given a right of way over the yard of Block 1. If your client sells Block 1 before it sells Block 3, it must reserve a right of way over the yard of Block 1, so that the later buyer of Block 3 will inherit rights of way over the yards of Blocks 1 and 2. Got it?

Indemnity Covenants

1936 Covenants   There is no note on the proprietorship register to indicate that your client gave an indemnity covenant when it bought. As it is under no obligation to indemnify the person from whom it bought, it does not need a promise of indemnity from the people to whom it is selling. [However, remember that an indemnity covenant given by an applicant for first registration is not mentioned on the register (see section 12.10). You must check whether the title to Malherbe Grange was registered or unregistered when your client bought the Old Mill. If it was the latter, your client was an applicant for first registration and the absence of a note on the proprietorship register is not evidence that it did not give an indemnity covenant when it bought.]

1988 Covenants   Your client gave this covenant when it bought the Old Mill; it is the original covenantor. As it was the original covenantor, usually it would have acquired a perpetual contractual responsibility and therefore need an indemnity when it sold (see section 12.9). However, did you read the covenants carefully? Did you notice the words '*but so that the Buyer shall not be liable for a breach of this covenant occurring on or in respect of the Property or any part or parts thereof after he shall have parted with all interest therein*'? These words mean that your client's contractual liability as regards Block 2 will end as soon as he sells it. It will not, therefore, need an indemnity covenant.

Note

It is becoming increasingly common for restrictive covenants to be drafted in this way, so as to avoid the creation of chains of indemnity. It does not leave the person with the benefit of the covenant without remedy. Although he cannot sue the original covenantor once he has sold the land, the person with the benefit can enforce it against the current owner of the land under *Tulk* v. *Moxhay*. A positive covenant should never be drafted in this way. If the covenantee has no remedy against the person who first gave the covenant he will have no remedy at all. The burden of a positive covenant does not run with the land.

Other Special Conditions

As this is a sale of part of your client's land, there should be a special condition to say that the transfer will contain a statement negating any implied grant of easements.

You may also decide to include a special condition altering standard condition 5, and throwing the risk of physical damage on to the buyers.

VAT

Your client is making a standard rated supply, as Block 2 is a 'new' commercial property. If you incorporate the Standard Conditions of Sale into the agreement for sale that you are drafting, the purchase price will be exclusive of VAT. The buyers will have to pay £125,000 plus VAT at 17.5 per cent.

Now read the workshop to Chapter 14, where you will see a draft of the agreement for sale.

Chapter 14

Problem

Transfer of part	**HM Land Registry**	
of registered title(s)	*SPECIMEN DOCUMENT*	**TP1**

(if you need more room than is provided for in a panel, use continuation sheet CS and staple to this form)

1. Stamp Duty

Place "X" in the box that applies and complete the box in the appropriate certificate

☐ It is certified that this instrument falls within category ☐ in the Schedule to the Stamp Duty (Exempt Instruments) Regulations 1987

☒ It is certified that the transaction effected does not form part of a larger transaction or of a series of transactions in respect of which the amount or value or the aggregate amount or value of the consideration exceeds the sum of

£ 250,000

2. Title number(s) out of which the Property is transferred *(leave blank if not yet registered)*
SHU 123456

3. Other title number(s) against which matters contained in this transfer are to be registered *(if any)*

4. Property **transferred** *(insert address, including postcode, or other description of the property transferred. Any physical exclusions, eg mines and minerals, should be defined. Any attached plan must be signed by the transferor and by or on behalf of the transferee).*

No 2 Old Mill Offices, Malherbe Road, Malherbe, South Humberland, MA21 9MZ

The Property is defined: *(Place "X" in the box that applies and complete the statement)*

☒ on the attached plan and shown *(state reference eg "edged red")* edged red

☐ on the Transferor's filed plan and shown *(state reference eg "edged and numbered 1 in blue")*

5. Date

6. Transferor *(give full names and Company's Registered Number if any)*
Holt Development Ltd
Registered Office - Slingsby Business Park, Slingsby, South Humberland SL24 1RX
Company Registered Number - 666

7. Transferee **for entry on the register** *(Give full names and Company's Registered Number if any: for Scottish Co Reg Nos. use an SC prefix. For foreign companies give territory in which incorporated)*

John Able, Jack Bell and Jill Carter carrying on business with others in partnership under the name of "Spindles"

Unless otherwise arranged with Land Registry headquarters, a certified copy of the transferee's constitution (in English or Welsh) will be required if it is a body corporate but is not a company registered in England and Wales or Scotland under the Companies Acts.

8. Transferee's intended address(es) for service in the UK *(including postcode)* for entry on the register

No 2 Old Mill Offices, Malherbe Road, Malherbe, South Humberland, MA21 9MZ

9. The Transferor transfers the property to the Transferee

10. Consideration *(Place "X" in the box that applies. State clearly the currency unit if other than sterling. If none of the boxes applies, insert an appropriate memorandum in the additional provisions panel).*

[X] The Transferor has received from the Transferee for the Property the sum of *(in words and figures)*
one hundred and twenty five thousand pounds (£125,000)

[ ] *(insert other receipt as appropriate)*

[ ] The transfer is not for money or anything which has a monetary value

11. The Transferor transfers with *(place "X" in the box which applies and add any modifications)*

[X] full title guarantee   [ ] limited title guarantee

12. Declaration of trust *Where there is more than one transferee, place "X" in the appropriate box.*

[ ] The Transferees are to hold the Property on trust for themselves as joint tenants.

[ ] The Transferees are to hold the Property on trust for themselves as tenants in common in equal shares.

[ ] The Transferees are to hold the Property *(complete as necessary)* upon trust as an asset of the business carried on by themselves and others in partnership under the name of "Spindles" in accordance with their partnership agreement dated 9 September 1995.

13. Additional Provisions

1. Use this plan for:
   - *definitions of terms not defined above*
   - *rights granted or reserved*
   - *restrictive covenants*
   - *other covenants*
   - *agreements and declarations*
   - *other agreed provisions*
   - *required or permitted statements, certificates or applications.*
2. *The prescribed subheadings may be added to, amended, repositioned or omitted.*

Definitions

Rights granted for the benefit of the Property

A right over the part of No 1 Old Mill Offices, Malherbe Road, Malherbe, South Humberland, MA21 9MZ, that is coloured brown on the attached plan in common with the Transferor and all others now or at any future time authorised by the Transferor of access on foot and for private motor vehicles and light commercial vehicles only in a reasonable manner and so as not to cause any obstruction or undue interference with the rights of any person owning occupying or using the Property.

Rights reserved for the benefit of other land (*the land having the benefit should be defined, if necessary by reference to a plan*)

A right for the benefit of No 3 Old Mill Offices, Malherbe Road, Malherbe, South Humberland, MA21 9MZ (outlined in green on the attached plan) over the part of the Property that is coloured blue on the attached plan) a right of access on foot and for private motor vehicles and light commercial vehicles only in a reasonable manner and so as not to cause any obstruction or undue interference with the rights of any person owning occupying or using the Property.

It is hereby declared that the Transferees and their successors in title to the Property shall not be entitled to any easements or rights over No 1 and No 3 Old Mill Offices other than that expressly granted in this transfer.

298   *Conveyancing*

14. **The Transferor and all other necessary parties (including the proprietors of all the titles listed in panel 3) should execute this transfer as a deed using the space below and sign the plan**. *Forms of execution are given in Schedule 3 to the Land Registration Rules 1925. If the transfer contains transferees' covenants or declarations or contains an application by them (eg for a restriction), it must also be executed by the Transferees.*

(The transfer form would provide for execution by the Transferor and the three transferees).

Note: 1.   The transfer could not be made to all five purchasers, as a legal estate can only be held by four people. If it listed all five names as transferees, the legal estate would vest only in the first four named (see chapter 11.2). The choice of transferees is a matter on which we need instructions from our clients. We are imagining that we have received those instructions.

       2.   It would have been difficult to have a general definition of the retained land as the part burdened by the grant to the Transference differed from the part benefited by the reservation.

This form has been reproduced for educational purposes only by kind permission of The Solicitors' Law Stationery Society Limited

Chapter 16

Problem 1

(a) *Consents*
1. *Assignment*   The need for the landlord's consent for assignment is obvious. This will probably be obtained before contract, but could be sought after contract (see section 16.3).

2. *User*

    (a) The landlord's consent is needed.

    (b) We do not know whether this is a headlease (i.e. granted out of the freehold) or an underlease. If it is an underlease, we need to consider the user covenants in the superior leases. A superior landlord generally has no direct right of action against an undertenant if he breaks a provision of the headlease. An exception to this rule is a restrictive covenant. If the superior lease was granted before 1 January 1996, the superior landlord can obtain an injunction against a subtenant who breaks a restrictive covenant in a superior lease if the subtenant had notice of the covenant when he obtained his sublease. This is because of the rule in *Tulk* v. *Moxhay* (1848) which has the effect of making a restrictive covenant an encumbrance on the land enforceable against anyone who takes with notice. However, as Pamela, by virtue of s.44 of the Law of Property Act 1925 is not entitled to see the headlease, she cannot be taken to have had constructive notice of its contents. If the superior lease was granted on or after 1 January 1996, the superior landlord can obtain an injunction against any person who owns or occupies the demised premises. This is by virtue of s.3(4) Landlord and Tenant (Covenants) Act 1995. This point can be pursued in any land law textbook, but it is not the major point which is as follows.

        If the subtenant's activities on the premises cause the tenant to be in breach of the covenants of the superior lease, the superior lease may be forfeited for breach of covenant. Therefore, for practical reasons a subtenant has to observe the user restrictions not only in his own lease, but all superior leases, as the forfeiture of a superior lease causes the end of all inferior leases derived from it. It is for this reason that user-covenants in a superior lease are often reproduced in the sublease. The tenant, knowing he can be controlled by his landlord, needs the same sort of control over his subtenant.

        So, to return to Pamela, she should ask if the lease she is buying is the headlease, or an underlease. If Vera's landlord is not the freeholder, he can be asked if any consent to change of use is needed under the terms of his own lease, and if it is, it should be obtained. It is as much in the interest of the landlord that consent is obtained as it is in Pamela's.

        Of course, it is also possible that there is a covenant on the freehold preventing use as a shop. If this covenant is registered either under the Land Charges Act 1972 or under the Land Registration Act 1925, it will bind Pamela as she will be treated as having actual notice of it. The risk of an unknown covenant is diminished if the contract between Vera and Pamela provides for deduction of the superior titles (diminished, not removed, because of the spectre – if the freehold title is unregistered – of the pre-root land charge).

    (c) The proposed change of use will need planning permission. It is a change from one class of use to another within the Use Classes Order (see section 6.5).

3. *Alterations*   Pamela will probably want to alter the inside of the premises. The lease should be checked to see if the landlord's consent is needed to alterations.

(b) The Option

This answer is given on the assumption that the lease was granted on or after 1 January 1996 and is governed by the Landlord and Tenant (Covenants) Act 1995.

An option to renew a lease is what the Act calls a 'landlord covenant'. When a lease is assigned, the new owner of it automatically succeeds to be benefit of landlord covenants. Therefore, when this lease is assigned Pamela will automatically have the benefit of the option, unless it was expressed to be given only to Vera personally. If Len is still the landlord, the option will be enforceable against him and he will have to renew the lease. However, it is possible that Len has assigned the reversion to the lease. Let us assume that we check on this point and that we find that he sold the reversion to Mary last year. Can Pamela enforce the option against Mary? It is true that a purchaser of a landlord's reversion takes subject to all tenant covenants, but the option is affected by other rules as well. We need to know whether or not the reversion is registered under the Land Registration Act 1925. If the title is registered, Mary will have taken free of the option unless it was a minor interest that was protected by an entry on the register, or was an overriding interest. The option was probably overriding under s.70(1)(g) as an interest belonging to a person in actual occupation of the land. So s.70(1)(g) ensured that Mary was bound by the lease and by the option. It was also possibly overriding under s.70(1)(k) (see Chapter 3, section 3.15(e)).

If the title is unregistered, the option comes within the definition of an 'estate contract', and is registerable as a C(iv) land charge. If Vera did not register the land charge before Mary bought the reversion, Mary is not bound by the option and cannot be forced to renew the lease. The only remedy would be to sue Len for breach of contract. He promised to renew the lease if asked, but now cannot do so.

Notice that if Len sold to Mary under an agreement for sale incorporating the Standard Conditions, Len could claim an indemnity from Mary if he were sued in such circumstances. Condition 3.2 provides that a purchaser of property subject to a lease shall indemnify the seller against all claims arising under the tenancy 'even if void against a purchaser for want of registration'. Mary might prefer to renew the lease rather than face the cost of indemnifying Len.

Problem 2

She is entitled to see the assignment to Enid. She must always see the assignment to the seller. This assignment is not yet fifteen years old. So Pamela is also entitled to see the assignment by Carol to Deirdre. This is over fifteen years old. Enid therefore satisfies her obligations under s.44 of the Law of Property Act 1925 by producing the 1940 lease and the 1973 and 1988 assignments. Pamela has no right to insist on investigating ownership of the lease between 1965 and 1973.

Note   Pamela has no right to investigate the superior titles unless s.44 of the Law of Property Act 1925 has been altered by a term in the agreement for sale.

Chapter 18

Problem 1: Possible Solutions

You need to work out how much the Archers will need to buy Greenbank, and the money they will have coming in.

Coming in

A. *Sale proceeds*

Contract price		£40 000
Less		
● redemption of first mortgage	£10 000	
● redemption of second mortgage	(unknown)	
Solicitor's fees and disbursements in connection with sale, purchase and mortgages say	£ 400	
Estate agent's fees say	£ 600	
at least	£11 000	£11 000
Less than		£29 000

Urgent step – to confirm redemption figure on first mortgage and to obtain redemption figure on second mortgage.

B. *Net Mortgage offer*

Amount of loan		£32 000
Less retention moneys	£2000	£ 2000
		£30 000

So less (perhaps, *considerably* less) than £60 000 coming in

Going out

Purchase price		£60 000
Miscellaneous expenses, say		£ 200
Total – something over		£60 200

Note: as the price is £60 000, no stamp duty has to be paid.
There is a shortfall. There are possible solutions.

1. Your clients must reconcile themselves to remaining in 5 King Street.
2. The Grasping Bank might be willing to transfer its mortgage from 5 King Street to Greenbanks. It will not then be necessary to find money to redeem it. The fees of the Bank's solicitors will have to be paid. You must check whether the Building Society's mortgage contains a covenant not to create a second mortgage without the Society's consent.
3. Increase the size of the loan from the Building Society. Your clients, before seeking to increase their borrowing, must consider their ability to repay.

If the transaction can continue, you must think about the deposit of £6000 to be paid on the exchange of contracts for the purchase of Greenbanks. Your clients will want to use the £4000 coming in from the sale of 5 King Street so make sure that the 5 King Street contract incorporates standard condition 2.2.2 unaltered. This leaves £2000 to find. Your clients do not appear to have any savings. Possibly the seller can be persuaded to accept a smaller deposit. Otherwise, your clients will have to arrange temporary finance, or use the deposit guarantee scheme. Both involve expense.

The two sets of contracts must now be exchanged as simultaneously as possible. This can be done by arranging exchange over the telephone. A simple method would be this:

Suppose Q is selling Greenbanks to the Archers, and the Archers are selling 5 King Street to S. S's solicitors will send S's part of the contract concerning 5 King Street to the Archers' solicitors, together with the payment of the deposit. (If the standard conditions apply, this will have to be by way of banker's draft, or a cheque on the solicitors' clients' account.) The accompanying letter will make it clear that the contract is not sent by way of exchange, but that the Archers' solicitors are for the present to hold it to the order of S. The Archers' solicitors then send their clients' part of the contract concerning Greenbanks to Q's solicitor, and the deposit, again making it clear that it is not sent by way of exchange. This is necessary because otherwise Q could force a contract on the Archers by returning his part of the contract. When they are ready to exchange, the Archers' solicitors will phone Q's solicitors, to say that they are about to exchange contracts on 5 King Street, and asking if they will be able to exchange the contracts on Greenbanks immediately afterwards. If the answer is 'yes', the Archers' solicitors phone S's solicitors, and the exchange of the contracts on 5 King Street is agreed, and the Law Society undertakings given, in this case, according to formula A. The Archers' solicitors immediately phone Q's solicitors, and contracts are exchanged for the purchase of Greenbanks.

This method does not remove all risk. It is possible that at the last minute while the Archers' solicitors are exchanging contracts on 5 King Street, Q may telephone his solicitors and withdraw his instructions to exchange. The Archers' solicitors will then find that when they telephone back to Q's solicitors, exchange does not take place. The risk of this happening in the small amount of time involved is small, and possibly acceptable.

Notice the order of events. The contracts for sale are exchanged before the contracts for purchase, so there is no risk of the Archers being bound by a contract to buy, while not having disposed of their own house.

Problem 2: Possible Solution

The point about finances here is that Mrs Fawkes presumably owns part of the beneficial interest in The Plot, so *her* money will be partly financing the purchase of The Tower. If this is so, then The Tower should be conveyed into both their names, and the conveyance should declare how they hold the equitable interest.

Provided that there is no conflict of interest between Mr and Mrs Fawkes, you can act for them both, but you must receive Mrs Fawkes's instructions from her, not from her husband, and the point about the conveyance being to them both must be explained. If they cannot agree as to the ownership of the equitable interest there is a conflict between them, and you cannot act for them both.

Another reason why the conveyance should be to them both is that the mortgage to the Building Society should be by both of them. If the conveyance were to Mr Fawkes alone the Building Society would have to be warned that Mrs Fawkes contributed to the purchase price, and so has an equitable interest in The Tower. The Building Society would then be reluctant to accept a mortgage from Mr Fawkes alone, lest it be subject to the wife's interest.

An undertaking such as you have been asked for is common in chain transactions where a bridging loan has been obtained from a bank. If you are a solicitor or licensed conveyancer you are under an absolute duty to honour your professional undertaking, and any failure to do this would be looked upon as serious misconduct. For this reason you must only undertake to do what is within your own control. So the following precautions must be taken:

1. You must obtain your clients' irrevocable instructions to give the undertaking.
2. You must only undertake to the bank to pay the net proceeds of the sale to it if and when they come into your hands. This covers the possibility that you may never receive the proceeds, e.g. because your clients decide to transfer the transaction to another solicitor.
3. The undertaking is only in respect of the net proceeds after, e.g. deduction of your own costs, and redemption of mortgages, etc. Tell the Bank what deductions you will be making.
4. Undertake only to pay the proceeds into the account. Do not undertake to discharge the bridging loan from the proceeds. Otherwise, if the proceeds are insufficient, you may have to discharge the bridging loan from your own money. If the bank does not accept an undertaking in these guarded terms, you refuse to give an undertaking to the bank.

Problem 3

(a) Usually there is no conflict of interest between co-purchasers, and so it is possible to act for them all. However, if there is a conflict of interest the purchasers will have to be separately represented. So your answer depends on whether you can see the probability of a conflict of interest between the Savages and the Cowards. We will return to this point when we answer part (c).
(b) To begin with, check the overall position to see if there will be sufficient money to buy 'The Knoll'.

Coming in

A.	Net proceeds of sale of 22 Mount Road (This is an estimate made by the Savages, and should be checked.)	£ 50 000
B.	Contribution by the Cowards	£ 45 000
C.	The mortgage loan	£ 95 000
		£190 000

Going out

Purchase price of The Knoll	£190 000

(The expenses connected with the purchase, e.g. stamp duty and solicitors' fees and disbursements seen to have been taken into account in estimating the net proceeds of the sale, but this must be checked.)

The figures here seem to balance, but there is no surplus to meet any expenses that have been overlooked. The figure given for the net proceeds of the sale of Mount Road must be carefully checked to see if the Savages have foreseen all the expenses connected with both transactions.

Second, what about the position of the Savages? They have life savings of £70 000. They are going to contribute £45 000 towards the purchase and pay for the costs of conversion which are approximately £5000. This leaves them with only £20 000. They need to obtain firm estimates for the costs of conversion. They must also be sure that they will have sufficient income to live on after most of their capital has been tied up in the house. Apparently they will have little more than their old age pension. The problem could become even more acute when one of them dies, and the other is living on the reduced pension. It will be difficult to realise their capital investment if they need to do so, unless the Savages cooperate.

(c) A decision must be reached as to how the equitable interest in The Knoll is to be shared. There must be a division of it into two shares, one for the Cowards and one for the Savages. Each couple will then be a tenant in common with the other couple. The Cowards' share can then be held by them jointly. This ensures that when one dies, the entire share will be automatically owned by the survivor. When the survivor dies, the share will pass over the terms of his or her will, i.e. to Sara. This will carry out the Cowards' wishes that only Sara will benefit from their deaths. The Savages' share will also probably be owned by them jointly, as again the right of survivorship, which is inherent in a joint tenancy, seems appropriate to the matrimonial home. (Notice that even if the couples' contributions had been equal, it would have been wrong for the conveyance to them to declare that they held the whole as beneficial joint tenants. This would not have carried out the Cowards' wishes, as it would mean that after their deaths their interests would be owned by their son-in-law and daughter jointly, rather than entirely by their daughter.) The problem lies in deciding the size of the two shares. The Cowards are contributing £45 000 of the total purchase price of £190 000, so possibly should have a share in proportion to their contribution, i.e. a nine thirty-eighth share. They are also paying for the costs of the conversion, but it is debatable if this adds anything to the capital value of the house. On the other hand, the Savages are bearing the expenses of the purchase.

The mortgage is another difficulty. The understanding between the Savages and the Cowards is that the Savages are to be solely responsible for the repayment of the loan. However, as they are giving the legal estate as security, not just the Savages' equitable interest, they will all sign the mortgage and covenant to repay. In other words, as far as the Building Society is concerned, all four of them are responsible, and the Cowards could be sued for debt. What would certainly happen if the Savages failed to make the monthly repayments is that the Society would sell the house, and the Cowards would lose their home.

It is possible to draw up the conveyance so that the legal estate is conveyed to the Savages alone on trust for themselves and the Cowards. The mortgage of the legal estate would then also be solely by the Savages, and only the Savages would covenant to repay. This would mean that the Cowards could not be sued by the Building Society for debt, but it otherwise offers no solution, and indeed, creates other problems. The Cowards remain at risk if the Savages should fail to repay, as the Building Society would sell the property. The Cowards' equitable interests would not have bound the Building Society, as they would have been overreached by the mortgage (see *City of London Building Society* v. *Flegg* [1988]). It would be possible for the Savages to create a second mortgage without the concurrence of the Cowards. A safeguard against this in the case of registered title would be a restriction on the register, saying that no disposition by the registered proprietors would be registered unless the consent of the Cowards was obtained.

We can now see that the proposed arrangement is not completely satisfactory from the Cowards' point of view and as a result it is probably impossible for us to act for them as well as for the Savages without a conflict of interest. The Cowards should be separately advised.

Chapter 19

Problem

(a) Does the power authorise White to execute the conveyance? Yes. Re-read section 9.4(b).

White should hand over a facsimile certified copy of the power. Re-read section 9.4(e).

(b) This is not a security power, so death revokes it. More importantly, Green *knows* of the revocation, and for this reason any conveyance by White to him would be void. The person who will have the power to convey is Black's personal representative. He will be bound by the contract, as the contract for the sale of land is not discharged by the death either of the seller or of the purchaser. Can the personal representative convey *now* however? No. He must first obtain the grant, either of probate or letters of administration (see section 10.2). So there will be delay before the sale to Mr Green is completed.

(c) (i) The fact that his purchase may be delayed is no excuse for Mr Green to delay his sale. So he may decide to convey his present house on the agreed date, and find temporary accommodation. Mr Green may be tempted to stay where he is, and postpone completion of his sale until he completes his purchase. He may be thwarted by the purchaser, who can issue a writ for specific performance as soon as the agreed completion date has passed, or serve a completion notice and threaten to end the contract. If Green's purchaser is prepared to accept a delayed completion, when it takes place he may have a claim for interest under standard condition 7.3, or for damages.

(ii) It would be pointless for Mr Green to try to speed completion on by applying for a decree of specific performance. The personal representative cannot give a good title until he has obtained the grant, so the delay is inevitable.

If Mr Green does wish to discharge the contract, he could serve a completion notice. However, there are difficulties. It is not possible, whatever means are used, to serve notice on a dead man. Nor can the notice be served on his solicitors. A corpse has no solicitors, and death ends the retainer.

Service on a personal representative is not possible until he is identified by a grant of representation.

Sections 18 and 19 of the Law of Property (Miscellaneous Provisions) Act 1994 provide a solution. If a notice affecting land has to be served, but the person on whom it should have been served is dead and there has been no grant of representation, then the notice is treated as served if

1. it is addressed to 'The Personal Representatives of' the deceased (naming him) and is left at or posted to his last known place of residence or business in the United Kingdom, **and**
2. a copy of it, similarly addressed, is served on the Public Trustee.

Green could, therefore, serve a completion notice using this method, wait for it to expire, and then treat the contract as discharged.

Chapter 20

Problem

Presumably the contract does not repeat the statement as to the existence of the permission. So there is no possibility of action for breach of contract. Pauline will have to establish that the statement was a misrepresentation. If it is, the next question to decide is whether the representation was fraudulent or not, as this affects Pauline's remedies. To be fraudulent, the statement must have been made with the knowledge that it was false, or without belief in its truth, or reckless of whether it was false or true. A fraudulent misrepresentation could give Pauline the right to rescind the contract and to claim damages for the fraud. It seems difficult here for Pauline to prove fraud. Her remedies for non-fraudulent misrepresentation come from the Misrepresentation Act 1967. She has a right of rescission, (subject to the court's power under s.2(2) of the Act to award damages instead). She has a right to damages unless the representation was made without negligence.

The contract incorporates the standard conditions, and condition 7.1 restricts remedies for misrepresentation. (The condition has already been considered in this chapter in the context of misdescription, but it applies to misrepresentations as well.) When considering its effect, remember that a condition removing or restricting remedies for misrepresentation is void unless the condition is a fair and reasonable one to have been included in the contract having regard to all the circumstances known to the parties when the contract was made (s.3 of the Misrepresentation Act 1967). It is up to Roger to establish the validity of the condition. If he cannot do so, *or* if Pauline can establish that the misrepresentation makes a *substantial* difference, she will be able to rescind the contract. The right to rescission survives completion (s.1(b) of the Misrepresentation Act 1967) so it is possible that even if the house had actually been conveyed to Pauline, she could still ask for her money to be returned. This may make things very awkward for the seller, who may have used it to buy his new home, or otherwise put it beyond easy reach, and that sort of difficulty could be a reason for the court to exercise its discretion to award damages in place of rescission.

The remedy of rescission is an equitable one, and there are so-called 'bars' to obtaining an order for it. One is delay. Another is that rescission will not be awarded if it would prejudice innocent third parties who have acquired an interest in the property for value. If Pauline bought with the aid of a mortgage loan, rescission would destroy the mortgagee's security for repayment of the loan. This difficulty should be solvable by an arrangement being made for redemption of the mortgage when Pauline reconveys the land to Roger, in return for the purchase price.

If the exclusion clause is valid, and the misdescription makes a material difference, but not a substantial one, Pauline could not rescind, but could only claim damages.

Index